ROUTLEDGE LIBRARY EDITIONS: FAMILY

I0028154

Volume 1

CHANGING PATTERNS OF EUROPEAN FAMILY LIFE

CHANGING PATTERNS OF EUROPEAN FAMILY LIFE

A Comparative Analysis of 14 Countries

Edited by
**KATJA BOH, MAREN BAK,
CRISTINE CLASON,
MAJA PANKRATOVA,
JENS QVORTRUP,
GIOVANNI B. SGRITTA
AND
KARI WAERNESS**

Routledge
Taylor & Francis Group

LONDON AND NEW YORK

First published in 1989 by Routledge

This edition first published in 2023
by Routledge
4 Park Square, Milton Park, Abingdon, Oxon OX14 4RN

and by Routledge
605 Third Avenue, New York, NY 10158

Routledge is an imprint of the Taylor & Francis Group, an informa business

British Library Cataloguing in Publication Data
A catalogue record for this book is available from the British Library

ISBN: 978-1-032-51072-9 (Set)
ISBN: 978-1-032-53630-9 (Volume 1) (hbk)
ISBN: 978-1-032-53644-6 (Volume 1) (pbk)
ISBN: 978-1-003-41293-9 (Volume 1) (ebk)

DOI: 10.4324/9781003412939

Publisher's Note
The publisher has gone to great lengths to ensure the quality of this reprint but points out that some imperfections in the original copies may be apparent.

Disclaimer
The publisher has made every effort to trace copyright holders and would welcome correspondence from those they have been unable to trace.

CHANGING PATTERNS OF EUROPEAN FAMILY LIFE
A COMPARATIVE ANALYSIS OF 14 EUROPEAN COUNTRIES

Edited by Katja Boh, Maren Bak, Cristine Clason,
Maja Pankratova, Jens Qvortrup, Giovanni B.
Sgritta and Kari Waerness

For the European Co-ordination Centre for
Research and
Documentation in Social Sciences

R

ROUTLEDGE
London and New York

First published in 1989 by Routledge
11 New Fetter Lane, London EC4P 4EE
29 West 35th Street, New York, NY 10001

© 1989 European Co-ordination Centre for Research and Documentation
in Social Sciences

Printed and bound in Great Britain by
Biddles Ltd, Guildford and King's Lynn

British Library Cataloguing in Publication Data

Changing patterns of European family life: a
   comparative analysis of 14 European
   countries.
   1. Europe. Family life
   I. Boh, Katja II. European Coordination
   Centre for Research and Documentation in
   Social Sciences
   306.8'5'094
   ISBN 0-415-00513-2

Library of Congress Cataloging-in-Publication Data

Changing patterns of European family life : a comparative analysis of
   14 European countries / edited by Katja Boh . . . [et al.].
      p. cm.
      1. Family—Europe. 2. Work and family—Europe. 3. Sexual
   division of labor—Europe. I. Boh, Katja, 1931- . II. European
   Coordination Centre for Research and Documentation in Social
   Sciences.
   HQ612.C47 1989
   306.8'5'094–dc19

   ISBN 0-415-00513-2   88-39976
                                          CIP

Contents

Foreword

This book reports on an international comparative research project on 'Changes in the life patterns of families in Europe' accomplished under the auspices of the European Co-ordination Centre for Research and Documentation in Social Sciences (Vienna Centre) in the years 1979-86 with the participation of researchers from 14 Eastern and Western European countries. The project director was Katja Boh from the University of Ljubljana.

The Vienna Centre, an independent non-governmental institution created in 1963 as a result of a UNESCO General Assembly decision, aims to promote co-operation in comparative social science research, including both Eastern and Western European countries.

The Joint Committee of the Nordic Social Science Research Councils, initiator of the project, has given considerable economic and moral support to the project. National research councils, academies of science and funds have helped finance the national research teams. We wish to thank all these funding agencies for their contribution to the project.

We also wish to express our gratitude to Margaret Sierakowski from England who did the linguistic editing and to Peter Tamási from Hungary who accomplished the stylistic editing of the manuscript. Thanks are due also to Waltraud Salimi and Joanna Ambrus, staff members of the Vienna Centre, for their careful setting of the manuscript.

The Editors

Introduction

Maren Bak

Background of the project

In 1976 a group of Nordic family researchers and the Nordic Social Science Research Councils argued for the need and relevance of a comparative research project to assess the very important changes going on in the family in rapidly modernising European countries. The broad background for the study of the family was the macro-changes in production and working life, when agricultural and handicraft production changed into industrial production and the production of services. We intended to study the interaction between these changes and family and individual life. But two recent social changes must be understood as having immediate external influence on the present study: the changing position of women and the redefinition and challenge of the welfare state.

In the Nordic countries the strong and powerful wave of women's research emerging after the mid-1970s brought into focus the importance of women's entrance into the labour market for both the family and society. It showed a gender-segregated labour market and it focused on the emergence of the post-industrial service society, in which a major part of the service work is performed by women. Feminist research also raised challenges to social research, urging it to become aware of its blindness so far to the situation of women, and it called for more comprehensive research into those social structures which are of vital importance for the fate of women and in which women play an important role - the family being in this respect a very essential unit for research. Feminist research called for attention to structures of power and oppression between the sexes operating on all levels of society, including, of course, the family.

The interest in family research reflected in the present project should be seen in this historical context. Many of the researchers are part of or have created women's research milieux and all of them are of course responding to those societal changes which brought women much more into the focus of research interest.

The other major societal change which is challenging family research and which is a background to the present project is the economic recession and the retrenchment and redefinition of the whole system of social welfare which has taken place in most Western European countries since the late 1970s.

The belief that the state and its institutions could and should provide the bulk of caring, reproductive and socialisation work in society was deeply challenged. The economic recession and cuts in welfare expenditure and the growth in the number of people needing care or support, both as a result of unemployment and of the ageing of the European populations have created a whole set of new questions and solutions to the welfare systems in the European countries. 'Getting back to the people' has been a formula for satisfying the needs and standards of living even in advanced societies through re-establishing the responsibility of individuals, families and local communities for their own well-being. Especially the role of the family in caring for its individual members and raising and redistributing resources became crucially important.

Main research questions and ways of analysing the family

With regard to the changing position of women and the redifinition of the social welfare system - two recent social changes to be paid specific attention to - a group of researchers from fourteen Eastern and Western European countries set out to conduct a comparative study of the interrelationship between changes in production and working life on the one hand and changes in family life and reproduction on the other hand, roughly covering the period from 1945 up to the present. These 14 countries were Belgium, England, Finland, France, Federal Republic of Germany, German Democratic Republic, Hungary, Italy, the Netherlands, Norway, Poland, Sweden, USSR and Yugoslavia (Slovenia).

Of basic interest for this study were the changes which have been produced by the division of functions between family and work, and problems which have arisen as a consequence of the sometimes incompatible and even conflicting demands of the two institutions. Some forces operating in the sphere of work gave rise to work patterns which were not adapted to family life and vice versa, changes in family relationships were not always attuned with the organisation of work. This has created problems for family members in both their working and their family roles.

The main research issue of this study, put in general terms, was this: how do people cope with a growing number of partly new problems imposed on them because of the extended role of working life and public intervention?

This general problem was made more explicit in three basic questions, which served as the framework of the study presented here:

1. What is the interrelationship between the development of new forms of organisation of work and the development of new life patterns in the family at different times and in different social settings?
2. What are the points of compatibility (incompatibility) and what kind of problems arise out of incompatibilities between the world of work and the family? How do the family members perceive and cope with these problems and how does this influence family behaviour?
3. What are the formal (institutionalised) and the informal (non-institutionalised) strategies and arrangements for care and reproduction and their differentiated use by families in various cultural and social systems and economic conditions?

Since the very first proposals for this research project there has been a point of departure remaining unchanged and having been a common view of the involved researchers in spite of the many differences in their theoretical and methodological approach. Namely, the family is seen as a very important social unit. In opposition to the 'withering away theory' which assumes that the family is becoming gradually emptied of its functions and importance and might disappear altogether, we see it as a changing but not disappearing unit which is reacting to but also influencing other social institutions, i.e. the state, the market (especially in the form of the labour market and work) and mediating structures (like kinship and friendship networks, voluntary organisations, etc.) constituting the triangle within which we analyse the family (see Table 1 in

G.B. Sgritta's chapter, which shows the frame of analysis). We do not understand the family as a 'victim' of development but as a social unit reacting to contradictions and pressures towards change and still fulfilling important social functions.

The investigation centres on the family's role in the strains and contradictions between production and reproduction. Whereas theories and policy relating to production are quite well developed, adequate and comprehensive theories of reproduction (where the family is the central institution) are still lacking. One of the project's aims is to contribute to the conceptualisation and further development of a theory of reproduction. This approach requires the rethinking and refinement also of the classical theories of production and work since these exclude the whole reproductive sphere as non-work and non-production.

When we are analysing work here it is in the sense of both paid and unpaid work, thus stressing the interdependence and indispensability of the two and uniting the analysis of production and reproduction. We wish to bring to light the changes in reproductive work and to conceptualise as work many of the functions assumed to be no more than an expression of the emotions and love between family members. The concept of caregiving as work was developed in this project for the first time and the analysis of caregiving constitutes another important part of the study.

The study thus focuses on the family as one playing a part in societal changes, on pressures and contradictions in the situation of the family and of its individual members and on resources and solutions to problems generated in and used by the family. It tries to give an understanding of the general functioning of the family as well as of the social reality of the great number of intertwined, conflicting, differentiated elements which constitute the family.

To meet the purpose of the study, two main types of information have been utilised in the analyses. National statistics and documentary material have been used in writing the national background reports in the first phase of the research. Structured interviews conducted personally with samples of urban population have furnished the new empirical data for the second phase of the research.

The structure of the present book follows the main issues of the research as they were presented above. The first theoretical part gives a deeper presentation of the ways of analysing and reflecting on the family. The following two parts focus on the empirical findings of the research. The part on paid and unpaid work relates to the first two main research issues, analysing the interrelationship between the world of work and the family. The third part moves the analysis from the world of work and production to the world of reproduction and tries to give answers to the third issue, namely the changing family strategies and responsibilities for care and reproduction in various social and cultural systems. Finally the conclusions in the last part give a reappraisal of both the changing patterns of European family life and the methodology used in the analyses.

Theoretical background

The universality of the family as an institution in all societies, and yet the wide variety in its concrete forms and functions throughout history and across cultures, makes it challenging to assess the particular and the universal in family patterns by means of comparisons.

Comparative family research is not a novel phenomenon. Anthropology has already made classical contributions in the field and family history has given insights into the mechanisms of changes in family forms. Also comparative family sociology has its tradition. Many so-called comparative studies, however, appeared in the form of a series of 'parallel' studies of different countries, with the actual comparative work left to the reader.

It is attempted in this project to handle the comparative aspect in a much more ambitious but also in a more risky way: to compare contemporary European family patterns by analysing each of the crucial ones cross-culturally, through trying to assess differences and similarities between nations on each pattern and to come up with system-bound explanations for the differences found. It is an attempt at finding typologies or clusters of the involved nations, by way of linking family patterns to other important social, economic or political patterns.

The conditions of this approach to comparative research are investigated from the point of view of the theory of science in the chapter by Jens Qvortrup. He stresses the need for all the research teams to adopt a common research problem, which is at the same time a comparative problem, relating to those systemic differences which are supposed to be relevant for the patterns to be compared.

Such an attempt is of course daring and ambitious. To unite researchers with different cultural and scientific traditions and backgrounds in identifying and working on a common research problem is very difficult to fulfil in practice. The shortcomings of our results give testimony to the difficulties. We have not always been able to raise the analysis from the level of 'parallel' descriptions and to incorporate relevant explanatory systemic variables, though it has been attempted in every chapter.

The theoretical chapters give an outline of the theories and ideologies of family functions, family forms and the place of the family in society, and they give the theoretical framework for our research. All the three authors have diachronic as well as synchronic comparative perspectives, emphasising historical changes in the theories of the family as well as the differences and similarities in the theories and ideologies across the East-West dimension. The interaction between the development of society and family forms on the one hand and theories and ideologies about the family on the other is of central interest in this part. It shows the controversies between different theories of the family and their implications for the understanding of the future of this institution as well as for social policy and practice.

In the West the Parsonian structural-functional concept of the ideal family under industrial conditions has been extremely influential. It emphasised as functional the complementarity of the gender roles and thus idealised the nuclear family with the instrumentally oriented man-father-provider and the expressively oriented woman-mother-caregiver. This theory and concept of the family is now heavily criticised from a number of aspects to such an extent that we can talk of a changing paradigm in family research.

In the East we can similarly recognise a traditional idealised notion of the family based on the assumption that as a society moves from a capitalist to socialist form of political and economic organisation, the family will automatically evolve correspondingly. This notion has also been criticised.

Edmund Dahlström, Rhona Rapoport and Giovanni Sgritta all formulate their criticism of these kinds of idealised concepts of the family and the related traditional research paradigms and emphasise the theoretical foundation of the research presented here in opposition to the structural-functional school of thought.

Dahlström goes into a penetrating analysis of dominant ideologies and theories of the family in the democratic capitalist countries and in the socialist countries, especially enlightening the controversy between the 'withering away' theory and the 'indispensability' theory. This controversy is of course linked to the notion of the family as either passive or active partner in the process of social change, where the emphasis in our understanding is on the family as an active social unit.

Dahlström and Rapoport emphasise the present development towards an accepted diversity in family forms in both the West and the East. Rapoport stresses that there has always been diversity in the course of history and the family has continually changed. The present changes involve a diversity in structures, for instance non-married couples, one-parent families, reconstituted binuclear families, etc., and a diversity in the roles of the household members.

Dahlström shows that the change towards diversity in family life relates to the changing conditions of and contradictions in the family. He identifies four main contradictions of contemporary family life: (1) the contradiction between production and reproduction, which is reflected in the difficulties of combining parenthood with gainful employment; (2) the attempts of political-ideological institutions to regulate and influence everyday life and the practices/protests and reactions against these attempts; (3) the contradiction between the increased freedom of choice and change in conjugal relations and the need for stability in the children's lives; (4) and finally the contradictions between a patriarchal heritage and ideals of gender equalisation.

Sgritta traces the new paradigm in family research by relating the change in research interest to changes in the social structure, first and foremost to the crisis of the welfare state. He outlines the main features of this new paradigm, which is also the paradigm of the research presented here: linking the behaviour of the family to larger social institutions; greater concreteness in the analysis of the family through growing interest in the private sphere, in everyday life and everyday consciousness, i.e. in subjectivity in the sense that the family is not just analysed as a solid unit but also as a meeting point of different, sometimes conflicting, individuals with different needs, interests and perspectives.

Paid and unpaid work

This empirical part investigates the complicated interrelationship between work and family life from a number of different angles and perspectives. Of importance is the conception of work encompassing paid work as well as unpaid work, whereby we understand all activities classifiable as work but not measured in economic terms when carried out by household members. Unpaid work includes household tasks, caregiving, work done for kinship and community groups, voluntary organisations, etc.

The part starts by a macro-perspective relating modernisation theory to empirical data on family life and women's work-life careers. It then proceeds to describe and analyse the qualitative differences in content and amount of men's and women's work, paid as well as unpaid, and looks into the mechanisms of tension between working life and family life and strategies for overcoming the incompatibilities between the two spheres. In spite of important cross-national differences, a common picture also appears clearly. A patriarchal heritage is still prevalent in all the European countries researched, with women given lower wages and having poorer conditions in the labour market while at the same time having an overburden of domestic unpaid work compared with men.

Riitta Jallinoja starts with the macro-perspective. She develops a typology of national patterns relating the three variables: the modernity of society, the modernity of family life and women's work-life careers. She shows very interestingly that there is no necessary correlation between the modernity of society and a modern family life. All the countries can be called modern but there are great differences especially concerning the life situation when children are small. The ideal of housewife is still prevalent in some modern countries while in others, on the same level of modernisation, it is not valid any more.

Elina Haavio-Mannila describes the type, extent and consequences of gender segregation in paid and unpaid work, seeing the division of labour between men and women as a social and cultural phenomenon which is possible to change. Functional segregation is common all over Europe. The segregated women's work is connected with low education, employment status and wages. It means more often part-time or shift work and strict control. In all countries segregated women's work is related to human reproduction and service.

In unpaid work there also appears a clear gender division of labour, but there is more variation between the countries compared. The North-South difference is more remarkable than the East-West divide in this respect.

In Nevenka Černigoj-Sadar's investigation of the psycho-social relations between paid work and family life, the focus is on the subjective experiences and feelings of men and women. Her thesis is that from the subjective point of view the two life spheres are strongly interrelated, no matter to what extent family life and paid work are formally segregated. Perhaps her most striking result from the empirical data is that among negative and positive influences the transfer of personal satisfaction from work to family life is most often mentioned and that women more often experience positive influences than men. This experience is shared in all the examined countries.

In the negative or conflicting relations between paid work and family, for the women the family is the source of conflict whereas for the men it is the job. In the women's experience of conflicts there are important differences between countries.

When discussing the uneven share of domestic work and possible mechanisms for furthering a more egalitarian share of responsibilities within the family, a general shortening of working hours has been one of the main requests. Rosemarie Nave-Herz tests the 'time available' hypothesis derived from this argument, namely that the inner familial division of labour is dependent on the married partners' employment and the length of their working hours.

She comes forward with the striking result that the hypothesis cannot be maintained at the general level because it does not apply to both sexes to the same extent.

There was no correlation between the length of working time for men and the degree of their participation in family activities. In contrast, women's working time seems to play some role. The chance of higher participation of men increases with full-time working women, but not with part-time working women.

Andrée Michel finally uses the empirical material to test the hypothesis that marriage and children reinforce the traditional gender role division of labour between the spouses. Her point is that division of work between the sexes need not automatically imply inequality but that patriarchal mechanisms in the present society both capitalist and socialist are still operating and causing inequality between the sexes, which can be noticed in both paid and unpaid work.

Reproduction and caregiving

This part focuses on the empirical findings of our project relating to the most basic functions of the family: reproduction of life and caring for the growing generation as well as for other dependants. It analyses the changes in reproduction and caregiving as they are influenced by changes in work and employment structures, and by the changing welfare policies and strategies.

The concepts of caregiving and reproduction actually belong under the concepts of paid and unpaid work. They constitute another angle for the analysis, taking the family as a point of departure.

Angelo Saporiti starts by analysing the fundamental reproductive pattern: the reproduction of life through childbirth. His aim is to analyse the changes and decline in fertility in relation to social change, to see which level of analysis (a macro-, meso- or micro-level) is the most fruitful and to investigate what probably the determining factor of contemporary reproductive behaviour is. He points to the importance of looking not only at the macro-level (i.e. national) but at the meso-(homogeneous groups) and micro-levels (family, individuals) as well, since the family is the locus of biological reproduction. At these levels he combines the theory of the transition in the value of children for the parents with the changes in familial power structures accompanying the changes in the mode of production, changes which imply an overthrow of the older male generation's monopoly of power in production and reproduction matters.

Finally Saporiti relates the recent decline in fertility to these explanations of 'the fertility transition' of the last century, and offers the hypothesis that in present day society the status of women has to be introduced as a major explanatory variable.

The changing status of women, especially expressed through married women's permanent presence in the labour market and the consequent internal changes in family relations, is also in the centre of analysis of caregiving in the next two chapters. The expansion in female employment is intimately linked to the expansion of the encompassing societal institutions of service of care, which according to the 'withering away' theory tend to take over more and more of the caring and service functions of the family.

The analysis here goes into a close examination of the caregiving work actually performed by the family and it looks at the possible changes in gender roles in relation to caregiving. Kari Waerness defines caregiving work as caring for dependants on a consistent and reliable basis, whether it is paid or not, no matter whether it takes place in the private sphere or not. She analyses changes in caregiving work in the case of children and that of the elderly family members, as well as those institutions and persons from whom the spouses get help in problem situations.

The analysis reveals quite striking similarities in the countries compared. Both in the East and the West there is a high acceptance of professional care of children over three, while for smaller children it is still mothers who give up work and provide care, maintaining that this is what they want to do.

Looking at the elderly, Waerness states the fact that contrary to common belief even in the states with the most developed public care systems most dependent adults still live in their homes and are taken care of by - almost exclusively female - family members. In problem situations it is again the informal family network and close friends who are relied upon - not professional help in the first place.

Proceeding from this knowledge of the family as a resource in caregiving, Hildur Ve poses the issue of possible changes in the gender roles relating to care, keeping in mind the aim of gender equality and the liberation of both women and men. She states that with few exceptions neither liberal nor Marxist traditions have regarded the ability to care for children as having liberating dimensions. Equality between the sexes must mean not only the extension of men's rights and opportunities to women but also the taking over of women's obligations by men. The possibilities of such a take-over are examined by analysing men's actual share of household chores and the national policies concerning fathers rights to care for small children.

Conclusions

Katja Boh gives a reappraisal of the changes in European family life patterns in the 14 countries as they emerge from the national reports, written for the first phase of the project, and from the empirical data gathered in the second phase.

This chapter is an attempt to give a macro-level picture of the simultaneous variation of three central family patterns: changes (1) in work patterns, (2) in marriage patterns and (3) in the reproductive patterns and forms of parenting. By casting more light on changes in the marriage and reproductive patterns, it fills some of the gaps which were still left in the two empirical sections.

In her analysis the author uses a scale for each of the patterns, placing every one of the 14 countries with a low, medium or high score; and with this scaling as a basis is the convergence and divergence in the changing patterns discussed and analysed in relation to possible explanatory variables (such as economic, socio-political, cultural and religious differences).

The last part of the chapter unites the analysis of the work, marriage and reproductive patterns in an 'integrated' family life pattern. Katja Boh has given this part the heading 'Towards convergence in diversity' and thereby she indicates her major conclusion regarding the changes in European family life patterns.

She identifies three clusters of countries based on their integrated patterns; however, her conclusion is that there are very few common background variables uniting the countries in each cluster. She suggests that variation in family patterns (in toto) cannot be predicted directly from differences either in political systems, economic development or cultural traditions, and that the patterns do not change by following some universal rule. Changes in one aspect of family life may occur independently from developments in its other dimensions, since each pattern might be influenced by specific internal and external forces.

The chapter stresses the complexity of change-promoting factors as well as the complexity and variation of family life patterns.

The common trend in all the 14 countries studied here is, however, the growing acceptance and legitimation of a diversity in family life patterns.

By the analysis and the material presented here and by the conclusions drawn from it we hope to have contributed to new knowledge and understanding of contemporary European life patterns and to the theories of social change as well as to methods of comparing national variations.

The research team is aware of the shortcomings of and gaps in this ambitious project. Many questions could be raised regarding the selection of variables, the validity and comparability of the national data, the selection of samples and the methods of comparison. The final chapter on methodology gives the background information on the organisation, the research plan and the work procedures as they emerged when the scientific ideals met with the reality of conditions for international comparative research. This chapter is intended to make understood the decisions and compromises which are inevitable in a big research project and to assess the empirical foundations for the trends presented in the book.

The diversity which characterises the subject studied here is also a characteristic of the research team that created the project and of their individual contributions to this book. The chapters reflect the diversity in national scientific traditions as well as in individual ways of thinking and writing. We hope that this book will contribute both to the recognition of the fruitful and inspiring qualities in this scientific diversity, which is a characteristic of international comparative research, and to a recognition of the qualities of scientific co-operation across borders.

Part One

Theoretical Background

1

Comparative Research and Its Problems

Jens Qvortrup

Introductory remarks

Comparative research has a heritage which dates back to the founding fathers of sociology and philosophy, although it can hardly claim to have constituted itself as a scientific discipline proper. One of the barriers is the belief which holds that 'all social research is comparative research' and which seems to indicate that there is nothing new or specific about what is called comparative research.

Much discussion has been devoted to that topic, discussion which in itself is not without interest in the sense that it has tried to elucidate whether comparative research has its own specific methodology or research techniques (see e.g. Mokrzycki, 1979). On the other side I do not feel very much inclined to challenge the statement that 'all research is comparative research' since it is nothing but a truism in the form it is put and thus neither interesting nor fruitful. It only forces us to distinguish between different kinds of comparative research as far as the level is concerned in order to come to the conventional meaning of comparative research, which is research crossing boundaries either in time or in space. Even then it may still be argued that cross-boundary research does not require methods different from other kinds of 'comparative' research. But although the discussion then starts to gain in quality, the main point is missing. The main point is namely not whether a new method can be ascertained or proven, but rather whether the involvement in cross-boundary research promises new insights. That comparative research understood as cross-boundary research does enhance our understanding of social processes appears to be beyond any doubt, and in view of this it is of secondary importance whether new methods have been applied, or whether we want to name comparative research itself at this level a new methodology.

But what does 'level' mean? It is not enough to say that comparative research in its conventional meaning is conducted at a macro-level, while 'intra-boundary' research is done at a micro-level. In fact, both micro- and macro-phenomena can be dealt with in national as well as in international research, and it is quite possible that both the dependent and independent variables may belong to either level. In order to elucidate this problem, one may refer to the classical canon of comparative research, namely that by John Stuart Mill (1950, p. 211) while distinguishing two fundamental methods of comparison: 'One is by comparing together different instances in which the phenomenon occurs. The other is by comparing instances in which the phenomenon does occur with instances in other respects similar in which it does not. These two methods may be respectively denominated the method of agreement and the method of difference.'

The crucial concepts in this quotation are 'phenomenon' and 'instance'. Broadly speaking, 'phenomenon' is here taken to mean the 'dependent variable' while 'instance' must be understood as the 'independent variable', or, more generally, the causation. The phenomenon is thus something which must be explained by reference to the instance, either directly if the instance constitutes a 'cause' (method of agreement) or indirectly, which is the more complicated case (method of difference). The best known application of the method of difference has been demonstrated by Max Weber - and his conclusion is still much debated. Weber (1904-5) endeavoured to prove that capitalism in Europe originated as the result of a Protestant ethic, which was not found in the Orient, where - e.g. in China - the necessary conditions for establishing capitalism were present, but capitalism did not develop. So the initial 'instances' being approximately similar, the main difference between the two instances - Protestantism - counts as the explanation of the development of capitalism.

Irrespective of the soundness of the substance or the validity of the argument, the methodological importance remains for comparative analysis, namely that the causal factor could only be perceived by recourse to knowledge of other societies. One could have thought of a hypothesis relating 'saving' - *die innerweltliche Askese* - to capitalism, but the hypothesis gains its strength only by reference to other instances where this factor was absent.

Weber's comparative theory is not typical. First, because the method of difference is rather the exception than the rule; secondly, because it moves at the macro-level as to both the independent and the dependent variable. But in principle it is a feasible approach. Much more representative for the mainstream of comparative research is the formulation by another famous comparativist, the French historian Marc Bloch, who states: 'Thus two conditions are necessary to make a comparison, historically speaking, possible: there must be a certain similarity between the facts observed - an obvious point - and a certain dissimilarity between the situations in which they have arisen' (Bloch, 1967, p. 45). So - in Mill's vocabulary - the *phenomenon* must exhibit some similarity, while the *instances* must show a certain dissimilarity. We have to do here with the method of agreement, and at a level which will typically be macroscopic for the instance and microscopic for the phenomenon.

There is obviously no watertight borderline between what are regarded as macro- and microscopic variables, so I choose here the functional definition by Etzioni (1968, p. 49). 'Macro-units (of sociology) are defined as all those units the majority of whose consequences affect one or more societies, their combinations, or their sub-units.' Etzioni allows for intermediary cases, but in general micro-units are then units which do not have societal consequences, but only consequences at the micro-level. This definition is functional in the sense that it takes account of the *consequences*, which means that a unit which nominally may count as a micro-unit, e.g. a family, may be a macro-unit, for instance if it is a royal family or another influential family.

Whether we denote the variables macro- or microscopic, the important thing in comparative analysis seems to be that the 'instance' stands in supra-sub relationship to the 'phenomenon', that we, in other words, have to do with a *hierarchical relationship*, theoretically speaking. In comparative research, according to the conventional definition as cross-boundary research, the instance will typically be society, system, culture, historical period or the like, while the phenomenon may be any kind of sub-unit *vis-à-vis* this instance.

Europe's homogeneity and heterogeneity

For some, talking about Europe would be an impermissible abstraction. And yet it may sometimes be scientifically justified. In a number of sociologically relevant respects Europe can be regarded as an entity. Compared with other parts of the world Europe is a continent whose similarities are more conspicuous than the differences between its countries. Demographically, economically, educationally and socially it distinguishes itself together with other industrialised countries from those of the Third World, but at the same time the history of Europe sets it apart from other industrialised countries outside Europe. When North Americans, for instance, speak about Europe, they have this historic continent in mind rather than its internal differences. And in current political parlance it makes sense to speak of 'the American challenge to Europe' or vice versa.

Speaking about Europe in this abstract way is a way of setting the limits for what we talk about. Globally and historically Europe has so much in common that it would be justifiable to define it as an 'instance' (Mill) or a 'situation' (Bloch) in comparative analysis. This has significance in comparative research not only as a warning against exaggerations of the differences which certainly are there, but more because it may help us define the purpose of comparing Europe's countries along certain dimensions.

As was said above, the general purpose of comparative research is to enhance our cognition, or - more specifically for our study, as was said in the project's proposal - 'the aim of this study is to deepen and refine our understanding of social processes and problems which have emerged as a consequence of the interrelationship between family and work and help to improve programmes and services for the family'. In the proposal - as an argument for making an inter-European project - the differences between the countries are stressed, i.e. the heterogeneity of the area. I will come back to that, but I think it is worthwhile first to dwell on its homogeneity.

There is no contradiction between hetero- and homogeneity, it is only a question of perspective. The very concrete setting, where programmes and services for the family have to be implemented, appears as very complex and heterogeneous, but looked upon from a bird's-eye view it is homogeneous. One mode of production, feudalism for instance, is from one perspective very complex, but in a long historical perspective it certainly exhibits some typical features, which - and this is important - can only really be perceived when compared to other modes of production.

Claiming that Europe is homogeneous therefore amounts to postulating some factors defining the 'instance' or the 'situation' as parameters. It means that we postulate them to be constant or at least to have exerted approximately the same influence in the different cases. If we, for instance, think of two examples related to our study: birth rate and women's employment rate as our dependent variables (facts or phenomena), both - especially women's employment - show a certain variation among the European countries. The relativity of this impression is, however, immediately seen if the levels of the variables' values are compared to those of the 'instances' of Africa or Asia. In this comparison the variability appears as rather belonging to the same level. The instance of Europe exhibits one level, the instances of Africa and Asia belong to another level. This is all well-known substance, but from a methodological point of view not as trivial as it may sound, since only by means of comparison are we able to give meaning to any notion of level of variable value, and only comparative analysis enables us to locate the parameters which produced the different levels, and which therefore contribute to a social scientific characterisation of the instance. By means of the 'method of difference' we can suggest that 'industrialisation' is the parameter we are looking for, in the sense that certain levels are found where industrialisation is absent, and other levels can be observed where it is not. The instance or the situation of Europe has in this way assumed 'quality': we have located a parameter with explanatory power and presumably with predictive power as well; and we have substantiated the abstraction 'Europe' so that we can claim its homogeneity more meaningfully.

In a comparative study including only European *industrialised* countries it is thus not scientifically productive to stress the similarities among them as far as, for example, birthrate and women's employment-rate are concerned. The similarities are there, but they are demonstrated merely by reference to a parameter, the relative, but approximately common, value of which could only be shown in comparison with non-European countries. It thus gives no more insight to ponder on an explanatory parameter, which in fact only demonstrates Europe's homogeneity. This is thus the importance of Europe's homogeneity: some factors can be kept constant and even if they are very significant in explaining a trend towards similarity in a global perspective, they are of less scientific

importance when it comes to explaining the intra-European variability. The comparison with non-European areas has helped us to
reach a *limited generalisation*, which appears to hold for Europe.
(It must be said, of course, that even if this is true, the factor 'industrialisation' is not totally ruled out, since *degrees* of industrialisation may still have considerable importance.)

When we turn from Europe's homogeneity to her heterogeneity
we shift position from speaking about Europe as one 'instance' to
talking about a number of different 'instances', represented for
example by culture, common history, political system or by country. This shift has importance in the sense that it will help us - not
in explaining the *general* trend common to all of the instances -
but rather in *specifying the limited generalisation*, i.e. under what
conditions and according to which supplementary factors do our
dependent variables differ? Marc Bloch's conditions cited above
seem to be appropriate for this situation: Europe's homogeneity
makes sure that a certain similarity of the *facts* are found, while
her heterogeneity accounts for a certain dissimilarity among the
situations.

As was the case with the 'instance' of Europe, the different instances within Europe are also as such *abstractions*, but to a lesser
extent, since we are now able to speak of, for example, 'the industrialised country X' and 'the industrialised country Y', etc. A
further specification of the relationship between instance and
phenomenon would amount to finding another parameter which
would systematically explain the variance of the phenomenon.

In general terms it is quite easy to think of such parameters,
whether we speak of different geographical-cultural areas, historical-cultural areas, areas under differing religious influence or systems under varying political-economical character, or simply national states. The difficulty is of course to formulate operationali-
sations of parameters so as to bring them to bear scientifically on
our common problem. 'Culture', 'history' and 'country' are instances which cannot as such be handled scientifically, it is necessary to translate them into concepts which are measurable or at
least open to interpretation. This question is, unfortunately, very
often bypassed in studies with comparative pretensions. Too often
we learn about variable-differences between countries without
being informed about the factors which produced these different
results in these countries. A widely used procedure, which may be
labelled the 'juxtaposition approach', puts side by side results of
variable values from different countries. To the extent, however,

that it is suggested that this procedure is comparative in the real sense of the term, it indeed presupposes a similarity between 'instances' which in most cases is presumptive and unwarranted. It is in fact begging the question: what is it about the instances, e.g. the countries, which are so similar as to make a comparison between phenomena meaningful?

Nation-states, or countries, do not always coincide with cultural or historical entities, but at least in a short-term perspective they very often do constitute a meaningful common unit, which *vis-à-vis* a problem or a phenomenon through its political and economic structure is making its influence noticeable in more or less the same way. In comparative research such structures are 'disturbing' factors contributing to heterogeneity. But it is possible to think of countries which are clustering around one type of political-economic structures and others which have another built-up in that respect. In the European context one example should be mentioned here, since in an especially pertinent way it illustrates Europe's heterogeneity.

The East-West divide

The division of Europe into countries of socialist and capitalist ones has occasioned quite a number of studies which may be called comparative, although their main target has been the characterisation of the new socialist societies which came to compete with those of the capitalist world. In this context, they are interesting in so far as they paradigmatically underline certain aspects as preponderant in societal development.

The 'totalitarianism/pluralism' paradigm accounts for some differences, the explanatory level being primarily the political one. Stressing the importance of the political level and given the differences between totalitarianism and pluralism, the conclusion is hardly surprising that the way of life in the two systems must be very different. Pluralism will as a matter of principle allow people as far as possible to lead their own lives, which gives way to a great variety of behavioural forms. Totalitarianism, on the other hand, is moulding people to fit its own demands - according to this paradigm. 'Even the socializing functions of the family have been shaped to the regime's demand', it is said (Feldmesser, 1960, p. 252). Under totalitarianism - this paradigm holds - individual behaviour is fully subordinated to the regime's demands. Thus the interesting level to study is *the political level*.

The other paradigm, the convergence paradigm, stresses the similarities rather than the differences. The claimed similarities are said to be the result of similar assumptions in both systems, namely, the 'assumption that economic development is fostered by emphasis on "other-directedness"; and the one that egalitarianism, universalism, and achievement appear to be congruent with the success of major protagonists in today's world' (Smelser and Lipset, 1966, p. 45).

Contrary to the paradigm of totalitarianism, the paradigm of convergence deduces the differentiation of society from the individuals' behaviour, from their rational response to given opportunities in the economic sphere. The economic realm through the technological requirements of modern society so to say gains supremacy over any political pretension. Thus *the economy has primacy* and forces any modern system to converge.

Finally, a third model of socialist origin moves at the level of the *mode of production*, and stresses the importance of (1) the ownership of the means of production, (2) the correspondence of the means of production with the relations of production, and (3) the influence of the relations of production on the social consciousness of the people. Since it is especially the relations of production that are stressed, the differences between the systems are underlined.

My intention is not to discuss the validity of these paradigms. They are mentioned only for the purpose of exemplifying ways of characterising systems or 'instances', which may be helpful in explaining differences or similarities in countries belonging to one or the other system. Are family life patterns different in socialist countries compared with capitalist countries? Did they change in another way and at another speed? Or - following the above-mentioned paradigms - are politics, economics or relations of production determining factors in shaping family life patterns?

Since all industrial countries are very complex units, it may be difficult to judge the weight of each factor, but looking at the dependent factors it may be possible to approach this problem in an effort to formulate some hypotheses.

If we consider again the example of birth rate and women's employment rate in the countries participating in the project it appears that the birth rate generally speaking is slightly higher in socialist than in capitalist countries, but the difference seems not to be significant. The women's employment rate, on the other hand, is undoubtedly higher in the socialist countries. Even the highest employment rate for women in the capitalist countries does not reach the lowest rate in the socialist countries. This is particularly interesting since women's employment is usually treated as one of the indicators of modernisation; and since the capitalist countries, generally speaking, have a higher score on most modernisation indicators, this finding seems to be a powerful one. It suggests that - as far as this factor is concerned - the primacy of politics is stronger than the primacy of economics, or if you like, socialist planning is stronger than the inertia of industrialisation. Another theoretical possibility - according to the socialist paradigm - could be that women's 'socialist consciousness' has been positively provoked as a response to the new relations of production. However, it should not be overlooked that in the first decades of socialist societies a state of emergency to a large extent forced women to be gainfully employed outside their homes.

Be that as it may, there is no doubt that within the instance of Europe, which globally speaking is relatively homogeneous, her division into a socialist and capitalist part makes an excellent case for testing specific parameters.

The ambiguity of the concept of change

So far our discussion has focused on locating properties for our instances at the cross-sectional or the synchronical level, and I shall return to that later. I want, however, to invoke another dimension of utmost importance for comparative analysis and the interpretation of findings, namely the diachronic or the historical dimension, even if this increases complexity and thus amplifies our difficulties.

The title of our project indicates that we want to study 'changes' in family life patterns. But what is meant by 'changes'? The term is ambiguous: it is the antonym of the concept of 'stability', while 'discontinuity' is one case of change. But at the same time there is no necessary contradiction between 'change' and 'continuity', while of course 'continuity' and 'discontinuity' are terms which cannot be reconciled. It makes, indeed, sense to speak of a continuous change.

In much theorising about the family, it has been regarded not only as a fundamental group in society, but also as a *stable* and stabilising entity in a *changing* society (cf. Lasch, 1979), and yet, the family has itself undergone dramatic changes. It has been a group exhibiting change and stability at one and the same time. But while its changes have been acknowledged primarily in its internal structures and as far as the importance of the functions of its members are concerned, its stabilising significance is seen in relation to the society.

It is therefore of special pertinence for a comparative study aiming to account for macro-influences - or influences of 'macro-instances' - on family life to elucidate its position in relation to other societal forces, and not least: the varying rate of change under different conditions.

What appear to be more or less unanimous trends in an all-European setting, declining family-size, more and more dual-career couples, growing divorce-rates, etc., may in fact assume different interpretations depending on (1) the starting point and the duration of the trends, and (2) their rates of change in relation to other societal changes.

The present project has endeavoured - as a preparation for its empirical, cross-sectional parts - to make 'national reports', which, however, go back only to 1945. Although very rich in contents and most informative, the reports cover scarcely more than one generation, which historically speaking is a very short period for explaining deeper changes. The apparent converging trends which can be traced during recent decades must be seen on the background of the historical development before that period.

In that respect it becomes important that - in addition to what was said above - a historical divide is found which geographically more or less coincides with the socialism/capitalism divide. (From a family-history point of view, moreover, this divide also largely coincides with the Hajnal-line accounting for changes in marriage ages, see Hajnal, 1965.) Apart from the GDR, the socialist countries in our study began their industrial development at a much later date than the capitalist ones. This 'lag' combined with a change to socialism seems to have prompted an unforeseen rapidity in social development, which no doubt must have influenced family life much more deeply than did the smoother development which could be observed in Western Europe.

It is, for instance, in countries of the capitalist West more or less taken for granted that a correlation exists between the number of children and women's employment; there is a strong argument for regarding the latter as having greatly influenced the decline of the birth rate. This argument can, however, not be substantiated by data from socialist Eastern Europe. Already in the mid-twenties women's employment in the Soviet Union was at a level which was reached only in the sixties by a number of Western countries (e.g. the Netherlands and Italy). Nonetheless, the birth rate in the Soviet Union and other socialist countries (excepting the GDR) during this whole period has been higher than in the Western countries - even today when almost all women in the socialist countries are gainfully employed.

This is only one example among others which tells us that although certain trends in different countries seem to converge, their order and rapidity may have been at variance (cf. Garnsey, 1982; Konrad and Szelenyi, 1977). Different historical experiences are therefore part of Europe's heterogeneity and must be taken into account in any comparative analysis. In this respect it is worth remembering Scheuch's warning that 'similar indicators in different countries may be interpreted as functionally different and different indicators as functionally equivalent' (Scheuch, 1969, p. 173).

Acknowledging that all European countries are industrialised, the foregoing considerations would induce comparativists to make an analytical division of countries into those with an industrialisation process of long duration, and those with one which has lasted for a relatively short time. Studies during recent years of life-histories have proved the importance of differential life-experiences, and there is good reason to suspect the pace of change as having a deep impact on family life patterns.

Many critics of civilisation have been concerned as to whether the family could catch up with other societal changes; others, however, have seen the family as part and parcel of all these changes.

Goode (1963, pp. 22 ff.), for instance, regards the conjugal family as having been conducive to the development of a modern industrial system. On the other side, Hobsbawm (1975, p. 239) observes for a period as early as the mid-nineteenth century that 'the crucial point is that the structure of the bourgeois family flatly contradicted that of bourgeois society. Within it freedom, opportunity, the cash nexus and the pursuit of individual profit did not rule'. Parsons (1949, p. 187), finally, appears to be worried about the autonomy of the family when he states that since the family structure and sex roles are of 'crucial functional significance to the motivational economy of the occupational system', 'the family cannot be left uncontrolled and must in some fashion be integrated with the instrumental system'.

No doubt, it is extremely difficult to measure the extent to which the family has itself been an agent of change or to the extent to which it has been the victim of other societal changes. Has it been changing at the same rate as the rest of society, or has it relatively speaking been a stable element in processes of centrifugal forces? One which has been more reactive and adaptive than initiative?

No immediate clue appears on the horizon to answer these questions. The comparativist might resort to factors like family ideologies and their influence on family policies. Distinctions could possibly be made between countries with different approaches to a family policy (remembering that no family policy is also a family policy!).

Context and comparison

I have been discussing how to characterise our 'instance' so as to delineate parameters measurable or interpretable along certain dimensions. However, intra-country differences sometimes raise unsurmountable problems in cross-national comparative research.

It is true that in some countries differences are so large that even a national study may be difficult to undertake. Italy is one case. It is well known that the general level of development in southern Italy is much lower than in the northern part of the country. And in another country of our study, the Soviet Union, differences are in almost every respect very huge indeed. Think of, for instance, family life patterns in Soviet Central Asia - a Muslim area with families that on average have between five and seven children - compared with, for instance, the Baltic parts of the same country.

The general problem is: what can be done from a comparative perspective if intra-country differences are greater than the inter-country differences? In this case, one might initially suggest giving up 'country' as the prime determining factor, but this would probably be premature. What this situation tells us is that other forces are in play than those which we believed were the main determinants of our phenomenon. To discover this is already a useful insight to be exploited in further national or comparative studies. It is one thing to become attentive to the fact that family life in the Soviet Union is very varied, quite another to conclude from that knowledge that socialism did not have a noticeable impact on family life in Soviet Central Asia (or in Transcaucasia for that matter if we want to stay in Europe). Or in other words: it is important to sort out or become aware of what are the common influences in a particular country on the problem in question.

The complexities of the world are hardly surprising for any social scientist. They only have to be faced as they are found. From a methodological point of view the crucial thing is that in the different instances we have a *common problem*. As Marc Bloch has put it: the unity of place is only disorder; only the unity of the problem makes a centre.

This must be our point of departure. In the project on changes in family life patterns of families in Europe the common problem is formulated as one which hypothesises that family life patterns are the product of the interrelationships between family, gainful work and state intervention. In any of the countries involved in the project this problem is very complex and the national studies sought to consider as many factors as possible pertaining to it. At the national level high priority is given to peculiarities of time and place. This procedure is necessary and justified in a *specific context*. In comparative research the idea is of course not to ignore the context; it is, however, necessary to make conceptualisations which capture the quintessence of each of the cases. Therefore pre-knowledge is indispensable. But the conceptualisation must be 'guided' by the common problem, and not by the varied contexts, which - as Bloch indicates - in this connection are disturbing conditions. A too close look at the context will prevent us from making the necessary abstractions of our supra-units, independent variables and 'instances' without which no common concepts can be developed. And without common concepts describing parameters applicable to all cases, no comparison is possible.

It may be argued that the benefit of comparative research is primarily cognitive in the sense that it furthers the opportunity to make generalisations. On the other hand, we must never forget the final purpose of any science, namely to improve living conditions for ordinary people, or as it was said in our project proposal, 'to improve programmes and services for the family'. Comparative research cannot achieve this directly, since its abstract concepts are not immediately translatable to the specific contexts in each country. What it can do, however, is to 'teach' national researchers and practitioners which factors are more relevant than others, and thus enrich research and practice, and help to cure a short-sightedness which I think befalls all of us if not acquainted with systematic knowledge of other 'instances' (Qvortrup, 1984).

References

Bloch, M. (1967): 'A Contribution towards a Comparative History of European Societies'. In: M. Bloch: *Land and Work in Mediaeval Europe*. Routledge & Kegan Paul, London

Etzioni, A. (1968): *The Active Society*. The Free Press, New York

Feldmesser, R. (1960): published in: Black, C. (ed.): *The Transformation of Russian Society*. Cambridge Mass., Harward University Press

Garnsey, E. (1982): 'Capital Accumulation and the Division of Labour in the Soviet Union'. *Cambridge Journal of Economics*, No. 6, pp. 15-31

Goode, W. (1963): *World Revolutions and Family Patterns*. Free Press, New York

Hajnal, J. (1965): 'European Marriage Patterns in Perspective'. In: Glass, D.V. and Eversley, D.E.C. (eds): *Population in History*. London

Hobsbawm, E. (1975): *The Age of Capital*. Weidenfeld and Nicholson, London

Konrad, G. and Szelenyi, I. (1977): 'Social Conflicts of Underurbanization'. In: Harloe, M. (ed.): *Captive Cities*, Wiley and Sons, Chichester, pp. 157-173

Lasch, Ch. (1979): *Haven in a Heartless World*. Basic Books, New York

Mill, J.St. (1950): *Philosophy of Scientific Method*. Hafner, New York

Mokrzycki, E. (1979): 'On the Adequacy of Comparative Methodology'. In: Berting, J. et al. (eds): *Problems in International Comparative Research in the Social Sciences*. Pergamon Press, Oxford

Parsons, T. (1949): *The Social System*. Free Press, New York

Qvortrup, J. (1984): 'Is Comparative Research Basic or Applied Research?' Paper presented to the IVth International Training Seminar on Cross-National Comparative Research. Evitskog, Finland, June 15-20, 1984

Scheuch, E. (1969): 'Methodologische Probleme gesamtgesellschaftlicher Analysen'. In: Adorno, Th. (ed.): *Spätkapitalismus oder Industriegesellschaft?* Ferdinand Enke, Stuttgart

Smelser, N. and Lipset, S.M. (1966): *Social Structure and Mobility in Economic Development*. Chicago, Aldine

Weber, M. (1904-05): *Die protestantische Ethik und der Geist des Kapitalismus*. Archiv für Sozialwissenschaft und Sozialpolitik, XX-XXI, 1904-05

2

Theories and Ideologies of Family Functions, Gender Relations and Human Reproduction

Edmund Dahlström

Family functions

The functions of the family have been a controversial issue in both political ideologies and social science. The emergence and development of encompassing economic, political and cultural-ideological institutions implied a modification of family functions and a new division of labour and exchange between the family system and the encompassing institutions.

These changes of family functions generated opposite ideas of the future role of the family. The withering-away theory assumes a continuous decline and loss of family functions to encompassing institutions. The indispensability theory asserts that the family has indispensable contributions to offer that no other institution can provide and that the encompassing institutions can and should relieve and support the family but not substitute it. The controversy has both descriptive and normative aspects. There is disagreement both about the extent and character of family contributions and about the value of these contributions. There are reasons for alternative arrangements when the contributions are conceived as negative, whereas positive evaluation of family functions is an argument for maintaining them as well as for the existing family forms.

The disagreement about the family functions goes deeper. Some thinkers conceive the family as a passive recipient of economic and political changes and processes. Other thinkers believe that the family system is an active participant in the process of social-change (Berger and Berger, 1983).

Function here refers to objective consequences of a given pattern or institution for different parts or the totality of society. These consequences or contributions may be positive or negative with respect to given parts or wholes and given goals and values.

So both functions (positive contributions) and dysfunctions (negative contributions) need to be considered.

There is an ambiguity in the use of the term 'family functions'. A distinction should be made between the functions of a specific form of family and the functions of the family institution in general. Most theories of family functions concern the former, though the specific family form is often not satisfactorily defined: extended family, nuclear family, bourgeois family, authoritarian family, democratic family, socialist family, diversity model family, etc. Theories of family functions in general raise controversial issues of the universality of family and what non-family societies would look like (Bell and Vogel, 1960).

Functional analysis should be distinguished from functional sociology. Functional sociology of the post-war type has been inclined to focus on the positive contributions of the family and has disregarded dysfunctions (Nimkoff, 1965). Marxist, feminist and critical sociology have considered the dysfunctions of the family, e.g. the class-generating functions of the bourgeois family, the gender-exploitive functions of the patriarchal family and the prejudice-generating functions of the authoritarian family.

The notion of family forms and their specific functions have changed in the post-war period as will be discussed in this paper. Changes in family forms and their consequences have influenced political and scientific notions of family functions. There has been mutual influence between political and scientific ideas.

It is the intention of this paper to elucidate some of the conditions and reasons for changing notions about the family and its functions.

Ideologies of family functions and gender relations

The changing functions of the family and the gender relations have been differently viewed in the various dominant political ideologies. 'Ideology' is used here in the sense of a belief-system, whereas 'political' refers to political parties, interest-organizations and social movements. I shall discern four political ideologies, taking the view of family functions and gender relations as the main point of departure. I shall limit the exploration of political ideologies to three dominating ideologies in the democratic capitalist countries and the dominating ideology of the socialist countries.[1]

Conservative ideologies favour the maintenance of existing structures and order. In the post-war period the conservative-democratic ideology has been a proponent of a bourgeois-democratic society, private markets and electorate systems. The traditional family is seen as an indispensable institution in need of protection against state intervention and an expanding public sector. The freedom of markets and families is contrasted to state coercion and tutelage. The gender asymmetries of the traditional family are seen as functionally complementary and the positive aspects of gender peculiarity are emphasised. The conservative ideology questions radical gender equalisation and the support of mothers' gainful employment by means of collective service, e.g. day-nurseries; conservatism claims the importance of reproductive work in the families and that this should be appreciated and acknowledged by society.

The liberal-democratic ideology in its social-liberal form sees the free-market forces as the motor of societal development and recommends a balance of public policy and free-market processes. The traditional authoritarian family is conceived as an obstacle to progress and modernisation and the goal of gender equalisation by means of legislation and public policy is a central theme. Liberal-democratic ideology has been rather unclear about family functions now and in the future. The freedom of the family and markets have to be defended against collective encroachments.

The social-democratic ideology in its German and Nordic versions has maintained a reformistic strategy of the transformation of capitalistic society in stages: political democracy, social democracy with equalisation of living conditions between classes and economic democracy with increased public and popular control of the production system and an expansion of the public service sector. These societal changes are supposed to bring about changing family functions, family forms and gender equalisation. Gender equality is one of the main goals of social-democracy, and the transformation is seen as a condition for gender liberation ('gender liberation' is understood as the liberation of both women and men from the traditional roles that have been formed in the course of patriarchy). Social-democratic ideology has been rather unclear about family functions. It has been generally assumed that family functions will decline in the long run and the public sector will take over important family functions. However, the actual policy has been split between conflicting views about to what extent public policy should support family functions or substitute family through public-service arrangements.

These ideologies dominate the political scene in Northern and Western Europe at present but there have been and are other influential ideologies that were more important in the pre-war and middle-war period: conservative-authoritarian, fascistic, and different kinds of anarcho-democratic and populistic thoughts. The latter have influenced the present 'green' movement or 'third wave' with self-reliance theories (mentioned later). The left-socialist and Marxist thoughts have been influential especially after 1968 and will be presented in the form they have been forged in the East European socialist countries.

It is important to make a distinction between ideologies and programmes on one side and actual politics on the other. Capitalist democracies have often displayed compromises in family and gender policies. Family and gender policies cover policies in many fields that often have very mixed motives and can only indirectly (implicitly) be labelled as a family and gender policy.[2] A conservative government may support collective service arrangements to increase women's gainful employment in situations of insufficient labour force supply, while a socialist government may carry out a conservative family policy to accomplish certain short-run goals such as budget cuts.

The scientific thinking about family life in the post-war period, has been deeply rooted in political-ideological assumptions. There was a strong radical thrust after the Second World War in the capitalist countries, conceptualised in 'the democratic family'. The authoritarian family with father suppressing the wife and children was associated with fascism. The new democratic family was to be an egalitarian companionship with indulgent upbringing of children. Liberal-democratic and social-democratic intellectuals included gender equality, a kind of free form of socialisation and sexual liberation in the concept of the democratic family. The notion of declining family and kinship functions suited this picture. Some of the observations made in the US can also be found in Europe (Berger and Berger, 1983). There has been a negative evaluation of the family in its traditional sense and a rather unclear wishful thinking about the 'democratic family'.

The criticism of the authoritarian family was more founded on ideological presumptions than on scientific evidence (Lasch, 1977). The proletarianisation process had already stripped the father of his authority. Studies of fascism have not given evidence for the destructive role of the authoritarian family (Larsen, Hagtvet and Myklebust, 1980). The professional tutelage of the family was questioned in the seventies as was the late capitalistic state in general. There emerged a more positive view of the family as a resource of resistance against pressures from the market and the state.

There has been a corresponding change of view among Marxian intellectuals in capitalist countries and their notions of the family (Holter et al., 1975). There was a prevalent negative view of the family in the fifties and sixties, perceived as a source of exploitation. The privatisation of the family prohibited radical class struggle, class consciousness and made the wife dependent on the husband. A more positive picture of the family emerged in the seventies; the family should not be made responsible for the contradictions of capitalism and the proletarian family is a resource for the worker in his/her struggle against the hardships of capitalism.

'Socialist ideology' will be used in the sense of the dominating ideology of the Soviet Union and its allied socialist countries in Europe. Other terms have also been used to describe the same meaning for instance, state-socialist ideology and vanguard-democratic ideology. This ideology makes a strong distinction between socialism and capitalism and between the family structures in these different formations. It is generally assumed that the democratic family (socialist family) and gender equality presuppose a socialist transformation of society. The socialist transformation of society is a period of transition leading to communism.

The original socialist ideology as it was expressed by Karl Marx and Friedrich Engels and the early socialist parties in Germany, the Nordic countries and Eastern Europe assumed that the existing forms of the family under capitalism would disappear gradually and be replaced by a socialist family in a socialist society. The family form would be determined by the mode of production. Marx and Engels were cautious about predicting how things would turn out in a socialist society but some traits of the future family were obvious: the privacy of the bourgeois family would be transcended through public arrangements and women and men would participate in the expanding public life on equal conditions (Engels, 1884).

The socialist visions of the future emphasised the importance of public life. Women's drudgery and slavery in housework would be replaced by public-collective arrangements where men and women participated freely and symmetrically and love would in the future be liberated from restrictions and be based on free choice. There were very optimistic visions of how reproductive work of the family would be replaced by public work (Bebel, 1878). Notions of the withering-away theory may be found among the socialist classics. Family was infected by its association to bourgeois family.

The social policy (including family policy) of the Soviet Union focused in the first decade after the revolution on establishing gender equality and creating collective institutions for human reproduction, e.g. day-nurseries, educational systems, organisations in the workplaces and in residential areas for supporting the underprivileged and women. Many measures were taken to support the public participation of women in work and politics. There was an intensive discussion of the role of family and gender relations in the transitional period, e.g. concerning family and inheritance, the responsibility of parents in the upbringing of children and 'free' sexuality (Geiger, 1968; Chartschew and Golod, 1972). The actual policy and official ideology of the thirties implied that both the socialistic family and gender equalisation were given high priority.

The important role granted to the socialist family in the transitional period has been confirmed in the post-war discussion and actual politics. The family is supposed to grow stronger during the transition to communism and communism will lead 'to an increase in the role of the moral factor in family life' and will present 'the most complete development of family life' and 'stable monogamy'.[3] The indispensable role of the family in rearing the children has been stated by leading family experts (e.g. by Kharchev).

There has been a corresponding development of family and gender policy in the other socialist countries of Europe. During the first decade the urgent priority of family policy was to do away with the underprivileged status of women and the distorted family relations which had been directly inherited from fascism.[4] This policy included the protection of mothers and children and the promotion of women to help them to co-ordinate their professional work with duties in the family.

Some of the socialist countries showed a certain 'suppression of family policy': activities in the public sphere in politics and in the 'construction of socialism' were seen as more important, and existing families were perceived as the stronghold of private life and individualism. The 'retrograde' features of the traditional family gave reasons for such priorities. Mass education and propaganda stressed the image of the citizen as a member of collective work teams rather than as a member of the family. There was a change in these socialist countries at the end of the fifties. The private and the public sphere were seen as complementary rather than conflicting. The conclusion was that the family, its stability and well-being was extremely important for the individuals as for society as a whole. The family has partly replaced the work team in mass education and propaganda. Programmes directed to the family 'meet a warm response from the population'.

Today it is generally assumed that there is an objective agreement of interests in socialist societies between family and society (the state?).[5] It is also assumed that capitalism furthers antagonism in the family whereas socialism helps to overcome the inconsistencies.[6] Statements like these raise some interesting questions about the meaning of objective interests, conflicts and contradictions and how one can study these phenomena by comparative research.

Radical ideologies (socialist, social-democratic and liberal-democratic) are all for gender equalisation in the sense that men and women should share equally roles of participation in private and public areas, welfare and power. This does not principally exclude acknowledging gender particularities and for instance considerations of men's and women's different biological conditions and roles in reproduction. However, there was a period in the fifties and the sixties when radical ideology in capitalistic countries emphasised equality at the expense of feminine particularity; women had to show the same efficiency as men in the occupational and political fields, in spite of their double burden in the homes. There was a feministic reaction against this thinking in the seventies and eighties emphasising that this policy implied equalisation on the conditions of patriarchal capitalism and it demanded a more radical 'liberalisation' giving more room for feminine values and reproductive welfare (Liljeström, 1983b). The equalisation in the socialist countries gave more consideration to the particular requirements of gender roles in the reproductive process. The conservative-democratic view has paid more attention to gender particularities and taken them as a rationale for gender segregation without paying due interest to the effect of this for women's access to welfare, independence and power.

There is need to distinguish here between two concepts of gender equality: equality of sameness and equality of inter-dependence and balance (Sandy, 1982, p. 170). There exist gender peculiarities and asymmetries in the reproduction process that should reasonably come out in the overall division of labour. We find these asymmetries reflected and reinforced in the existing division of labour in the families. We need not require total sameness to accomplish overall equality. The main thing is that there is a balance and interdependence when considering all life-spheres and the total life course.

Family, everyday life and encompassing institutions

Sociological theories of modern societies usually differentiate three encompassing institutional sub-systems; the economic, the political and the cultural-ideological institutions. The market, the state and the Church of the nineteenth-century capitalist society illustrated these sub-systems. Institutions have been conceived of as regulating and controlling sub-systems, organised around basic societal and/or human needs and functions (International Encyclopedia, 1968; Hertzler, 1961).

The existing institutional framework should be related to the hierarchical structure of society with a centre and periphery, and ruling classes and subordinated classes. The economy forms the base for class structure and the state is an area for class struggle and tensions between the centre and the periphery.

These society-encompassing institutions may be contrasted to institutions of a more local character. It is common to discern the family-kinship institution as a universal institution. The family-kinship institution regulates the relations of descent and in-heritance, the gender relations, spouses and parent-children, and the sexual, reproductive and procreative functions. The family-kinship institution is an archaic and primordial institution that may be seen as the most original and universal of all institutions.

There is need to develop a broader concept covering all human relations on a local level, in contrast to the encompassing institutions.[7] This concept should include the totality of people's relations on the local level with the reproductive functions in the core, in contrast to the wider, political economic and cultural-ideological institutions built around the core in the centre. The term 'everyday society', or 'everyday life', is introduced with reference to this level. The family has been a basic unit in everyday life but not the only focus for it. To what extent the family unit dominates everyday life varies in different historically given societies. The workplace or other local collective arrangements have offered alternatives for the productive and reproductive functions of everyday life. Those who have been for the withering away of the family have conceived collective alternatives to the family. Everyday life cannot be treated as an independent system: there is no independent history of everyday life alone. We cannot understand and explain changes of everyday life in modern time without taking into account wider institutions, national history and relations with world society.

There has been an increased tendency among historians to deal with everyday life in historical processes.[8] Historical research has turned to a more theoretical and comparative approach during the last decades and macro-sociology has come closer to historical research. There are signs of a merger of comparative history and historical sociology (Abrams, 1982, pp. 301 ff.; Burke, 1980; Giddens, 1982, p. 165; Tilly, 1981, Ch. 1). This is the intellectual background for elaborating the concept of everyday life in this paper.

Political-evaluative considerations may give reasons for thinking about everyday life. Established political and economic institutions have set criteria for evaluations of social relations, processes and products in terms of economic growth, economic efficiency, income distribution, consumption and living standard, governmental control, parliamentary democracy, bureaucratic efficiency, etc. These societal goals have been criticised as too narrow and broader welfare considerations have been demanded to be elaborated, to include such values as 'love' (*Gemeinschaft*, social integration, social community, etc.) and 'being' (collective identification, self-realisation, autonomy and meaningfulness of life in contrast to alienation, reification, anomie and apathy (Allardt, 1975). The life-concept has been central to these elaborations of the welfare concept, that try to take into account the individual or collective totality of everyday life in terms of quality of life, ways of life, forms of life, life-style or patterns of life (Björnberg et al., 1980; Roos and Roos, 1977; Zetterberg, 1977).

Everyday life embraces elementary cyclical processes through which life is created and recreated. The word 'life' in 'everyday life' refers to something fundamental. Life has biological and ecological aspects that are interwoven with social and cultural patterns and meanings. The socio-biological reproduction goes from generation to generation, from one period of the life cycle to the other, from season to season and from day to day. Life comprises birth, growth and death, sexuality, procreation, nurturance of the small, sick and old, the struggle for health and survival, and the phases of the life-course. The words 'gender' and 'sex' have been proposed to emphasise the cultural and biological aspect of the same totality. Bio-social life and production work constitute the material basis of society.

New ideas about civilisation, society, history and future have provided reasons for interest in everyday life. They have questioned the overall political, economic and cultural institutions with their large-scale and hierarchical structure and proposed an alternative road with small-scale, less hierarchically organised institutions and with more local co-operative participation (Gorz, 1980; Toffler, 1980). The 'formal sector' of the state and the corporations is contrasted to the 'informal sector' of households, social networks and mutual-help organizations, small enterprises, voluntary co-operative arrangements and voluntary associations. This 'informal sector' is seen as a possible basis for a future development transcending large-scale industrialism and centralised state power (Ingelstam, 1980). The Third World has a more extensive 'informal sector' in the traditional subsistence economy. The strategy of self-reliance suggests a revitalising reinforcement of this sector, creating a larger degree of independence in relation to the core area of the capitalist world economy, thus reducing international dependency, exploitation and inequality (Friberg and Galtung, 1983, 1984; Hettne, 1982). Political ideas of self-reliance may be seen as new trends in political ideology, questioning conservative, liberal, social-democratic and socialist ideas (see below). Critical attitudes towards academic disciplines, towards intellectuals and professions have emerged in the recent decades (Illich, Foucault and Galtung) and the superiority of scientific knowledge and expert knowledge in relation to common sense has been questioned (Dahlström, 1987).

The functional importance of the family

The transfer of productive tasks from families to enterprise has generated some rather simplified notions of linear change and overall declining functions of the family (Elder, 1981). The expansion of intermediate institutions has not stripped the family of its functions. The overall institutions are rather relieving the families of certain functions and sharing its functions than substituting the family. The serving institutions are dependent upon activities that go on in the family. The bureaucratic service institutions cannot provide the primary-group functions of the family. The service society has not radically reduced the reproductive subsistence work of the family; on the contrary, there has been an increase of do-it-yourself activities in the homes (Gershuny, 1978; Liljeström and Dahlström, 1981, pp. 177 ff).

Studies in several 'modern' capitalist countries show that kinship ties are both extensive and intensive in people's lives (Gaunt, 1983, pp. 267 ff; Litwak, 1965, p. 190; Sussmann, 1970). The term 'modified extended family' has been suggested for the network and community between nuclear family related members (grandparents-parents-grandchildren).

The national reports of the present research all bear witness to the importance of families and kinship relations with respect to reproduction and no evidence is given for declining functions.[9] There are differences between socialist and capitalist countries, e.g. with respect to the proportion of women in paid employment. But this does not greatly affect the importance of family functions. The increase in women's wage work does not reduce the reproductive functions of the family. The expansion of service facilities in the seventies relieved the reproductive work of families but did not substitute it.

Some of the national reports from Western countries (Netherlands, Sweden, Finland and Norway) present changes in public opinion from a strongly pro-nuclear-family view of life and society in the fifties and sixties when there was a strong marriage and birth boom, to a more balanced and partly critical view on family life in society in the seventies and eighties when marriage and birth rates declined somewhat and employment rates of married women increased. The opinion changes concerned more the form than the functions of the family, giving more support to the dual-career- family form (with two or more breadwinners) or to the diversity model of the family. The importance of family

41

functions and the value of family life in general was not seriously questioned.

The ideological discussion has often contrasted the privacy of family life in relation to the public life outside the home and raised the question of whether there is a trend towards more or less privatisation. The Finnish report questions this way of approach. The authors find two main tendencies in the new life pattern that are opposite to a great extent. On the one hand, they notice a tendency of socialisation of many activities through the state apparatus and private capital; on the other, they find the tendency of 'privatisation, i.e. many phenomena connected with marriage have become more and more private and are no longer so much controlled by the authorities'.[10] This challenging observation questions basic concepts of ideology and social science and calls for further elaboration.

It is sometimes stated that the family institution is passive, adaptive and 'lagging behind' in the societal processes of change. This notion needs to be questioned. It neglects the important functions of subsistence reproduction; the expansion of capitalism required a viable family system. The bourgeois family was an active component in the transformation process that generated mature capitalism (Berger and Berger, 1983, Ch. 4). The nuclear family preceded capitalism and facilitated its growth. The family system should be seen both as an agent and as an outcome of larger change.

Some socialist thinkers have conceived family relations as directly determined by economic relations. This view has been criticised by a leading Soviet sociologist, Kharchev: 'The complexity of the mutual link of marital-family relations with social life has as its consequence the relative independence of the development of marriage and the family in respect to changes in the economic base of society'.[11]

The notion that the nuclear family was created by capitalist industrialism because this fitted best to industrialism as well as the notion that the nuclear family was preceded by an extended family with many cohabiting generations need modification. This theory has not been confirmed by several studies in the Western part of Europe. The nuclear family was a common pattern far back in the Middle Ages in England, France, Austria, and Scandinavia (Flandrin, 1979; Gaunt, 1983, pp. 186 ff; Laslett, 1972; Mitterauer and Sieder, 1982).

It seems important to acknowledge the complexity of the family change processes and avoid polemic simplifications. This applies to some recent challenging theories of the 'social construction' and 'invention' of certain family-patterns in modern times; they need to be elaborated and in some points modified: childhood, sexuality, love, etc., were given new meanings in modern times as has been argued by Ariès (1979), Foucault (1979), Shorter (1976), Stone (1979) and Mount (1984) but the theory of 'invention' or 'construction' tends to exaggerate the significance of these changes.

Contradictions of family life today

The continued importance of the family-household system in its subsistence-reproduction function gives a false impression of survival and stability of traditional and primordial patterns. The family bears the stamp of being a subsistent reproduction system for the overall capitalist institutions (Wallerstein, Martin and Dickinson, 1982). The forms of the family have radically changed from a nuclear family model of the pre-war period to a diversified model of today.[12] Family life is also characterised by contradictions that have changed in content and proportion.

The family system of late capitalism is characterised by four basic contradictions. Two of these have their roots in the incompatible requirements of the overall institutions in relation to the demands of human reproduction of families.

1. The organisation of production and industrial society has been mainly determined by interests in capital accumulation and the reproductive subsistence system has had to adjust itself to these conditions. We all know the high 'social costs' of the reproduction of wage-earners when married women and children had to work for wages in early industrialism. The reproductive resources increased with rising real incomes and public welfare measures, but the organisation of everyday 'time-space' is still primarily determined by the interests of capital. Today this appears as difficulties of combining parenthood with gainful employment.

2. The contradiction between production and reproduction is also found in the contrast between bureaucratic culture and primary-group culture. This has been conceptualised by sociologists in the patterned variables: universalism versus particularism, specificity versus diffuseness, affective neutrality

versus affectivity, and achievement versus ascription (Holter, 1970, Ch. 2). The culture of production and market stands for subordination, interchangeability, anonymous standardisation, measurable results, payment for performance per unit of measurable time, competition, mobility, future uncertainty, compartmentalisation of work, human values dependent on payment and self-interest of man (Liljeström, 1981; 1982). The culture of reproduction on the other hand stands for personal involvement without pay, little interchangeability, self-managed personal and intimate relations, immeasurable results, unpaid work with low status, cyclical perception of the life process, priority to the weak and those who need help, co-ordination of needs, interlocking tasks, a future resting on inner loyalty, and work, the value of which cannot be quantified, based on moral and ideological incentives.

Political-ideological institutions have been eager to control and regulate forms and functions of everyday life and the family, and people have resisted these attempts. In order to acquire land the Catholic Church forbade marriage between close kin, and the adoption or legitimation of illegitimate children (Goody, 1983). The priest and the doctor have had important institutional roles in 'the policing of families' (Donzolet, 1979). Maternal welfare has been a hidden cover for an extensive public regulation of motherhood for nationalistic and sometimes even racist purposes (Lewis, 1980).

The family policy that emerged in the inter-war period in Europe was motivated by different objectives. Conservative forces referred to political-national goals relating to population and labour market as a reason for family policy while radical forces emphasised gender equality, distributive justice (between families with and those without children) and general quality-of-life considerations (Kammermann and Kahn, 1978, pp. 476-603). Nationalistic opinions saw the family as a vehicle for external goals and emphasised quantitative population and labour-force goals while radical opinions were inclined to take family welfare as an end in itself and point to qualitative problems concerning the children's health and care, the mothers' situation, the need of different kinds of services, better housing conditions, maternal care, etc. (Myrdal, 1944). But, in spite of benevolent goals, the measures of family policy have implied control and policing of families and the families have become subordinated to professional groups, that put 'public interest' in front of the 'particular' interest of human reproduction.

3. The third contradiction of the family system has a more internal character in the sense that it is an unintended consequence of what people strive to accomplish rather than enforced by market processes or political pressure. The increased freedom of conjugal choice (marriage partner or cohabiting partner) contradicts requirements of those growing up who need stability in parenthood and simplicity in family relations. The contradiction is tied to well-known changes in family life: a more hedonistic view of marriage and love, marriage seen as a contract, 'contraceptive revolution' and birth control, premarital and experimenting sexuality, higher instability in cohabitive relations, decreasing fertility, changing family and life-course patterns with shorter child-caring periods, women as permanent bread-winners, legal gender-symmetry patterns, etc.

The contradiction has its roots in two basic elements of the nuclear family: the husband-wife relation and the parent-child relation; and the married couple functions as the cement between the generations (Liljeström, 1984). However, high death rates made this arrangement unstable in earlier times. The dominant instability of cohabiting and high divorce rates have transferred the linking of generations to single parents. The single parent is usually the mother, which means a new type of matrilinearity. This takes us to the fourth contradiction of family life, that is linked to gender.

4. The fourth contradiction of everyday life and family has its roots in the patriarchal heritage and ideals of gender equalisation and gender liberation of the enlightenment, liberalism and socialism. The patriarchal heritage contained a paternal order, regulating marriage, kinship and sexuality and a master's rule with power over household members and domestic work. Capitalist industrialism transformed the personal rule of the father-master to the impersonal male rule, resting on markets and politics and beliefs in technological and scientific progress (Dahlström and Liljeström, 1981, 1982). Men dominate public life while women take care of most reproductive work in the private households. Women's main 'responsibility' for the reproductive work is a serious restraint for them in competing on the economic and political markets. Men tend to join in exclusive practices to maintain the impersonal male dominance.

The issue of gender liberation is broader than gender equalisation. Equalisation concerns the distribution within the existing structure, i.e. a structure marked by male rule. Male rule implies the suppression of female values of human reproduction, procreation, care and love. Women's liberation implies realisation of feminine values of human reproduction and life.

Gender relations are rooted in archaic relations of father, mother, son and daughter and are continuously reproduced in the socialisation process. Our notions of gender and sex are thus formed during pre-verbal and pre-rational periods of our lives. This gives a deep and irrational meaning to gender and sex; gender and sex are thus tied to the creation of our Person and Self. The asymmetric gender structure of the socialisation process reproduces basic emotional tensions between men and women that will have negative effects upon their later marital and erotic relations. The asymmetry of father- and motherhood lays the foundation for the 'erotic war' between men and women and thus for a human malaise (Dinnerstein, 1976; Chodorow, 1979; Liljeström, 1983a).

The national reports of the project 'Changes in the Life Patterns of Families in Europe' give rather uneven evidence of the contradictory relations of family. Interpretations of contradictions are tied to assumptions of values, interests and power. To what extent a scientific elucidation will discern relations of conflict and contradiction is dependent upon the critical stance of the scientist. However, there are some general observations in the project reports that confirm some of the above-mentioned contradictions.

1. There exist conflicting demands of family (reproduction) and work (production) in all countries. The increase of public and private services has not been able to satisfy the needs of the reproductive functions of the families. New tasks and burdens have arisen. The socialist countries have developed a broader public service system. To what extent the more efficient private service system in the capitalist countries compensates this is difficult to judge.
2. Women's position has been considerably strengthened in the post-war period and implied a radical change in many respects, e.g. with respect to civil rights, different legal protections, increased resources, opening of new fields, increased participation in many fields, extended service facilities, etc.
3. The routine household work has remained the main responsibility of the women though there has been a trend

towards its more symmetric division. This responsibility of women in the home hampers her in the competition on the labour market, in the workplace and in politics.

4. There is a trend towards higher instability in family relations in all countries and the pattern of 'cohabitation' is spreading. The increasing instability seems to be a concern in all countries.

The possible contradictions between family and public interests are not considered in some reports. It is generally assumed that increased public service and control is only to the benefit of families; some reports, however, raise some critical thoughts about this public control and this reflects differences in political-ideological presumptions.

Notes

1. I made an analysis of family and gender ideologies in the beginning of the sixties and I discerned there moderate, radical-liberal and radical-socialist views (Dahlström, 1967). Recently I have worked with a simple ideal-type kind of typology of political ideologies: social democratic, liberal democratic and vanguard-democratic (East-socialist) ideologies. This ideological analysis concerned the organisation of the production process. There is hardly any difference in Sweden between conservatives and liberals in this issue. There are, however, differences between conservatives and liberals in family and gender issues, so I have extended the typology in this paper, including a conservative-democratic variant (Dahlström 1983).

2. Kammermann and Kahn (1978) suggest a distinction between explicit and implicit family policies. It is mainly in the post-war period that there has been an explicit family policy in the capitalist democracies.

3. See e.g. Geiger, 1968, p. 114. References must be made to several important works by A.G. Kharchev (1959, 1963, 1964, 1969); see also Kozyrev (1969) and Kharchev's mimeographed paper to the Vienna Centre project 'Changes in the Life Patterns of Families in Europe': Changes in the Family Pattern in the USSR.

4. For the family and gender policy in the other socialist countries see e.g.: *Zur Gesellschaftlichen Stellung der Frau.* Verlag für die Frau, Leipzig, DDR, 1978. See also Ferge's chapter on Hungary and Sokolowska's chapter on Poland, both in *Family Policy, Government and Families in Fourteen Countries*, published by Columbia University Press, New York in 1978. Cf., too, the national reports from Hungary by Sas, from Poland by Kurzynowski and from the German Democratic Republic by Gysi and Speigner in the Vienna Centre project 'Changes in the Life Patterns of Families in Europe'.

5. See p. 11 of Gysi's and Speigner's national report from the German Democratic Republic in the Vienna Centre project 'Changes in the Life Patterns of Families in Europe'.

Edmund Dahlström

6. See p. 5 of Kharchev's mimeographed paper for the Vienna Centre project 'Changes in the Life Patterns of Families in Europe': Changes in Family Patterns in the USSR.

7. I have made an exploration of everyday-life notions in a paper 'Everyday-life theories and their historical and ideological contexts' published in Himmelstrand, U. (ed.): *The Multi-paradigmatic Trend in Sociology*. Acta Sociologica Uppsaliensis, 1987.

8. Everyday life has become a usual word in historical monographs in the last five decades. See, e.g. Braudel (1979), Carcopino (1939), Daniel-Rops (1961), Willets (1969).

9. See K. Boh's mimeographed paper 'New Trends and Changes of Family Patterns in 12 European Countries' written for the Vienna Centre project 'Changes in the Life Patterns of Families in Europe'.

10. See E. Haavio-Mannila's and R. Jallinoja's national report on Finland written for the Vienna Centre project 'Changes in the Life Patterns of Families in Europe'.

11. Reference is made by Geiger (1968, p. 114) to p. 37 of Kharchev's (1959) work.

12. See Rhona Rapoport's chapter 'Ideologies about Family Forms: Towards Diversity' in the present volume.

References

Abrams, P. (1982): *Historical Sociology*. Open Books

Allardt, E. (1975): *Att ha, att älska, att vgara. Om välfärd i Norden* (To have, to love, to be. About welfare in the Nordic countries). Argos, Lund

Ariès, P. (1979): *Centuries of Childhood*. Pelegrine, London

Bebel, A. (1878): *Die Frau und der Sozialismus*

Bell, N.W. and Vogel, E.F.A. (eds) (1960): *Modern Introduction to the Family*. The Free Press of Glencoe, Illinois, Ch. 1, 5 and 6

Berger, R. and Berger, P.L. (1983): *The War over the Family*. Hutchinson, London

Björnberg, U., Bäck-Wiklund, M., Lindfors, H., Nilsson, A. and Rundblad, B. (1980): *Livsformer i en region* (Life-forms in a region). Gotab, Kungälv

Braudel, F. (1979): *Les Structures du quotidien. Le possible et L'impossible*. Librairie Armand Coli, Paris

Burke, P. (1980): *Sociology and History*. George Allen & Unwin, London

Carcopino, C. (1939): *La vie quotidienne à Rome à l'apogée de l'Empire*. Librairie Hachette, Paris

Chartschew, A.G. and Golod, S.I. (1972): *Berufstätige Frau und Familie*. Dietz Verlag, Berlin

Chodorow, N. (1979): *The Reproduction of Mothering. Psycho-analysis and the Sociology of Gender*. University of California Press, Berkeley

Dahlström, E. (1967): 'Analysis of the Debate on Sex Roles'. In: Dahlström, E. and Liljeström, R.: *The Changing Roles of Men and Women*. Gerald Duckworth Co. Ltd., London

Dahlström, E. (1983): *Bestämmande i arbete. Några idékritiska funderingar kring arbetslivets demokratisering* (Control of work. Some critical reflections on democratisation of working life). Sociologiska institutionen, Göteborgs universitet

Theories and Ideologies

Dahlström, E. (1987): 'Popular Beliefs and the Intellectual Power of Dominant Ideas. A Conceptual Analysis'. In: Eierman, R. (ed.): *Intellectuals, University and the State*. University Press of California

Dahlström, E. and Liljeström, R. (1981): 'Det patriarkala arvet' (The patriarchal heritage). *Sociologisk forskning*, 1981/2

Dahlström, E. and Liljeström, R. (1982): *Working-Class Women and Human Reproduction*. Department of Sociology, University of Gothenburg

Daniel-Rops, A. (1961): *La Vie quotidienne en Palestine au temps du Jésus*. Librairie Hachette

Dinnerstein, D. (1976): *The Mermaid and the Minotaur: Sexual Arrangements and Human Malaise*. Harper & Row, New York

Donzolet, J. (1979): *The Policing of Families*. Pantheon Books, New York

Elder, H. (1981): 'History and the Family. The Discovery of Complexity'. *Journal of Marriage and Family*, August 1981, pp. 489-519

Engels, F. (1884): *Der Ursprung der Familie, des Privateigentums und des Staates*. Im Anschluß an Lewis Morgans Forschungen. MEW Bd. 21

Flandrin, J.L. (1979): *Families in Former Time, Kinship Household and Sexuality*. Cambridge University Press, Cambridge

Foucault, M. (1979): *The History of Sexuality*. Allen Lane, London

Friberg, M. and Galtung, J. (1983): *Krisen* (The crisis). Förlaget Akademilitteratur AB, Stockholm

Friberg, M. and Galtung, J. (1984): *Rörelserna* (The movements). Förlaget Akademilitteratur

Gaunt, D.L. (1983): *Familjeliv i Norden* (Family life in the Nordic countries). Gidlunds, Malmö

Geiger, K. (1968): *The Family in the Soviet Union*. Harvard University Press, Cambridge Mass., Ch. 3

Gershuny, J. (1978): *After Industrial Society. The Emerging Selfservice Economy*. Humanitarian Press, New Jersey

Giddens, A. (1982): *Sociology. A Brief but Critical Introduction*. Macmillan, London

Goody, J. (1983): *The Development of the Family and Marriage in Europe*. Cambridge University Press, Cambridge

Gorz, A. (1980): *Adieux au proletariat au de la du socialism*. Edition Galilée, Paris

Hertzler, J. (1961): *American Social Institutions. A Sociological Analysis*. Allyn and Bacon, Boston

Hettne, B. (1982): *Development Theory and the Third World*. SAREC Report R2

Holter, H. (1970): *Sex Roles and Social Structure*. Universitetsforlaget, Oslo

Holter, H., Ve, H., Gjertsen, A. and Hjort, H. (1975): *Familien i klassesamfunnet* (Family in class society). Pax forlag A/S, Oslo

Ingelstam, L. (1980): *Arbetets värde och tidens bruk - en framtidsstudie* (The value of work and the use of time - a futuristic study). Liber förlag, Stockholm

International Encyclopedia of Social Sciences. Macmillan and the Free Press, New York, 1968, pp. 409-429

Kammermann, S.B. and Kahn, A.J. (eds) (1978): *Family Policy. Government and Families in Fourteen Countries*. Columbia University Press, New York

Kharchev, A.G. (1959): *Marksizm-Leninizm o brake i Semia* (Marxism-Leninism on marriage and family). Moscow

Kharchev, A.G. (1963): 'O roli semi v kommunisticheskom vospotanii' (The role of the family in communist education). In: *Sov. Ped.*, No. 5

Edmund Dahlström

Kharchev, A.G. (1964): *Brak i semia v SSSR* (Marriage and family in the USSR).
Moscow

Kharchev, A.G. (1969): 'Marriage Motivation Studies'. In: *Town, Country and People. Studies in Soviet Society.* Tavistock Publications, London

Kozyrev, J. (1969): 'The Family and Family Relations'. In: *Town, Country and People. Studies in Soviet Society.* Tavistock Publications, London

Larsen, S.U., Hagtvet, B. and Myklebust, J.P. (eds) (1980): *Who Were the Fascists - Social Roots of European Fascism.* Universitetsforlaget, Oslo; see especially the papers by Bernt Hagtvet and Reinhard Kuhnl

Lasch, C. (1977): *Haven in a Heartless World.* Basic Books, New York

Laslett, P. (1972): 'Mean Household Size in England since the Sixteenth Century'. In: Laslett, P. and Watt, R. (eds): *Household and Family in Past Time.* University Press

Lewis, J. (1980): *The Politics of Motherhood, Child and Maternal Welfare in England 1900-1939.* McGill-Queens University Press, Montreal

Liljeström, R. (1981): 'Time Aspects of Production and Reproduction'. In: Gardell, B. and Johansson, G.: *Working Life. A Social Science Contribution to Work Reform.* John Wiley & Sons, New York

Liljeström, R. (1982): 'Planning and Organizing Alternatives Stemming from the Sphere of Reproduction'. *Acta Sociologica,* 1982 (25), pp. 47-55

Liljeström, R. (1983a): *Det erotiska kriget* (The erotic war). Liber förlag, Stockholm

Liljeström, R. (1983b): 'Kan vi förena likhet och särart?' (Can we unite equality and particularity?). In: *Rapport från kvinnouniversitet. Vetenskap, patriarkat och makt* (Report from the women's university. Science, patriarchy and power). Förlaget akademilitteratur AB, Stockholm

Liljeström, R. (1984): 'Paret som kitt mellan generationer' (The couple as cement between the generations). In: Anderson, B.E. (ed.): *Familjebilder* (Family pictures). Studieförbundet, Näringsliv och Samhälle. Stockholm

Liljeström, R. and Dahlström, E. (1981): *Arbetarkvinnor* (Working class women). Tiden förlag, Stockholm

Litwak, E. (1965): 'Extended Kin Relations in an Industrial Democracy'. In: Shanas, E. and Streib, G.S. (eds): *Social Structure and the Family.* Prentice Hall, London

Mitterauer, M. and Sieder, R. (1982): *The European Family.* Basil Blackwell, Oxford

Mount, F. (1984): *Den samhällsfarliga familjen* (The subversive family). PA Norstedt och Söners Förlag, Stockholm

Myrdal, A. (1944): *Folk och familj* (Nation and family). Kooperativa förbundets bokförlag, Stockholm

Nimkoff, M.F. (ed.) (1965): *Comparative Family Systems.* Houghton Mifflin Company, Boston, Ch. 1

Roos, B. and Roos, J.P. (1977): *Välfärdsforskning och levnadssättsforskning* (Welfare research and way-of-life research). Sociologisk forskning

Sandy, P.R. (1982): *Female Power and Male Dominance. On the Origin of Sexual Inequality.* Cambridge University Press, Cambridge

Shorter, E. (1976): *The Making of the Modern Family.* Fontana Collins

Stone, L. (1979): *The Family, Sex and Marriage in England 1500-1800.* Penguin Books, Harmondsworth

Theories and Ideologies

Sussmann, M.B. (1970): 'The Urban Kin Network in the Formation of Family Theory'. In: Hill, R. and König, R. (eds): *Families East and West*. Mouton, Paris

Tilly, C. (1981): *As Sociology Meets History*. Academic Press, New York

Toffler, A. (1980): *The Third Wave*. William Morrow, New York

Wallerstein, I., Martin, W.G. and Dickinson, T. (1982): 'Household Structure and Production Process - Preliminary Thesis and Findings'. *Review* (Sage), Winter 1982, pp. 437-458

Willets, R.F. (1969): *Everyday Life in Ancient Crete*. Batsford, London

Zetterberg, H. (1977): *Arbete, Livsstil och motivation* (Work, lifestyle and motivation). Svenska arbetsgivareföreningen, Stockholm

3

Ideologies about Family Forms: Towards Diversity

Rhona Rapoport

Level of ideology regarding family forms

The term 'ideology' refers here to a relatively explicit and systematically organised set of ideas held with conviction. Ideologies occur in various spheres of life, e.g. in the economy, politics, religion, gender-roles, child-rearing and family life. They operate at different levels, from the macroscopic level of national or international policy (as with ideologies of capitalism, comunism, and other 'isms) down to individual systems of ideas according to which each person develops more or less systematic views on how to cope with issues of daily life. In between, there is an intermediate range of encompassing organisations, professions, and social institutions, which function in different substantive areas within a common culture.

Focus of the chapter

The focus of this chapter is on ideologies about *family forms*. Although West and East European countries conceptualise the issues of family forms differently and neither began by espousing diversity, it is toward a recognition of diversity that both sets of countries are converging. This point is emphasised in the chapter by Katja Boh.

Each country in both Eastern and Western Europe has always had diverse ideologies and forms. However, in each there has usually been a conception of the most valued, normative type of family form, associated partly with the particular culture and traditions of the country and partly with state ideology. In the West, the Parsonian (1942) concept of the ideal form of family life has been most influential under modern industrial conditions.

In this, basically the conventional division of labour is functional (with the male primarily oriented to 'instrumental' tasks outside the family and supporting the family through his participation in the labour force, and the female primarily oriented to internal 'affectional' tasks of home-making, child-rearing, and the provision of emotional support for the male). This structural-functional conceptualisation - reflecting and reinforcing traditional ideologies - has been criticised from a number of perspectives: Marxist, feminist, and 'critical' (cf. Dahlström's chapter in this volume). Within the structural-functional framework, the erosion of family functions has been considered, but primarily as a source of weakening the family as a social institution, rather than altering its form (cf. Ogburn, 1922).

Empirical research in Western European countries, generally conducted with a positivist orientation, has produced a conclusion which has not proved the traditional conceptions of gender differences. Though there are demonstrable differences between men and women, they are (a) overlapping rather than mutually exclusive on most variables not having directly to do with biological reproduction; and (b) they are increasingly irrelevant to the requirements of occupations in advanced industrial societies (Fogarty, Rapoport, R. and Rapoport, R.N., 1971). This evidence, taken together with the dominating value orientation of individual freedom of choice, has led to the situation, described below, of a pluralist conception of family forms (cf. Rapoport, R., Rapoport, R.N. and Strelitz, 1977).

In East European countries, where Marxist ideologies have provided the dominant value orientations, the criticism of the conventional model of the nuclear family stemmed from an idealist source, i.e. the social evolutionary orientation characteristic of nineteenth-century social philosophers. The assumption was that as a society moved from a capitalist to a socialist form of political and economic organisation, the family would evolve correspondingly. Engels (1902) contended that the monogamous form of nuclear family structure - far from being the highest form as the Victorian social philosophers had held - would give way to one no longer based on the private property concept. The specific form which the family would take under the new modes of socialist production was something that Marx and Engels were cautious about predicting. It was assumed that the existing form of the bourgeois family under capitalism would gradually disappear, and that some form of more public or communal life would emerge. However, the actual way how the family, like the state, would 'wither away' was not clearly formulated. What was clearly formulated as an ideal was a programme of guarantees of equality between men and women. This is perhaps best expressed in the Soviet constitution which in 1936 laid down that:

'Women in the USSR are accorded equal rights with men in all fields of economic, state, cultural and social life. The possibility of realizing these rights of women is ensured by affording women equally with men the right to work, payment for work, rest, social insurance, and education, state protection of the interests of the mother and child, granting pregnancy leave with pay, and the provision of a wide network of maternity homes, nurseries and kindergartens.' (Article 122)

In the USSR reformulations have led to a revision of earlier views and ideologies on the family. Results of empirical research suggested that the de-emphasis of the family unit was associated with a rise in juvenile delinquency, and in costly and damaging social problems, including divorce. This led to more positive orientation to the family as a social institution, though initially without any suggestion of a positive valuation of diversity other than in the ethnic forms of national minorities (cf. Karchev and Golod, 1971; Karchev, 1964).

Though the literature on family forms and associated ideologies is less voluminous in the Eastern European than in the Western countries, there is an impression that in both sets of countries there has been an increasing recognition of the existence of diversity, and that a new stance toward such diversity is appropriate.

The ideological shift in family forms may be likened to the demographic transition in the period of early industrialisation. Just as there was a discernible shift away from large extended family forms to the small nuclear family as the functional (if not residential) unit, a shift is under way from the exclusive recognition of a specific form of nuclear family to a more differentiated and pluralist conception. Diversity prevails and, being seen to prevail, is being normalised.

Rhona Rapoport

The content of diversity

There has always been diversity in family forms; rich and poor families, one-parent families as well as two-parent families, large and small families, and families with diverse extensions and connections. The actual extent of these elements of diversity in the past will never be known because the data available for a historical study of family forms are limited, however creatively they have been mined, e.g. in the study of parish records by Peter Laslett (1972) and his colleagues. The question remains whether or not diversity has increased over the centuries. We do know from census data now available that there has been a change in the *demography* and also the *structure* of households over the past few decades. We also know from modern research data, including attitude surveys, that there has been a change in family *norms*.

Demographic changes include the shift in the familiar variables of age, longevity, fertility and household composition, but also some new factors.

Structurally, there has been an increase in households which represent variants in relation to classical definitions of the family: single individual households, couples living together not married, single parents, gay couples, 'reconstituted' families containing children of earlier unions of one or more of the adult members, and so on. Correspondingly there has been a decrease in the proportion of conventional households. Let us take a British example: census data of 1981 show only about 40 per cent of households containing conventional families of mother, father and at least one child compared with 48 per cent in 1961. Comparing 1945 with 1980 the data show that while the total number of households has increased by about one third, those representing conventional married couple families increased by only 10 per cent. The variant forms of household have increased much more sharply: single-parent female-headed households have increased by nearly 50 per cent, from 8.3 per cent of the households with children in 1971 to 12.1 per cent in 1980.

In general, the papers in this volume show that where we have trend statistics, there has been a demonstrable decrease in the proportions of households representing the classic nuclear family pattern - mother, father and at least one child. In Finland, this type of household decreased from 63.8 per cent in 1950 to 60 per cent in 1980; in Norway from 68.6 per cent to 60.1 per cent; in Sweden from 52.4 per cent to 42.6 per cent; in the GDR from 56.7 per cent in 1957 to 48.7 per cent in 1977; in Poland from 87.3 per cent in 1970 to 85.8 per cent in 1980.

This pattern transcends the major ideological regions, relating more to urbanisation/modernisation and the associated norms and laws relating to sexual relations, marriage and divorce (cf. Riitta Jallinoja's chapter in this volume; see also Cseh-Szombathy et al. 1985).

In addition to the basic demographic picture of family households there is diversity of structures as reflected in the roles taken by household members. Looking at *activity in the economy*, we have seen a massive trend in the past four or five decades in the proportion of married women in the labour force all over Europe. Some are disappointed that women still do not enjoy full equality with men in positions of power and responsibility in either East European or West European settings. However, there is no doubt that women have entered the labour force in greater numbers and for a wider range of occupations and a longer span in their life-course than at any other time since the Industrial Revolution. This affects the family structure in producing, on a widespread basis, a category of households with two rather than one economic provider.

Research on the changing roles of men and women has revealed a range of new family forms (cf. Fogarty, Rapoport, R. and Rapoport, R.N., 1971; Mitchell and Oakley, 1976; Dahlström, 1967). The term 'dual-career families', originated in Britain (Rapoport, R. and Rapoport, R.N., 1969, 1971, 1976, 1980), has become widely used. Gowler and Legge (1982) review the broad field of research on dual-worker families in Britain. As noted above, the ideologies associated with the statistical trends differ from East to West Europe. The emphasis on dual-working couples in the USSR has been on their contribution to the economy and on the liberation of women from domestic drudgery and exploitation. In Western European countries, most notably the Scandinavian countries, the emphasis has been on 'equality' between the sexes. In the UK there has evolved an emphasis on the diversity of individual motives and rewards (even within this family form) and a distinction is made between 'equity' and equality (Rapoport and Rapoport, 1975).

Dual-career families tend to be motivated by a mixture of idealism and the wish for self-realisation, but there is usually an economic motive as well, even where a second income is not essential to support the family. Dual-worker families lower on the occupational scale characteristically give primacy to economic reasons for going out to work. More recently it has been recognised that there are important non-economic motives, even where the wife's work is considered essential to maintain a standard of living. Even in unskilled jobs women also work for sociability and self-esteem. The relative lack of communication and confidantes in the domestic environment of working class women has been shown to be stressed (Gavron, 1966; Brown and Harris, 1978) and working outside the home can help.

In general the impression is that women can now admit the same range or mixture of motives for work as men. In the present volume, Cernigoj-Sadar's summary of responses on motives from seven countries shows this as a conspicuous finding. Both sets of motives are usually found. The type of motivation is seen to be a function of the country and its culture, rather than the gender of the respondent. In Slovenia all motives are rated high; in Poland all low; in Sweden, financial reasons are low for both men and women, and psycho-social ones high for both; and in Hungary the pattern is reversed, with financial reasons high for both and psycho-social reasons low for both - but particularly for women. This seems partly related to modernisation, as Jallinoja indicates, and partly to national characteristics; both Sweden and Hungary, for example, are rated among the 'modern' countries - having a high proportion of women in employment outside agriculture and a high divorce rate.

Within the broad category of dual-worker families, a distinction is relevant between full-time and part-time dual-worker households. The idea of part-time work for both husbands and wives was propounded early in the Scandinavian countries (Gronseth, 1975). Now there are in fact a variety of patterns of dual-employment households as far as the time dimension is concerned. This reflects labour market pressures and opportunities in relation to changing sex roles. There is now wide acceptance in both East and West European countries that married women are legitimately oriented to working outside the home. The differences are of emphasis - as to what sort of job, how long working hours and for what time periods in a woman's life the work should be.

Along with the trend toward more equal participation in the economy, another important element of structural change stems from the increase in the *divorce rate* (cf. Chester, 1977). The highest divorce rates in Europe are found in the USSR, Hungary, and Denmark, with the United Kingdom, Sweden, East Germany and Austria not far behind. In Britain the projection is that by the year 2000 one marriage in four can be expected to dissolve before one of the partners dies. In the higher divorce rate countries, like the USSR, it could be one in two.

This increase in divorce is associated with a *shift in norms*. Seen against the background of the traditional family norms, the rising trends in unorthodox households, in working mothers and in divorce tend to be seen as disastrous, indicating the erosion of the family institution.

But Arlene and Jerome Skolnick (1974, pp. 7-8) question the main assumptions underlying the traditional (Parsonian) model of the nuclear family. They summarise them as follows:

1. The nuclear family - a man, a woman, and their children - is universally found in every human society, past, present and future.
2. The nuclear family is the foundation of society, the key institution guaranteeing the survival and stability of the whole society.
3. The nuclear family is the building block, or elementary unit of society. Larger units - the extended family, the clan, the society - are combinations of nuclear families.
4. The nuclear family is based on a clear-cut, biologically structured division of labour between men and women, with the man playing the 'instrumental' role of breadwinner, provider and protector, and the woman playing the 'expressive' role of housekeeper and emotional mainstay.
5. A major 'function' of the family is to socialise children, that is to tame their impulses and instil values, skills, and desires necessary to run the society. Without the nuclear family, the adequate socialisation of human beings is impossible.
6. Other family structures, such as mother and children, or the experimental commune, are regarded as deviant by the participants as well as the rest of society, and are fundamentally unstable and unworkable.

The Skolnicks suggest that 'the problem with the nuclear family model is intellectual: it influences thinking in certain directions'. The assumptions give rise to a set of attitudes as well as definitions of the situation - making family forms that differ from the assumed natural one seem deviant. 'Advocates of this model promote not merely a view of how families are organised, but also a more or less rigid set of attitudes about what the function and role of parents *should* be'.

If one holds the above set of assumptions, family forms such as the one-parent family, the reconstituted family, the dual-worker family, etc., are seen as deviant, 'broken', deprived, or selfish. If, however, one accepts the diversity model, these are seen as options - even if not always voluntarily adopted.

The diversity model

With the diversity model, each particular family form - conventional, dual-worker, single-parent, reconstituted, etc. - is seen as providing the structure for a lifestyle. Within this structure there will be some who have chosen it and find it satisfying, and others who would wish to discard it if possible. Take, as an example, the family in which the husband works part time and the wife works full time. In one family, this structure might be a chosen one, for example, if the husband wishes to use part of his time for artistic pursuits, or is partly disabled. The wife might be a committed professional and love her work. Another family with the same structure might suffer from invidious comparisons, with the husband feeling a failure and the wife feeling exploited, wishing she could work less. The various responses involved depend partly on - cultural and personal - ideologies. In a culture with strong vestiges of conventional burgeois ideology, there might be a tendency toward the second orientation, while in a country with a 'modern' diversity orientation, it would be toward the first. In a culture oriented to classic Marxist ideology it might be felt that the man should either work as an artist or in his other job, but in either case he, like his wife, should work full time.

The essential point about the diversity orientation is that particular families need not fulfil the social functions of the family - e.g. reproduction and the socialisation of children. So long as these functions are fulfilled by sufficient families in the society, some families may choose not to do so while others may do so in double or triple measure. Evaluation of a particular family form, and the spread of family forms in the society, can be approached from two respects, from that of the individuals concerned and from that of society. If the individuals not having children wish to have them and feel abnormal if they do not, the correspondence between them and the family form is poor. Similarly, if a family has many children, but they are unwanted and poorly raised, neither they nor the society are well served.

A diversity model which cannot claim to be more free from ideological influences than any other is based on several overlapping conceptions. First, there are social trends at work which are global in character and are producing variation in family-household forms. The trends are in family size, household composition, linkages with the economy and dissolution/reconstitution. There are also trends towards ethnic pluralism, and this also affects family household forms - e.g. in relation to non-nuclear family kin residing in the household.

One position holds that these are due to forces of social change which it is futile to try to oppose, and therefore it is best to accept them as legitimate. This is the position implied in Jessie Bernard's concept of the 'tipping point' (Bernard, 1972) - the point beyond which a statistical trend produces a change which is then legitimated as normal.

Another position is that it is a human right to be able to choose one's form of personal domestic arrangements without interference from political, religious or other bodies with ideological positions. Examples of different bases for legitimating family forms is seen in the recent working group set up by the Church of England to consider whether marriage between affines - i.e. persons related through marriage (e.g. step-relations) should be allowed in law. Within the working group there were those who supported a change in the law which would allow this, as well as those who opposed it. The supporters did so on human rights grounds; the opponents on two kinds of grounds: possible psychological harm (which failed to get support from experts giving testimony); and on the basis of religious dogma (which failed to attract a majority).

The third rationale for the legitimation of the diversity model is that diversity allows individuals with varying personalities to realise their potentials. This is less possible where one pattern is supported as normal while others are stigmatised. Safilios-Rothschild argues this point in relation to personal identity and sex roles (1977, pp. 149-50).

Implications of the diversity model

The diversity model has implications both for policy/practice and for social theory. It has been persuasively argued in the area of national policy that stereotyped assumptions about families are undesirable (Kammermann and Kahn, 1981; Aldous and Dumon, 1980). As in organisational policy, the lack of an explicit family policy does not mean that there is none. Bailyn (1984) argues that when organisations act on the assumption of a standard nuclear family model, they fail to recognise that some people do not fit the model. If they disregard these people, they may fail to make the most out of their human resources. For example, if an organisation does not recognise the special needs of married women with children and thus does not provide the special supports needed, they might lose the contribution these women could make. This would be less likely to happen if there is an assumption of diversity instead of standardisation.

Rapoport, Rapoport and Strelitz (1977) argue that health and education policies and practices, social welfare policies, and practices in therapeutic fields are influenced by the model of the family. In Western European countries, an authoritative set of formulations emerged in the period following the Second World War, idealising a conception of the nuclear conjugal family described by the Skolniks. This conception viewed the family as having a relatively standard composition, division of labour and life-cycle timetable. This conception, with its expectation that 'normal', 'mature' men will be economic providers, and 'normal', 'mature' women will be housewives and mothers, was bolstered by clinical psychiatry (as in the work of Bowlby and Winnicott), medicine (as in the early work of Spock), sociology (as in the work of Parsons) and by authorities in the fields of law, education and social work. The conception was rationalised as 'natural', in the sense of biologically determined, universal amongst human societies and therefore reflecting a human imperative. It has been designated as functionally adapted to modern industrial society. This set of assumptions served as a basis for much expert professional writing and practice in the 1950s-70s. To the extent it was unquestioned, it could be regarded as quasi-ideological.

In the current decade this model of family life has been increasingly questioned. As Sgritta notes in his chapter in this volume, recent social changes have produced a powerful impact on existing theoretical framework for analysing the family as a social institution. The various disciplines bearing on the family have produced a wide range of perspectives. This creates a new awareness of complexities and diversity. Even more important is that the improved quality and quantity of empirical research - what he calls the greater *concreteness* of available knowledge - had made it clear that conceptions based on simple normative ideal types of family structure do not correspond to reality. They cannot, therefore, be accepted either as practical guides to families and policy makers, or as adequate conceptualisations for scientific explanation and hypothesis formation.

The contemporary predicament of the family as a social institution - for parents as well as experts who seek to guide them - has engendered a search for new models. This is important in a number of ways: first, because there are so many unknowns and so there is a challenge for research to produce new knowledge; second, since past ideologies about family forms have proved inadequate for understanding contemporary changes, there is a need for developing new positions for interpreting scientific knowledge as it becomes available. For this, something more flexible than the classic ideologies is called for.

An example of how a 'position' affects the analysis of 'facts' is in Michael Young's discussion of 'Some alternative types of family structure' (Young, 1970). He presents a continuum of family forms from the traditional nuclear household to the communal household. As an example of an intermediate alternative, he uses the dual-career family. However, in noting that research on this family form has revealed characteristic tensions, he does not conclude - as would someone with the conventional normative position - that 'it is therefore an undesirable form'. Rather, he states that 'few, if any, systematic attempts have been made to produce a design for living which would reduce tension for the dual-career family', and he asks for scientific information on new housing developments, informal living arrangements, or other devices for making such a new form work with less tension. Even with this information, however, he would require a value stance as to whether the level of tensions associated with this family form is acceptable. Many dual-career couples choose this form as having less tension for them than other options (Rapoport and Rapoport, 1976).

Another example of how ideologies affect the interpretation of variant patterns is seen in relation to the recent public debate in England over the birth of a baby by a surrogate mother. The quality of the debate took on dimensions termed by journalists as a 'moral panic'. The traditionalist reaction was that babies should not be 'for sale', women should not 'rent their bodies', and the baby should not be separated from its natural mother. On the other side, which prevailed in the legal proceedings, were the points that a woman had the right to use her body as she wished, the baby was not bought but a service was performed, not unlike that of an adoption agency which had its legitimate costs, and that the baby had a natural father as well as a natural mother, and the father and his wife were ready and able to provide a good home for the baby.

There is no clear relationship between these differences in orientation and differences in religious and political values. However, these differences do relate to conceptualisation of the family. Where the dominant conception is the diversity model, the assumptions and responses to the arising new situations are different from those based on the traditional model.

The main argument is that the conception of the family is to some extent a product of the forces of social changes, these forces being independent of political/economic ideologies. These same forces affect the development of social science. Oakley and Oakley (1979) have pointed out, for example, how public statistics reflect sexist biases. Brian Jackson (1982) has noted that the assumption that single-parent families are unfortunate or deprived is a product of a particular ideology. Though there is some factual basis for it, i.e. that many of them are economically disadvantaged and stigmatised, it is clear that some one-parent families have chosen that form of family structure deliberately and feel neither unfortunate nor deprived. The implication of this for social science is that we need to understand the processes involved as well as the form because previously held 'traditional' assumptions about the meaning of the form are no longer valid. The situation is different as to whether a given pattern is chosen as an option or arises through misfortune.

Some difficulties with the diversity model

There are problems associated with the diversity model at different levels: research, social and administrative.

First, as regards research: as Trost (1974) noted in relation to the family life-cycle stage theory there are a near infinite number of categorisations of family types possible, and thus a basis for selection is required. So the question arises for researchers: how to categorise family forms. As Trost pointed out, there are many dimensions which can combine and recombine in 'n ways' through the life-course. The proliferation of typologies presents a challenge to systematic comparative research.

Secondly, there is a social control issue. If the legitimation of the plurality of family forms gives rise to a completely *laissez-faire* attitude, problems may arise as regards limits. The norm of free choice may be applicable to adults, but where children are involved the main issue is to serve their best interests in some form of domestic arrangement.

Finally, there are policy and administrative difficulties as new ranges of family forms are recognised. A *laissez-faire* attitude is equated in some administrators' minds with a chaotic situation.

From the point of view of social theory, the diversity model may present problems in that there is a tendency to reduce analyses to a micro-sociological level. Individual and very small-scale interpersonal analyses are conducted and the importance of large social structural factors may be given little attention. This is, however, not intrinsic in the recognition of diversity. Eventually, both sociological and psychological factors will have to be combined in a multi-disciplinary ecological framework to provide adequate explanations of behaviour observed in particular family forms.

The future of the diversity model

The numerical shift in the direction of diversity is now well documented. Less well documented but argued here on the basis of certain indicators is the emergence of a new norm which accepts diversity not only as a fact, but also as a valuable social condition. This 'diversity model' is at present what might be called a scientific postulate - different from an ideology in that it is more open to empirical test and revision. What evidence do we have from the studies reported here supporting the idea that the existing diversity is recognised as valuable? Elina Haavio-Manila, for example, differentiates among the types of caring. The need to match a family form to the requirements for care is an obvious implication and as different families have different care requirements, the 'responsible rationality', as she calls it, varies.

However, this model is not accepted by everyone. One form of non-acceptance is 'lag', i.e. traditional models and ways of viewing the world continue to be held. Individuals retain conservative attitudes and social institutions in the same way as the Church remains dogmatically attached to traditional norms. 'Lags' are also found in professional practice and in government and organisational policy.

Quite another phenomenon is *backlash*. This is found where new forms have been tried but disapproved. In such situations a resurgence of conservative orientations can be found.

What will the future pattern be, and what issues will merit study? Forecasting is risky, and there are many possible readings of contemporary data. In spite of this, we suggest to deal with three conceptions of family forms, vying with one another for dominance.

1. The *traditional position* will continue to hold among conservative-oriented people. And the conservative-minded families may be strengthened by a backlash of revivalists. The revival will involve male domination and female domestic focus with a return to firm social control in child-rearing. This is seen among some young people who are disenchanted with egalitarian and permissive ideologies.
2. The *social orientation*, generally associated with strong central state policies, will emphasise firm social control over the range of family forms that will be tolerated. Social utility, social cost and social responsibility themes will be salient in public policy formulations about the family in such matters as fertility planning, strengthening of the family for primary care functions and the prevention of social problems such as crime and delinquency.
3. The *secular pluralist orientation*, characterised by tolerance towards the diversity of family forms, will be followed by people advocating human rights. Free choice and the value of self-fulfilment are important in this, but so is competence and the capacity to deal with stress. This is associated with a de-emphasis of explicit social policy at the state level, and the assumption that socially costly family options - e.g. teenage motherhood - should be dealt with by private or local interventions.

We have recently experienced a phase of emphasis on expert opinions - about how to raise children, how to resolve marital conflicts, how to achieve sexual fulfilment and so on. Though based on a variety of credentials and the mystique of various disciplines, these experts reflect the cultural ethos within which they are trained and working. In the future we expect greater emphasis on self-sufficiency and the adaptation of expert information to the various situations of diverse family forms.

The new orientation is described by Scanzoni (1983) as 'progressive':

> 'In rejecting both traditionalism and an "expertism" that fails to question the conventional family fundamentally, progressives assert that "neither is it acceptable that parents should simply do as they feel; the vulnerabilities and difficulties of such a course are too great... What is required... is a cultivation of the capacity to work with and resolve problems of living as parents in today's society" (Rapoport, Rapoport, and Strelitz, 1977, p. 364). This "capacity"... is the core of the progressive vision of egalitarian marriage and family.'

For the next few decades, all three orientations are likely to co-exist in the developed world, with different emphasis in different countries. Each will be seen as 'semi-equitable', because there will be disappointment with failing to match ideologies - of the social nature of family forms in the East, and of the individual 'self-realisation' in family forms in the West. There will likely be greater recognition of democracy requiring tolerance towards the 'clash of equities'. While specific countries may experience backlash revivals of traditional norms and structures, it is likely that diversity will be increasingly tolerated within the limits set by what is actually harmful to family life. This conclusion is very much in keeping with Boh's analysis.

References

Aldous, J. (ed.) (1982): *The Two Paycheck Family*. Beverly Hills/London, Sage Publications

Aldous, J. and Dumon, W. (eds.) (1980): *The Politics and Programs of Family Policy*. University of Notre Dame, and Leuven

Bailyn, L. (1984): 'Issues of Work and Family in Organisations: Responding to Social Diversity'. In: Bailyn, L. (ed.): *Working with Careers*. New York, Columbia University School of Business

Berge, A. (ed.) (1977): *Être parent aujourd'hui*. Paris, Privat

Bernard, J. (1972): *The Future of the Family*. New York, World

Brown, G.W. and Harris, T. (1978): *Social Origins of Depression*. London, Tavistock

Chester, R. (ed.) (1977): *Divorce in Europe*. Leiden, Martinus Nijhoff

Rhona Rapoport

Cseh-Szombathy, L. et al. (1985): *The Aftermath of Divorce - Coping with Family Change.* Akadémiai Kiadó, Budapest

Dahlström, E. (ed.) (1967): *The Changing Roles of Men and Women.* London, Duckworth

Engels, F. (1902): *The Origin of the Family, Private Property and the State.* Chicago, Kerr

Fogarty, M., Rapoport, R. and Rapoport, R.N. (1971): *Sex, Career and Family.* Beverly Hills/London, Sage Publications

Gavron, H. (1966): *The Captive Wife.* London, Routledge & Kegan Paul

Gowler, D. and Legge, K. (1982): 'Dual Worker Families'. In: Rapoport, R.N., Fogarty, M. and Rapoport, R. (eds): *Families in Britain.* London/Boston, Routledge & Kegan Paul

Gronseth, E. (1975): 'Work-Sharing Families'. *Acta Sociologica,* Vol. 18

Jackson, B. (1982): 'Single Parent Families'. In: Rapoport, R.N., Fogarty, M. and Rapoport, R. (eds): *Families in Britain.* London/Boston, Routledge & Kegan Paul

Kammermann, S. and Kahn, A. (1981): *Child Care, Family Benefits and Working Parents: A Study in Comparative Family Policy Analysis.* New York, Columbia University Press

Karchev, A.G. (1964): *Brak i semia v SSSR* (Marriage and family in the USSR). Moscow

Karchev, A.G. and Golod, C.E. (1971): *Professional Working Women and the Family.* Academy of Sciences, Leningrad

Laslett, P. (1972): *Family and Household in Past Time.* London, Penguin

Mitchell, J. and Oakley, A. (eds) (1976): *The Rights and Wrongs of Women.* London, Penguin

Oakley, A. and Oakley, R. (1979): 'Sexism in Official Statistics'. In: Irvine et al. (eds): *Demystifying Social Statistics.* London, Pluto

Ogburn, W.F. (1922): *Social Change.* New York, Viking

Parsons, T. (1942): 'Age and Sex in the Social Structure of the United States'. *American Sociological Review,* Vol. 7, No. 5, pp. 604-616

Presvelous, C. and de Bie, P. (1970): *Images and Counterimages of Young Families.* ICOFA

Rapoport, R. and Rapoport, R.N. (1969): 'The Dual Career Family: A Variant Pattern and Social Change'. *Human Relations,* 22, pp. 1-96

Rapoport, R. and Rapoport, R.N. (1971): *Dual-Career Families.* London, Penguin

Rapoport, R. and Rapoport, R.N. (1975): 'Men, Women and Equity'. *Family Coordinator,* Vol. 24, p. 421

Rapoport, R. and Rapoport, R.N. (1976): *Dual-Career Families Re-examined.* London, Martin Robertson; New York, Harper & Row

Rapoport, R. and Rapoport, R.N. (1980): 'Three Generations of Dual Career Family Research'. In: Pepitone-Rockwell (ed.): *Dual-Career-Couples.* Beverly Hills/London, Sage Publications

Rapoport, R., Rapoport, R.N. and Strelitz, Z. (1977): *Fathers, Mothers and Others.* London, Routledge & Kegan Paul

Rapoport, R.N., Fogarty, M.P. and Rapoport, R. (eds) (1982): *Families in Britain.* London/Boston, Routledge & Kegan Paul

Safilios-Rothschild, C. (1977): 'Les Rôles Futures des Parents'. In: Berge, A. (ed.): *Être parent aujourd'hui.* Paris, Privat

Scanzoni, J. (1983): *Shaping Tomorrow's Family.* Vol. 143 of the Sage Library of Social Research, Beverly Hills/London, Sage Publications

Skolnick, J. and Skolnick, A. (1974): *Intimacy, Family and Society.* Boston, Little Brown

Trost, J. (1974): Published in Cuisenier, J. (ed.): *The Life Cycle in European Communities.* Brussels, Mouton

Young, M. (1970): 'Some Alternative Types of Family Structure'. In: *ICOFA Conference Proceedings*, Rennes

4

Towards a New Paradigm: Family in the Welfare State Crisis*

Giovanni B. Sgritta

The argument

For many years social scientists attributed the changes in the structure and functions of the family to the larger economic and social transformations occurring with the transition from traditional society to the complex society of the modern age. As long as the family was the dominant unit of subsistence, its functions were all predisposed to ensure the survival of its members, secure their existence, and counter the threat of adversity; but with the increasing progress of industrialisation, urbanisation, and market production, most of the traditional family's responsibilities in the religious, judicial, economic and cultural spheres disappeared and were transferred to other social institutions. The family turned inward and assumed domesticity, intimacy and privacy as its major characteristics, while its tasks were limited primarily to consumption, procreation and childrearing.

The retreat of the family from the outside world and its consequent gradual and continuous loss of functions were further strengthened by the proliferation of welfare policies. As these policies covered ever more basic needs - needs which in the past had been taken care of within the family - the responsibilities of the family in terms of satisfying the needs of its members became proportionately fewer. And, as Habermas (1971, pp. 187-8) points out, the family 'increasingly loses, with the formation of capital, the functions of childrearing and education, of protection and support, of guidance and even the most elementary tradition and orientation. It loses the power to mould behaviour in areas which

* This study is part of a wider research carried out by the author on a grant of the Italian Consiglio Nazionale delle Ricerche.

were considered by the bourgeois family to be the innermost recesses of private life'.

In the course of many years, these ideas have assumed a dominating position in the panorama of contemporary sociological thought. In terms of public opinion, this thesis was generally accepted as an accurate description of the 'grammar' of lifestyles characteristic of modern society. At the government level, a considerable part of social policy passed at this time was explicitly or implicitly related to the thesis of the functional crisis of the family.

A significant confirmation of the importance given to this interpretation by social policy is represented by the move in the policy of public intervention from the 'residual' model to the 'institutional' model (Mishra, 1977, p. 91). Historically, most social welfare programmes were developed on the premise that the family and the immediate neighbourhood would support their dependent members. As Moroney (1976, p. 4) puts it, however, 'this residual approach has gradually been replaced with the philosophy that society, especially as represented by its government, should assume more and more direct responsibility for assuring that the basic social and economic needs of its members be met'.

Most of the institutional services (for the elderly, children, the handicapped, etc.) were enacted and eventually translated into operational programmes on the principle that the family was unable to fulfil its main functions of care and support for its dependent members.

From the end of the Second World War until the end of the sixties, the objective of the progressive expansion of collective services was followed without any apparent opposition in all modern countries. This programme was certainly helped to be carried out by the growth of resources, by the expansion of the basis of production and by an increased employment of labour in the industrial and tertiary sectors of the economies of these countries. But beyond these favourable circumstances, the surrender of familial functions to public service institutions constituted a real political choice for the governments of the highly industrialised societies. For over 20 years this direction of social policy and this collective commitment represented the dominant expression of a certain way of perceiving social life.

The theory, according to which there exists a direct relation between the loss of functions by the family and the urban-industrial development of society, retained a leading position in social thought at least until the end of the sixties. In the years immediately following this period, however, this interpretation underwent a serious process of critical review. The attention of scholars was first directed at the assumptions of this interpretation regarding the change of the extended family into the nuclear family. Between the end of the sixties and the middle of the following decade, numerous studies and research challenged these assumptions on the basis of a considerable amount of demographical and historical data (Laslett, 1968; Laslett and Wall, 1972; Mitterauer and Sieder, 1982; Hareven, 1982).

Subsequently, the attention of economists and sociologists focussed on the functional characteristics of the modern family. As a result of this interest, new approaches and integrations affected both the theoretical framework and the methodological procedures used in the study of the family. On the one hand these new ideas led to the progressive abandonment of the thesis of functional deprivation; on the other, the main contribution of these analyses can be recognised in the attempt to recover the functional value of the tasks and activities carried out by families.

But, despite the criticism which was directed at the thesis of the decline of the family in modern society, most of the contributions could not deny the importance of the changes in the functioning of the family as a result of the modernisation process. The effects produced by industrialisation and urbanisation on the role of the family is carefully borne in mind in these analyses. Similarly, proper consideration is given to the impact on social reality of those social-policy measures which can be understood as compensating intervention with respect to the traditional tasks of the family.

The purpose of these contributions is rather that of redimensioning the thesis which gives the family the role of a 'dependent' variable within social change. From this point of view, what they propose to establish is the fact that the family cannot be assumed as a linear function of social change. In opposing the classical functional thesis which restricted itself to considering the influence of changes in the main institutions of the economy and government on family behaviour, these contributions support the interdependence of the actions of the various institutions in society. The social environment can no longer be considered as the only source of change, and therefore as something given upon which the behaviour of families must be dependent. The family itself is capable of actions and modifications which in turn produce a transformation in its environment. The market as well as the public social-service institutions or the voluntary solidarity agencies do not in any way operate independently of the action and reaction of families.

The family, in other words, is itself taken as an 'environment' with respect to the remaining institutions of society. And it is this conclusion which most certainly constitutes the main innovation introduced by most recent studies and research. It demonstrates, in effect, how the family's role of being a dependent variable was excessively overestimated and in final analysis mythologised by the classical functionalist theory (Berger and Berger, 1983, Ch. 4).

The fact of considering family behaviour in 'strategic' terms rather than 'functional' terms (Elster, 1979) is not without important consequences for theory and methodology. One early result is certainly represented by the considerable advance which is produced in the general framework of research. The fact that the family is attributed a theoretical status equal to that of other economic and political institutions inevitably implies the need for a more careful and detailed analysis of the mutual relations among the various parts of society.

In the research conducted in the past ten years, this necessity presents itself in two distinct ways. On the one hand, scholars tend to refer to various contributions coming from other social disciplines when analysing the family; that is, different disciplinary approaches enter an arena which until a short time ago was considered to be the exclusive competence of sociology. On the other hand, the role of families in the process of satisfying basic social needs increasingly tends to be taken into consideration.

In the analysis conducted in this period, this tendency can easily be documented in a series of attempts to specifically examine the material and non-material services carried out by the family in everyday life, the circumstances in which these services are carried out, the individuals who have the tasks of furnishing these activities, and those who benefit from these activities. In this case, the qualitative rise which occurs with respect to the traditional paradigm is also evident.

The new orientation of the knowledge of family phenomena constitutes a considerable advance in comparison with a previously widespread 'aristocratic' attitude of social researchers with respect to the issues and problems of family life. In the traditional approach, these problems were deemed to be trivial, excessively limited to everyday life and to mere subsistence and therefore scarcely worth scientific attention.

The attention given to the concrete aspects of everyday life is related to a more general interest in the subject of the social division of the responsibilities among the various institutions competing to satisfy the needs of individuals, families and social groups. From the theoretical point of view, this analysis, therefore, assumes fundamental importance. It marks a change from a conception which was limited to considering the general functions of the family within the social system to one that also takes into consideration the ways in which these functions are concretely accomplished in the dynamics of institutional relations. The analysis of the ways of acquisition, transformation and use of resources by families, the interest in the division of labour between partners, the reconstruction of family and occupational biographies of both sexes and the behaviour strategies in a plurality of spheres linked to the satisfaction of needs and the care of different members of the family: all these constitute some of the main interests of the 'new course' of the sociological analysis of the family. At the same time, they also involve the introduction of new research instruments which are certainly more suited to describing the complex reality of modern society.

A close examination of the sociological literature of the past ten years furnishes wide evidence to support this modification in the theoretical framework. The same comparative research referred to in this volume can be appropriately cited as evidence of the change occurring in the conceptual and methodological apparatus of the study of the family. The scheme shown in the following table offers a synthesis of the main aspects of family life and of the most significant relations between the family and other social institutions which were considered in the research on 'Changes in the Life Patterns of Families in Europe'.

Table 4.1. *Outline of social resources according to the main institutional frameworks and different areas of analysis*

Area of analysis	Institutional framework		
	Family and mediating structures	State	Economy
A. Reproduction:	Individual and family characteristics: reproductive history, education, women's status and role, expectations, aspirations, income, perceptions of children, family lifestyle; budget constraint: fertility regulation costs, direct and indirect costs and benefits of children; pressure and support by kinship and other informal groups	Legislation on family and marriage; policy and programmes (family planning, health care system, maternal and child services, etc.), education and information about services, ideologies	Occupational welfare system structure of the labour market (women's labour force participation and sector of activity), women's working conditions
B. Caretaking: Pre-school children	Mother and/or other family caretakers, voluntary help, neighbourhood, kinship and friendship caretaking inside and outside family, religious institutions	Public crèches, kindergartens	Nursery in factory/industrial premises, private nursery, day nursery, paid child minder, play group, kindergarten, private house
School children		State school, full or part time, extra school activities	Private school, extra school activities
Sick persons Elderly	Informal help, assistance and care in the family, voluntary services, religious groups, neighbourhood and ethnic community, kinship and friendship network, health service alternatives, charity organisations	Statutory health and social services, public home help services, residential care	Private health and social services, private home help services, institutions

| C.
Work:
Paid | Choices and constraints determining the need to appropriate resources in the economy | Incomes, transfer incomes or subsidies, family allowances, social and personal services | Incomes, employee benefits (pensions, life insurance, sick pay, vacations, supplementary unemployment benefits, fringe benefits (goods and services) |
| Unpaid (domestic) | Resources derived from the division of labour in the family, kinship and friendship network, mutual aid | Norms on sex equality, social and personal services, home helps | Social and personal services, domestic gadgets, private home helps, housemaids |

We refer to the single chapters of this volume for a deeper examination of the contents relating to each of the aspects which appear within the scheme. The purpose of this chapter is rather to furnish a preliminary clarification of the theoretical and methodological framework of the research. The fundamental issue this analysis is concerned with, therefore, is the reasons which have caused the abandonment of the traditional paradigm of knowledge and led to the introduction of the new orientation in the analysis of families as well as the relations between families and the other main institutions of society (market, state and intermediary structures).

The assumption of this chapter is that we can conceive only abstractly of the existence of an autonomous and independent development of knowledge. The very history of scientific thought demonstrates that the innovations decisive for the progress of knowledge and for the affirmation of new orientations of thought definitely deviate from this pattern. They rather emerge from the need to incorporate a new dimension of reality into our knowledge, which then might entail a change in the organisation of social life. More specifically, the transition to the new paradigm cannot be considered the result of pure speculative interest. It presupposes an equally profound change in the articulation of the relations between the family and other political, economic, social and cultural institutions. Thus, the structure and the contents of the new paradigm must be considered to be the reflection of the relations of push and pull, being present among the various fundamental institutions of society. The theoretical frame of reference of knowledge reflects the real structure of these relations or the changes in this structure.

Like any other aspect of knowledge, empirical research, too, is placed within the social context by which it is determined. As Rein and Peattie (1981, p. 531) point out, 'both the categories of description and the lines of investigation we pursue are shaped by our experience of trying to act on the world and limited by the sort of actions we see as possible'. Immobility as well as change in the models and the orientation of research are the expression at the symbolical level respectively of the permanence or the transformation in the main elements of the social organisation. And the whole picture of social knowledge and research is therefore constantly 'influenced by practice in the social and economic realms and not only by the conceptual and methodological paradigms of their disciplines'.

The theme of our analysis can substantially be understood as a particular aspect of this relation between reality and social knowledge. The understanding of the reasons that have solicited in recent times the development of new perspectives for research on the family presupposes the understanding of the structural changes which are found at the basis of this development. Our attention must therefore first be directed to the identification of the changes occurring in the structure of society during this period.

The welfare state crisis

In principle the array of causes which might have produced the change in the interpretative schemes of the family is undoubtedly very wide. A proper explanation of the causes to be found at the basis of the adoption of the new paradigm must take into consideration a plurality of factors, and at the same time integrate these factors in a single explanatory principle.

A common point of reference for the development of our analysis can be singled out in the economic-social crisis which, since the beginning of the mid-seventies, has affected all European countries. Among these countries there exist notable differences both historically and in terms of their social, political and economic organisation.

The character and intensity of the crisis have surely been different in the individual national contexts (Eisenstadt and Ahimeir, 1985; Flora, 1985; McAuley, 1982). The national reports for our project confirm that the impact and the significance of this crisis have been anything but uniform in the participating European countries (National Reports, 1982-84).

If, however, we avoid going too far beyond the examination of the peculiarities characterising the state of the crisis in individual national contexts, there emerges a situation which presents significant common traits. For example, more or less similar are the difficulties which, in the period under consideration, have inhibited the growth of GNP and the redistribution of resources in these countries. Other interesting common elements can be singled out in the increase in the discrepancy between the fiscal revenues and the social utilisation of resources (a problem of structural imbalance in the public household or the so-called fiscal crisis of the state); in the growth of serious problems in the area of employment; and above all in the difficulty of maintaining the steady growth of social expenditure that characterised the twenty years following the Second World War.

But it is not exclusively for these reasons that we can justify the adoption of the socio-economic crisis of the seventies as a suitable point of reference for our analysis. Along with these, several surprising formal coincidences deserve to be mentioned. In the first place, a singular parallel exists between the development of the crisis and the emergence of new theoretical orientations in the analysis of the family, which we have referred to in the preceding paragraphs. In the second place, the consequences of the crisis affect just those fundamental institutions of society to which the latest studies and research direct their attention most. Finally, it is no less surprising that, as we shall see later, a correspondence in timing can be noted between the transformations of social policy adopted by the individual national governments as an answer to the crisis and the changes produced in family life during the same period.

Any attempt to assign a precise date to a social event means a simplification of social reality. This is also the case with the winter of 1973-4, fixed as the turning-point of the great wave of post-war expansion. But taking as reference the oil crisis of 1974 we can identify fairly closely the ten-year period of 1974-84, which presents characteristics totally different from those of the previous twenty-year period. As noted above there are significant differences between the European countries with respect to the problems they encountered and the ways in which they reacted to them. In some cases the crisis cut seriously into the growth of the economy.

There were changes in the policies of social intervention which took on the form of real neo-liberalist policies. In other cases, the slowdown in economic growth was less dramatic. The adoption of adequate strategies of crisis management helped to avoid too drastic modification in the development of public expenditure in general and of social security expenditure in particular. In the Scandinavian countries, for example, economic growth was certainly slower after the oil crisis in 1974 than in the preceding period, still they experienced hardly any cuts in their welfare programmes (Johansen and Kolberg, 1985, p. 167). In others (as in the case of the socialist countries), the peculiarities in their economic-political order do not permit us to judge the situation having recourse *sic et simpliciter* to the same indicators.

The differences with respect to the capitalist countries seem, however, more apparent than real. Undoubtedly in these countries, too, we find a worsening of economic difficulties (McAuley, 1982). The growth in social consumption expenditures in the last decade has been modest in comparison with the past. Official documents make more and more frequent mention of a 'slowdown' in the accomplishment of anticipated social programmes, of the need for an 'improvement of relations of production', or of the appearance of 'new contradictions' between the changes occurring in the development of the forces of production and the criteria which govern the reallocation of resources among the various factors of production.

Nevertheless, there exist some traits common to the majority of the European countries. One of these common aspects is that the consequences of the crisis have caused the governments to review their programmes of social expenditure and introduce corrective measures. As P. Flora (1985, p. 23) puts it, 'the period since the mid-70's has not ... been characterized by a dismantling of the welfare state but rather by attempts to limit its further expansion in a period of economic restraints'.

Another common aspect is that the economic recession and the ensuing insecurity and vulnerability among the citizens has engendered popular discontent. In the messianic framework within which the first concrete signs of the welfare state began to appear in the wake of the Second World War, the achievement of widespread social equality and of a better quality of life was assumed by the governments as irrevocable and irreducible objectives of their national policies. The failure or partial accomplishment of these objectives has consequently given rise to an articulate series of protests, which changing according to the circumstances, have ranged from anti-tax to anti-welfare sentiments or the search for private alternatives in order to reach or maintain higher levels of welfare (in the 'second economy', for example).

But the most interesting aspect common to the various countries is the change in institutional relations. As Flora (1985, p. 25) points out, the essential meaning of the changes produced by the crisis 'may be found much less in the threat of an *historical regression* of the European welfare state, and much more in the break of the past *growth patterns* which will require a readjustment of major institutitons'. It is, therefore, to the examination of this process of reshaping the relations among institutions that we direct our attention in the following paragraphs.

The place of the family in the social division of welfare

As a result of the crisis, the institutional framework began to change. The effect of the recession, as the preparatory reports of the research amply show (National Reports, 1982-84), made it imperative to search for different organisational forms. The need to justify a progressive withdrawal of the role of the public sector in managing services and in maintaining adequate levels of welfare for the citizens, was generally expressed in the form of a re-negotiation of the division of responsibility among the various institutional spheres. The role of the institutional agents entrusted with the regulation of social welfare would have to undergo relevant changes.

In these conditions, the interrelationhsip between family, market and the state grew more complex. The assignment of new responsibilities to the family for meeting the needs of its members appears, in fact, as a development common to most European countries. The recovery of traditional areas of social solidarity, the implementation of new ways of producing services and income, the restoration of models of assistance and subsistence which seemed to have been abandoned, constitute some signs of manifestation of the economic and social consequences of the crisis in the various national contexts.

The role of the family as a producer of a 'composite income' and of labour and services was stressed in both the capitalist and the socialist countries. The role of 'informal' economy was also stressed (or at least tacitly approved) as an important element of flexibility in the social organisation and/or as a mechanism for easing the overload of collective demand addressed otherwise to the public institutions.

The impossibility of adopting a solution which entrusts either the state or the market with the task of satisfying needs implied, in these circumstances, that a large part of the responsibility for the maintenance and care of the family's various components was moved to the family itself. In the overall process of producing and reproducing resources it is in fact the family that assumes the job of compensating for that part of social demand for goods and services, which the state and the market cannot provide or are no longer able to supply.

Our research confirms that the role of the family in production, transformation and utilisation of resources remains of paramount importance for the realisation of an adequate standard of living even in the advanced welfare societies. As Moroney (1976, p. 4) puts it, the entire structure of these societies 'depends on a set of implicit or explicit assumptions concerning the responsibility which families assume, or are expected to assume, for their members and the conditions under which this responsibility must either be shared with or taken over by society through its public or voluntary organizations'.

Thus, despite the contributions of resources and services coming to the family from the market (income) and public institutions (transfers and social services), the family still remains primarily and predominantly responsible for meeting individual needs. As the main seat of the highest degree of affective and material solidarity, it is the structure within which most needs that arise in the social sphere are ultimately felt, if only indirectly. At the micro-level of the organisation and utilisation of resources, the family represents the social locus where needs are specified and become manifest, even though they may originate, wholly or partly, outside its realm.

But the micro-levels are encompassed within larger, also interlinked, macro-structures (Blumberg, 1984, p. 48), and in complex societies these macro-structures may be conceived as composed mainly of institutional services. Nonetheless, availability of social services that compensate for or replace services traditionally performed within the family does not necessarily bring a reduction of tasks and work loads for the family. In reality, it seems plausible that in some circumstances wider social rights of the citizens and the meeting of social demands by the state, far from producing a decrease in the functional contribution of the family, give the family new tasks and burdens. Given the organisation and working modalities normally present in institutional services, they usually allow only for a range or relatively rigid performances. Moreover, as they are uniformly based upon a hypothetical average demand, in many situations they appear inconsistent or at least non-respondent to the consumers' actual needs.

This inadequacy of public services to adjust supply to the variety of consumers' demands usually requires, as a matter of fact, a compensating or substituting action by the family. The request for compensatory interventions is directly proportional to the specificity of the consumers' needs. Thus, the more personalised the services required, the more inadequate, presumably, the services provided by the public structures are and the more indispensable the integrative and/or substitutive role of the family becomes. In a plurality of concrete situations, therefore, the utilisation of services entails supplementary work in which the family, temporarily or permanently, according to the type and magnitude of the need, takes over services institutionally entrusted to the formal sector.

A further important aspect of the changing context related to the restructuring of the institutional division of welfare, is the search for 'low-cost solutions'. A shift in social responsibility from the public sector back to families inevitably implies an increasing exploitation of family work, hence of women's work within the family (Sundström, 1982). According to the official expectation emerging from the decline of institutionally provided services it is up to the family and to the woman on its behalf to find 'naturally' the most convenient adaptations to the new situation; it is up to the family to bridge the gap between available services and consumers' needs, as well as to increase the flexibility of intervention so as to provide a timely and adequate response to individual needs.

In the face of a steep reduction in public expenditures and public welfare provision, the role of the woman - the 'designated career' - and some intermediary structures (neighbourhood and mutual aid groups, kinship and friendship networks, voluntary organisations, etc.) have been invested with growing responsibility in the management of a large range of care and assistance needed by dependent subjects.

At the same time, arguments for replacing the welfare state with more 'self-reliance' have loomed in various programmes to promote informal social care, which would, in effect, force people to rely on the family and the community rather than the state as the basic source of support (Goodin, 1985; Abrams and Bulmer, 1985; Lee, 1985). In fact, as J. Finch and D. Groves (1983, p. 5) point out, 'low cost solutions include a renewed enthusiasm for so-called community provision of various sorts and a reliance on the recently designated informal sector of welfare provision'.

In terms of the relationship between micro- and macro-levels, this emphasis on alternative policies leads straight to a recon-sideration of the economic and social value of the 'informal' sphere. Definitely, the giving of informal care means work - unpaid work - which is not always replaceable by the public sector.

For this reason, the fact that 'caring' is an activity which is culturally defined as being 'natural' for women and other volun-tary agencies, must not be allowed to hide the important reality that services given in this form - principally in the home and family context - represent an economic contribution essential to the functioning of modern welfare societies.

The 'game of subsistence'

The importance given to the mediating structures - 'the sort of groups and organizations found midway between the macro and micro levels' (Scanzoni, 1983, p. 225) - clearly expresses the need in advanced industrial societies to re-negotiate the social division of welfare which has characterised the expansive phase of eco-nomic growth. The national reports of our project illustrate the dif-fusion of this process within the political and social realities of the countries involved (National Reports, 1982-84).

The conclusion to which we come on the basis of this and other research can be symbolised through the image of a 'chess-board'. The interplay of different institutional agencies may be meta-phorically presented as an immense chess-board on which the great game of choices and strategies needed to guarantee the sub-sistence and the welfare of individuals, families and groups is played.

In this complex set of intricate relations, the women have an absolutely crucial role. They are in fact the principal mediators between the private market, public services and the concrete needs of their families. Through the 'servicing work' within the family and outside it, it is the woman who, as L. Balbo (1983, p. 229) notes, 'mediates between human needs, as they are perceived in daily life, and the external resources'. It is this work that permits the transformation, organisation and production of resources for the satisfaction of needs. And it is this work which helps us to understand the way in which the labour market is really structured (Federici, 1984; Barrére-Maurisson et al., 1984; Familie und Arbeitswelt, 1984); and even to explain the social division of work in the informal economy (Pahl, 1981), the employment structure in the specific sector of services (Pitrou et al., 1983), and the organisation of assistance for dependants (Waerness, 1984; Sundström, 1982; Finch and Groves, 1983; Sgritta, 1984).

The family-service society

Within the social division of welfare in modern societies, 'the private household and family continue to be the arena of an immense work effort, and it would not seem warranted to speak of any material weakening of this entity' (Dahlström and Liljeström, 1982, p. 92). Work done by women in the process of satisfying needs remains, all the same, predominant. Even though, in the face of retrenchment and other efforts to halt the expansion of the welfare state, an ever more important role is destined to be taken by the intermediate structures based on voluntary action, on the solidarity of individuals, the family as well as on the local network of neighbours (Kramer, 1985).

Expressions like the 'family-service society' (Dahlström and Liljeström, 1982), or the 'culture of service' (Bianchi, 1981) or the 'double presence of women' in the professional and family arena (Balbo, 1978) summarise in a particularly effective way the role of these structures in the maintenance of the present standard of living of the European populations. They emphasise the importance accorded to the family and the 'servicing work' done by women in welfare societies, both in the East and the West. They confirm, in other terms, that the networks of social relationships between the extended family, the kin and the neighbourhood continue to constitute an indispensable resource for the satisfaction of many of the basic needs. In many cases (such as the care of children and elderly people), the role of these voluntary non-profit

85

social structures and the service work of the family can be demonstrated as politically and economically crucial. As L. Balbo (1983, p. 239) observes, 'they permit that an enormous amount of needs, although legitimate, do not become political demand, capable of developing into pressure, tensions, and conflicts'. Thus, in the crisis of the welfare state they function as elements permitting a compensation for the existing gap between political objectives which should guarantee everybody an adequate standard of welfare, on the one hand, and the concrete answer which is frequently rigid, impersonal, strongly bureaucratic and definitely inadequate with respect to the needs of citizens on the other.

The crisis of the traditional paradigm

The arguments presented so far are sufficiently grounded as to cast serious doubts on the thesis that the family is progressively emptied of its functions in contemporary society. They are no less important, however, for the analysis of the causes which have produced change in the theoretical schemes of knowledge in the course of the last decade. Eventually, the possibility of knowing definite aspects of reality depends on the availability of adequate interpretative schemes capable of directing observation towards phenomena previously ignored.

Also in this case, the affirmation of the 'new grammar of institutions' resulting from the crisis in welfare society has therefore a precise correspondence in the conceptual categories employed in the most recent research on the family. At the symbolic level, these categories reflect the need to incorporate the set of changes taken place in the real structure of the institutional framework into social knowledge.

The main characteristics of the research of the last decade reflect precisely the necessity to represent these changes. Each of them mirrors the other thus the basic outline of research into the functional significance of the family and the organisation of the new social reality.

At the same time, however, the adaptation of this theoretical apparatus to the characteristics of the new social reality implicitly marks the abandonment of the traditional paradigm of knowledge. All things considered, the limits of these models or schemes of thought have become clear through their inadequacy to anticipate the marked shifts that have occurred in family behaviour and in social organisation. On the one hand, this paradigm proved unable to account for the increasing complexity of the relationships between different formal and informal welfare agencies. On the other, it was substantially inadequate for explaining the dynamics of these social processes which involved overcoming the discontinuity between different contexts in which the satisfaction of needs is accomplished.

Neither one nor the other of these two phenomena of the new social reality could have found recognition within the theories which dominated the sociological scene between the Second World War and the mid-1970s.

The structural-functional classical conception limited itself to considering the influence of the changes in the main institutions of the economy and of politics on the behaviour of families. The possibility of understanding the essential traits of the 'society in crisis' required, on the contrary, the availability of an apparatus of categories capable of connecting the links which formed among the various social actors in the process of satisfying needs.

The social changes produced by the crisis worked to upset the foundations of the theoretical framework of the structural-functional paradigm, and justified the difficulties which this paradigm faced in attempting to interpret the development of European society beyond the watershed of the socio-economic crisis of the last ten years.

From this point of view, the effect of the crisis was twofold. From one side, it produced a collective loss of faith in the possibility of an uninterrupted growth of the economy and disenchantment about the programmes and promises of the welfare society. On the other, it provoked a progressive 'demolition' of the scientific credibility of the traditional paradigm and its substitution with a new system of thought.

As regards the relationships between the family and other institutional agents, the inadequacy of this paradigm can be documented in one of its central theses, and precisely in the thesis which is related to the relationship between the productive and reproductive systems of society.

The foundations of this thesis lie in the assumption that there exists a substantial divergence of interests, aims and values in the organisation and functioning of these two sub-systems of society (Parsons and Smelser, 1964). According to Parsons this divergence should be kept under the control of one part of the society if one wants to avoid dysfunctioning consequences inside the whole system. In other words, it is indispensable that there be definite institutional mechanisms which permit solution to the problem of compatibility and of reciprocal adaptation between the productive sub-system and the reproductive one.

According to this conception, therefore, the most adequate solution to this problem has to be identified in the subordination of the family reproductive sphere, and its separation from the occupational productive one. This would be, in fact, the only solution able to guarantee that the essential functions of the social system are satisfying simultaneously and optimally the social needs.

The application of this thesis has consequences worth noting from the theoretical point of view. In the first place, it makes us consider the organisation of the family as a dependent variable in relation to the occupational and other sub-systems of society. In addition, it leads us to assume the relative independence of the two institutional contexts instead of their reciprocal influence (Brown, 1976; Moss and Fonda, 1980; Barrére-Maurisson et al., 1984).

Finally, a contemporary and inseparable element of this view is the specialisation of family functions: the male serves his family through paid employment, the woman serves through domestic work and childcare. In fact, as J. Scanzoni (1983, pp. 85-86) points out, 'specialization and ultimately (female) dependence is the essence of the conventional family. To many conservatives, specialization and social order go hand in hand'.

The consequences of these assumptions become clear in the empirical studies carried out in the period immediately following the Second World War. The results of these studies clearly express the limits of this conception as regards the relationships between the family and the world of work and production. Rarely is in this research domestic and family work taken into consideration as a theme which merits profound attention on the part of the sociologists. Instead, it was to be a *constant* of the female condition, so obvious as to be largely ignored or at most considered as belonging among the interests outside work of a woman employed in production. As M. Cacioppo (1982, p. 16) sums up, in the research conducted in this period, domestic and family work represents 'the antithesis to work for the market: non-work place to the extent that this appears ingrained in the female role'.

Evidently there are differences in viewpoint among the scientific contributions produced in this period. These should be carefully considered in a systematic review of the literature. It is a common characteristic of this research, however, that in most of it the relationship between family and work, between reproduction and production is not conceived as 'problematic'. Indeed, the traditional paradigm to which these contributions can be traced is not able to treat this relationship through the perspective of an organic interdependence of its elementary components.

Concluding remarks

The structural-functional paradigm was supported by the expansion of the welfare state just after the Second World War. Between the war and the mid-1970s, this paradigm gave coherence to sociological thought, organising it within some fundamental guidelines. The decline of this paradigm occurred side by side with the economic and socio-political crisis of the *ideal* of the welfare society; that is, simultaneously with the disillusionment created by the impossibility of achieving universal welfare and total equality.

Under these conditions, the continued recourse to this interpretative scheme unavoidably led to concealing wide areas of social and family reality.

In fact, the changes taken place in the institutional order of European societies could not be accounted for by traditional analysis. The recovery of the family's functional importance in the social division of welfare as well as the activation of new forms of solidarity and new ways and methods in the production of goods and services demonstrated the inadequacy of this paradigm and called for the modification of some of its fundamental premises.

The assumption that the family has an inferior status in the process of the production of resources and in the satisfaction of needs proved definitely inappropriate and misleading when interpreting the new reality. The presence of a plurality of institutional forms in which this process is actually accomplished, remained substantially extraneous to the theoretical framework of this conception. Nor did it permit the social analyst to understand the blurring of sectoral boundaries among these diverse institutional contexts.

The need to incorporate these relationships in theory led to recourse to a new paradigm of social knowledge. Thus, the aftermath of the welfare 'crisis' of the 1970s did not limit itself to the development of new ways of subsistence on the part of citizens. At the same time, these consequences presented a radical challenge to the traditional schemes of social knowledge.

From this point of view, studies and research on the family carried out in the last decade may be interpreted as an answer - in the area of knowledge - to the transformations that have occurred in the structure of society. In this same direction is the research on the 'Changes in the Life Patterns of Families in Europe' oriented.

As we have tried to demonstrate in this chapter, the formation of a new approach to the analysis of family behaviour can be traced back to the failure of a social promise. This promise inspired expectations that, in principle, it was feasible to delegate - either completely or in part - the satisfaction of the primary needs of the families to the public sector.

In a certain sense, therefore, the failure of this social policy may be interpreted as evidence of the impracticability of a solution that excludes the intervention of the family and intermediate agencies of voluntary solidarity from the process of satisfying basic individual and collective needs. It proves, as P. Rosanvallon (1981, p. 114) observed, that 'the development of collective services and facilities is no longer sufficient to compensate the effects of social atomisation. The hypersocialisation from above does no longer permit to respond to the demands arising from the desocialisation from below'.

In fact, the re-evaluation of the place of the family in the social division of welfare, and the recovery of interest in apparently minor themes such as 'daily life', voluntary and self-help initiatives, or collective movements of civic protest, constitute the most significant events to which many authoritative social analysts have recently directed their attention (Habermas, 1982; Hirschman, 1970).

Any further attempt to go deeper into the interpretation of these tendencies within the scope of the present chapter would inevitably be too short and too narrow. These tendencies represent unexpected and surprising results only if they are evaluated in the light of the theoretical conceptions having dominated the sociological scene in the past. If, however, they are linked to the background of the whole history of human society, they appear rather like a confirmation: an expression of a substantial continuity in the means by which humanity provided for the satisfaction of its actual needs, both emotional and material, with all that is both positive and unjust in what this perennial problem has posed and will always pose.

References

Abrams, P. and Bulmer, M. (1985): 'Policies to Promote Informal Care: Some Reflections on Voluntary Action, Neighbourhood Involvement, and Neighbourhood Care'. *Ageing and Society*, 5, 1985

Balbo, L. (1978): 'La doppia presenza' (Double presence). *Inchiesta*, 32, 1978

Balbo, L. (1983): 'Il lavoro di servizio delle donne nella società capitalistica' (Women's work in services in the capitalist society). In: David, P. and Vicarelli, G. (eds): *L'azienda famiglia: una società a responsabilità illimitata*, Laterza, Bari

Barrére-Maurisson, M.A. et al. (1983): 'Trajectoires professionnelles des femmes et vie familiale'. *Consommation*, 4, 1983

Barrére-Maurisson, M.A. et al. (1984): *Le sexe du travail. Structures familiales et système productif*. Presse Univ. de Grenoble, Grenoble

Berger, B. and Berger, P.L. (1983): *The War over the Family. Capturing the Middle Ground*. Anchor Press, New York

Bianchi, M. (1981): *I servizi sociali. Lavoro femminile, lavoro familiare, lavoro professionale* (Social services. Women's work, family work, professional work). De Donato, Bari

Blumberg, R.L. (1984): 'A General Theory of Gender Stratification'. In: Collins, R. (ed.): *Sociological Theory 1984*. Jossey-Bass Pub., S. Francisco

Brown, R. (1976): 'Women as Employees: Some Comments on Research in Industrial Sociology'. In: Barker, D.L. and Allen, S. (eds): *Dependence and Exploitation in Work and Marriage*. Longman, London

Cacioppo, M. (1982): 'La ricerca empirica sul lavoro femminile in Italia, 1950-1980' (Empirical research on women's work in Italy). *Inchiesta*, 12, 1982

Dahlström, E. and Liljeström, R. (1982): *Working-Class Women and Human Reproduction*. Forskingsrapport, Göteborgs Universitet, Göteborg

Eisenstadt, S.N. and Ahimeir, O. (eds) (1985): *The Welfare State and its Aftermath*. Croom Helm, London

Elster, J. (1979): *Ulysses and the Sirens*. Cambridge University Press, Cambridge

Familie und Arbeitswelt (1984): Bundesminister für Jugend, Familie und Gesundheit, Kohlhammer, Stuttgart

Federici, N. (1984): *Procreazione, famiglia, lavoro della donna* (Procreation, family, and women's work). Loescher, Torino

Finch, J. and Groves, D. (1983): *A Labour of Love. Women, Work and Caring*. Routledge and Kegan Paul, London

Flora, P. (ed.) (1984-85): *Growth to Limits. The Western European Welfare States, 1950-1980*. 5 vols, De Gruyter, Berlin

Flora, P. (1985): 'On the History and Current Problems of the Welfare State'. In: Eisenstadt, S.N. and Ahimeir, O. (eds): *The Welfare State and its Aftermath*. Croom Helm, London

Goodin, R.E. (1985): 'Self-Reliance versus the Welfare State'. *Journal of Social Policy*, 1, 1985

Habermas, J. (1971): *Storia e critica dell'opinione pubblica* (History and criticism of public opinion). Laterza, Bari, originally published in German: *Strukturwandel der Öffentlichkeit* (1962)

Habermas, J. (1982): *Theorie des kommunikativen Handelns. Zur Kritik der funktionalistischen Vernunft*. Suhrkamp, Frankfurt

Giovanni B. Sgritta

Hareven, T. (1982): *Family Time and Industrial Time*. Cambridge Univ. Press, Cambridge

Hirschman, A.O. (1970): *Exit, Voice, and Loyalty*. Harvard Univ. Press, Cambridge, Mass.

Johansen, L.N. and Kolberg, J.E. (1985): 'Welfare State Regression in Scandinavia? The Development of the Scandinavian Welfare State from 1970 to 1980'. In: Eisenstadt, S.N. and Ahimeir, O. (eds): *The Welfare State and its Aftermath*. Croom Helm, London

Kramer, R.M. (1985): 'The Welfare State and the Voluntary Sector: The Case of the Personal Social Services'. In: Eisenstadt, S.N. and Ahimeir, O. (eds): *The Welfare State and its Aftermath*. Croom Helm, London

Laslett, P. (1968): *The World We Have Lost*. Methuen, London

Laslett, P. and Wall, R. (eds) (1972): *Household and Family in Past Time*. Cambridge University Press, Cambridge

Lee, G.R. (1985): 'Kinship and Social Support of the Elderly: The Case of the United States'. *Ageing & Society*, 1, 1985

McAuley, A. (1982): 'Social Policy'. In: Brown, A. and Kaser, M. (eds) (1982): *Soviet Policy for the 1980s*. Macmillan, London

Mishra, R. (1977): *Society and Social Policy: Theoretical Perspectives on Welfare*. Macmillan, London

Mitterauer, M. and Sieder, R. (1982): *The European Family*. Basil Blackwell, Oxford

Moroney, R. (1976): *Family and the State*. Longman, London

Moss, P. and Fonda, N. (eds) (1980): *Work and the Family*. Temple Smith, London

National Reports (1982-84): 'Changes in the Life Patterns of Families in Europe'. Current Research Reports, Vienna Centre, Vienna, 3 vols

Pahl, R.E. (1981): 'From the Social Relations of Work to Household Work Strategies'. Fast, Marseille (mimeographed)

Parsons, T. and Smelser, N. (1964): *Economy and Society*. Italian translation by Angeli, Milano in 1970

Pitrou, A. et al. (1983): *Trajectoires professionnelles et stratégies familiales. Le cas des employés de la sécurité sociale et des aides-soignantes*, Cnrs-Lest, Aix en Provence

Rein, M. and Peattie, L. (1981): 'Knowledge for Policy'. *Social Service Review*, 4, 1981

Rosanvallon, P. (1981): *La Crise de l'Etat-providence*. Seuil, Paris

Scanzoni, J. (1983): *Shaping Tomorrow's Family*. Sage Publications, Beverly Hills

Sgritta, G.B. (1984): *Emarginazione, dipendenza e politica sociale* (Exclusion, dependence and social policy). Angeli, Milano

Sundström, G. (1982): 'The Elderly, Women's Work and Social Security Costs'. *Acta Sociologica*, 1, 1982

Waerness, K. (1984): 'Women in the Welfare State: The Case of Formal and Informal Old Age Care' (mimeographed)

Part Two

Paid and Unpaid Work

5

Women between the Family and Employment*

Riitta Jallinoja

Theoretical interpretations

When describing changes concerning the family, one of the most crucial phenomena mentioned is the participation of married women in the labour force. Interpretations have varied, but perhaps the most common explanation for the change has been found in industrialisation or, as it is often expressed, in the modernisation of a society (Goody, 1983, pp. 1-3; Morgan, D., 1980). Whatever concept in this connection has been used, the basic idea has been the same. The 'new' societal system has characteristics which foster the employment of married women. Most sociological traditions have adopted this type of interpretation.

Marxist theory relates the mode of production and the position of women very closely to each other. The connection between the private ownership of the means of production and the subordination of women has been regarded as direct (Engels, 1884/1902; Lapidus, 1979, p. 3) and in this respect the shift from capitalism to socialism is necessary, since it gives all women the opportunity to participate in social production and in public life, which in turn requires a shift of functions from the family to the wider society (Engles, 1884/1902; Rowbotham, 1976, pp. 82-3; Lapidus, 1979, p. 236); this type of shift was not considered to have been realised in capitalism. In the early seventies, when Western sociology was strongly influenced by Marxism, these interpretations were popular. They were not only accepted by openly Marxist-oriented researchers, but also by many others who preferred a materialist frame of reference.

*I would like to thank the Academy of Finland for funding the Finnish survey.

Many feminist-oriented researchers also adopted the interpretation. For them patriarchy was an essential part of capitalism and the former could not be eliminated without the abolition of capitalism (Allen, 1970, p. 13; Reed, 1971, p. 65; Rowbotham, 1976, pp. 65-6). Later on, the view became less popular among feminist researchers. Instead, patriarchy was seen as a more or less independent exploitative relationship which was in existence both in pre-capitalism and in socialism (Mitchell, 1966, pp. 12-17; Rowbotham, 1976, p. 45; Eisenstein, 1979, p. 25; Delphy, 1980, p. 1; Janssen-Jurreit, 1982, pp. 329-53). Experiences in the Soviet Union have dispelled the assumption that the liberation of women and the reform of the family go hand in hand in a socialist country. However, laying more stress on the role of the family was in contrast with the earlier view, according to which the liberation of women was accompanied by the loss of functions from the family (Lapidus, 1979, pp. 234-52).

Like Marxist theory, functionalist sociology has also had a strong tradition of the above-mentioned interpretation. Instead of the concepts of capitalism and socialism the functionalists have preferred the concept of 'industrialisation'. It has been regarded as a basic force, which drives all social institutions, habits and attitudes towards harmony with the total system. The conclusions drawn from this frame of reference have, however, been varied. Talcott Parsons saw that the new type of industrialised society with ever-increasing division of labour caused both the reduction of the family to a few specialised functions and the strong division of labour between men and women (Parsons, 1956; see also Goode, 1963, p. 16). Some other functionalists have, on the contrary, comprehended that the employment of women was one of the inborn products of industrialisation (Burgess, Locke and Thomes, 1963, pp. 349-50; Winch, 1963, pp. 399-405). In spite of conflicting conclusions, the basic interpretation remains the same. Women's role is more or less intimately connected with industrialisation (Parsons, 1956; Winch, 1963; Burgess, Locke and Thomes, 1963; Goode, 1963).

In addition to openly Marxist and functionalist researchers, many other sociologists have been very responsive to the view that there is a direct connection between industrialisation and patterns of family life. For example, Louise Tilly and Joan Scott have underlined the association of these areas. According to them, practically all changes and differences in women's participation in the labour force in Great Britain and France are explained by economic and demographic factors. As they say:

'An understanding of the position of women, in this case of their work-force participation, comes from an understanding of the economic, demographic, and family contexts within which they shape their lives. The history of women's work must be understood in terms of the history of changes in each of these variables and of changes in the relationships among them.' (Tilly and Scott, 1978, p. 215.)

But what is also significant is that, when it becomes difficult for them to interpret the employment rates of women through economic and demographic factors, other kinds of variables have to be found. These can then be, for example, religious and cultural values (Tilly and Scott, 1978, pp. 98 and 129). Louise Tilly and Joan Scott, however, only mention them, but they do not thoroughly analyse their real meaning.

The interpretation of the direct connection between the economic system and women's participation in the labour force is mainly based on aggregate figures, which evidently show parallel changes. In this way, at a very general level, tendencies in different countries appear to confirm the basic idea of the materialist interpretation. It is also supported by data on regional differences in each country. Married women are more generally in paid work in urban (i.e. more industrialised) areas than in rural (i.e. less industrialised) areas. The regional distinction is strengthened by data on family life in general. In the words of Gail Lapidus, there are thus two patterns of family behaviour (the case is from the Soviet Union):

'The limited impact of industrialization and urbanization on the local nationality and the persistence of traditional cultural norms are revealed on lower levels of female education, limited female labour-force participation outside agriculture and the predominance of early marriage and large families. A very different pattern of family behaviour characterized the urban and industrial regions of the USSR, particularly the Baltic and Slavic populations. High levels of female education and labour-force participation are accompanied by lower rates of marriage, later marriage age, high rates of divorce and declining family size.' (Lapidus, 1979, p. 262.)

The classification made by Lapidus is not at all uncommon for sociologists. As a result we have a popular and somewhat stereotyped view of two rather distinct modes or systems of production. The distinction is expressed by varied terms like pre-modern - modern, traditional - modern, pre-industrial - industrial, urban - rural, etc. These pairs are supposed to have corresponding patterns of family life, which can be characterised by a group of indicators, such as those mentioned above by Lapidus (see also Frykman and Löfgren, 1979; Goody, 1983, p. 3).

Economic conditions have not been regarded as the sole condition for the change. Edward Shorter emphasises the significance of values, though even he considers that 'market capitalism was probably at the root of the revolution in sentiment' (Shorter, 1977, p. 250). Lawrence Stones goes further in stressing the importance of mentalities. For him, the ideology (individualism) has been the crucial factor behind the change in family life (Stone, 1979, pp. 149-164). Applying this sort of interpretation to the labour-force participation of married women, one can say that they have been employed not only because they have *had to* do it for economic reasons, but also because it has become *acceptable* for married women to behave in that way. The question of acceptability refers to the ideological or cultural milieu, where the norms and values on human behaviour are expressed.

In order to understand the meaning of cultural milieu we must begin with the reasons behind women's participation in the labour force. National surveys carried out for this project show that the employment of women *per se* has not been unnatural. Only up to 5 per cent of urban women have never worked outside their homes. Most women have started their more or less permanent work before they were 20 years old (71-88 per cent). This was already common in the nineteenth century. The majority of the female labour force was young and single (Pinchbeck, 1969; Tilly and Scott, 1978, pp. 82-7; Jallinoja, 1980, pp. 228-9). It is then the family which has influenced the numbers of women in the labour market in a decisive way. This also came out in our surveys, where women and men were asked the reason for dropping out from paid work. Overwhelmingly the most often mentioned reason for women was *the care of children*. In the case of men, this was practically never mentioned as a cause for longer absence from the job. This kind of reason is related to the assumption that it is not only economic obligations which force married women into the labour market or allow them to stay at home. Though these factors are of importance, women's special relation to the family must also be taken into consideration.

To understand the real meaning of differences between the sexes in this respect, one must examine the ideologies which have formulated the idea of women's special relationship to the family. The relationship emerged in two contradictory views, in the ideal of housewife and in the ideal of the economically independent, i.e. employed, woman. Both of these ideals were formulated publicly in the nineteenth century. The ideal of housewife was expressed in the often-cited statement 'Family is the woman's natural place'. Many researchers believe this was originally the ideal of the middle class, from whom it spread out to the working class. This tended to distinguish between the role of husband and wife more sharply than earlier. Husbands became the sole breadwinners of the family, while wives devoted most of their time to childcare and household management (Tilly and Scott, 1978, pp. 6-145 and 176-7; Shorter, 1977, p. 261).

The ideal of the employed woman was presented publicly mainly by those women who struggled for their liberation and independence. For them, the family was not necessarily the sole life-sphere of married women. On the contrary, they insisted on the right of women to have both a family and paid work. Little by little the view received more and more popularity. This meant a change in the arguments for women's participation in the labour force.

The question of married women's participation in the labour force is thus not only an objectively defined fact but also an ideologically determined issue. In this respect, people have had varied opinions since the last century on women's relation to their family and paid work (Morgan, 1980, pp. 204-13; Jallinoja, 1984, pp. 37-57). The borderline between these opinions has not been clear, but at a general level the labour-force participation of married women has been an issue in which nearly everybody has tended to take a stand, often irrespective of his/her economic circumstances.

If the role of economic conditions in explaining the generality of married women's employment is not clear, the same can be said about the ideological factors. The only matter evident in this phase is that the role of the ideological and cultural milieu is at least of some significance. Its nature may even be of a different kind in socialist and capitalist countries. In capitalist countries, far advanced individualism and, its sequence, pluralism have together created an atmosphere of free choice. People are faced with a variety of alternatives, from which they are able to choose the most suitable one for themselves. In the case of married women, work-force participation could become a phenomenon of this sort (Berger, 1979, pp. 108-9; see also Rapoport's chapter in this book). In socialist countries, only one ideology has been prevalent, but it also has taken a stand on the matter. It has not so much emphasised free choice, but more the responsibilities of citizens, among which social labour, instead of private labour, is the dominant ideal (Lapidus, 1979).

Differences between socialist and capitalist countries also emerged from the surveys in our project to some extent. In capitalist countries, women who have stayed at home for a longer time, declared that they *wanted* to take care of their children (75-90 per cent: Finland, Sweden, Norway and the Netherlands). Only a small number of women felt that they were *obliged* to stay at home. The situation is somewhat different in socialist countries, where according to the survey data, women less often declared that the reason for staying at home was because they wanted to take care of their children (10-40 per cent: Slovenia, Poland and the Soviet Union).

These theoretical explanations were in my mind when I began to scrutinise the topic from a comparative perspective. In all 12 countries in this project the employment of women increased after the Second World War. In every country industrialisation has taken place, and finally, the family has changed in the direction which we generally call 'modern'. Divorces have increased in numbers, fertility rates have declined, cohabitation has become more common, etc. Changes like this support the relevance of the materialist theory mentioned above.

But in addition to these quite clear parallelisms, there are many data which distort the image of a direct relationship between these three spheres of life. For example, the rising standard of living mentioned by Tilly and Scott (1978, p. 142) was not only linked to the increasing number of housewives among working-class families in the 1920s and 1930s, but also brought about the decline in the proportion of housewives in the same social class in the 1960s and 1970s. Respectively, our survey data show that the proportion of housewives is not greatest among women with high social-economic status, but among women of the working class, which is a result contradictory to the materialist theory. Conflicting information gives good reason for a more detailed analysis. In other words, interpretations on a very general level are not sufficient for the comprehension of the tremendous differences between countries and of the nature of the change in the labour-force participation of married women.

The patterns

Differences between countries at the same moment in time and the direction of the change together reveal that changes in women's participation in the labour force has proceeded at varying speed. At the same time, the differences make manifest a kind of logic within which *the historically typical phases of the change* are realised. One can call them patterns or models, which indicate married women's special relation to the family and paid work. The patterns are here formed on the basis of real behaviour, i.e. according to how generally married women with children are employed. These patterns not only manifest real behaviour, but they also refer to certain ideologies, in which the conceptualisation of the family and women's relation to it are stipulated (Morgan, D., 1980, pp. 204-13; Rapoport's chapter in this book). These patterns are like ideal types.

The information used in the formation of the patterns is, first of all, from the data in Figure 1 (women's employment rate). The proportion of women who are economically active is not the best indicator for our purpose, because it includes single women, too. Employment rates by age groups (Table 5.1), however, reveal a tendency to drop out from the job when children are small. The proportion of part-time work is also of significance in forming the patterns (Table 5.2), and also important additional information is received from the national surveys made for this project.

Respondents were asked how the day care of their own and of their small children was arranged (Tables 5.3 and 5.4).

Table 5.1. Employed women as a percentage of all women according to age groups*

In 1960

Age group (years)	20-24	25-34	35-44	45-54
Soviet Union	86	75	79	71
Poland	68	63	68	67
Hungary	55	49	51	48
Finland	61	56	58	58
GDR	74	68	70	67
Slovenia	..	..	..	..
France	62	42	40	45
FRG	72	48	46	40
Norway	48	22	19	24
Sweden	57	39	36	36
Great Britain	62	38	42	43
Italy	41	29	27	24
Netherlands	53	19	16	16

In 1970

Age group (years)	20-24	25-29	30-44	45-49	50-54	55-59
Soviet Union		86	93	91	77	26
Poland	73	75	79	79	76	68
Hungary	66	65	70	64	57	29
Finland	63	68	68	64	59	49
GDR	75	79	80	80	74	62
Slovenia	..	..	..	..	..	..
France	62	51	42	45	45	42
FRG	67	51	46	48	43	35
Norway	48	35	28	35	35	32
Sweden	53	49	50	55	50	41
Great Britain	60	43	53	61	59	51
Italy	45	36	30	30	26	17
Netherlands	56	25	23	23	21	18

Table 5.1 continued

In 1980

Age group (years)	20-24	25-29	30-34	35-39	40-44	45-49	50-54	55-59
Soviet Union	..	..	..	..	..	..	..	..
Poland	68	75	79	82	83	78	72	58
Hungary	60	70	81	85	83	77	66	19
Finland	61	74	77	82	83	80	71	55
GDR	..	..	..	..	..	..	..	..
Slovenia	..	..	..	..	..	..	..	..
France	67	71	67	65	62	58	54	45
FRG	70	63	58	59	58	55	48	40
Norway**	65	68	71	75	79	80	71	61
Sweden**	71	74	75	79	83	83	78	66
Great Britain**	..	..	..	..	..	..	..	..
Italy	60	59	52	46	42	36	30	17
Netherlands	72	55	44	46	45	39	29	20

*For 1960 see *The Economic Role of Women in the ECE Region.* United Nations, 1980, pp. 7-8; for 1970 see *Yearbook of Labour Statistics 1975.* ILO, Table 1; for 1980 op. cit. 1984, Table 1.
**Countries with a high proportion of part-time work among females.

At first glance it seems to be difficult to construct any kind of classification on the basis of the information in Figure 1. This is especially true of the year 1960, when the dispersion of employment rates was quite even. In 1970, clustering is evident and it can also be seen in 1980. A kind of tripartition is apparent, which corresponds to the different ideals concerning married women's participation in the labour force. These ideals have been, firstly, that the family needs a woman's full-time participation, secondly that women are allowed to return to paid work after the children have grown up, and finally that all married women have a right to paid work. These ideals have historically followed each other in the above-mentioned order.

Figure 5.1. *Employed women as a percentage of all women according to age groups*

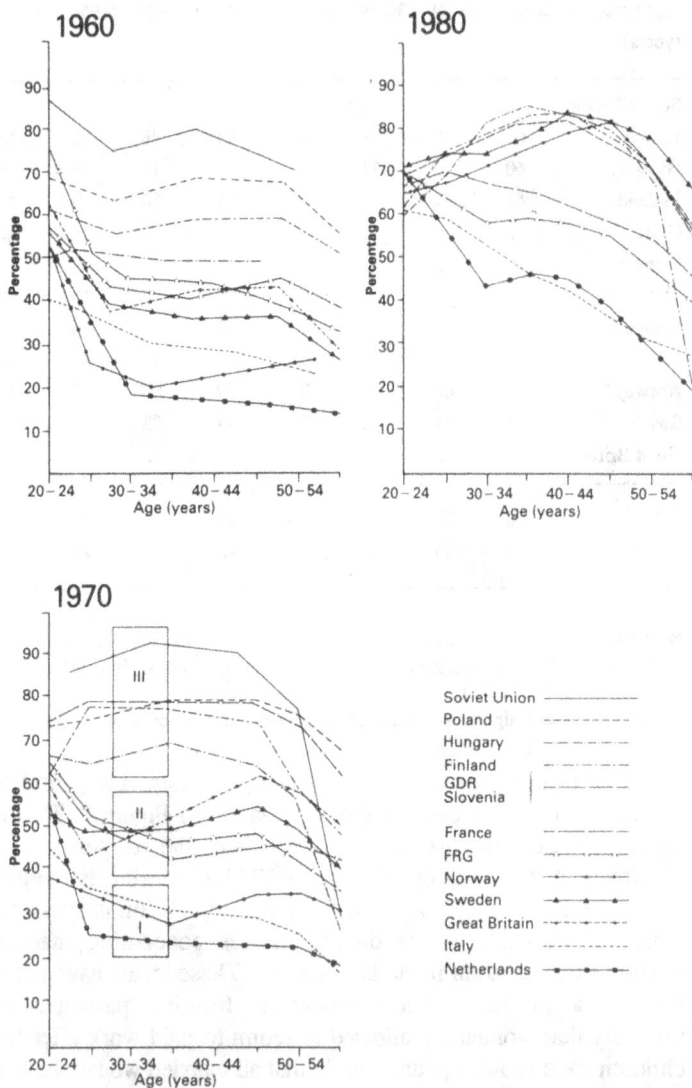

1960

1980

1970

Soviet Union	————————
Poland	————————
Hungary	————————
Finland	————————
GDR	
Slovenia	
France	————————
FRG	————————
Norway	—•—•—•—
Sweden	—▲—▲—▲—
Great Britain	—•—••—••—
Italy	————————
Netherlands	—●—●—●—

Women between Family and Employment

Table 5.2. Employment rates (%)

	Service sector as a proportion of the total non-agricultural labour force*	Females in the service sector*	Females of all university students**	Part-time employed of the total female labour force**
	(1980)	(1980)	(1975)	(1977)
Soviet Union	(38)a	(66)a	50	2b
Poland	36c	..	49	1d
Hungary	36	61	49	..
Finland	44	67	49	7
GDR	48e	60-70f	49g	..
Slovenia	38h	53i	44	5j
France	50	..	46	18
FRG	49	51	32	28
Norway	58	57	36	52
Sweden	58	62	37	46
Great Britain	55k	59k	34	41
Italy	43	43	39	12
Netherlands	55	44	25	28

*Yearbook of Labour Statistics. ILO, 1984, Table 2A.
**The Economic Role of Women in the ECE Region. United Nations, 1980, p. 93.
a In 1970. Suomen tilastollinen vuosikirja 1983 (Statistical Yearbook of Finland).
b Results of the survey made for this project.
c In 1975 (Morawski and Seppänen, 1978, p. 39).
d Results of the Polish survey for this project.
e In 1970. Suomen tilastollinen vuosikirja 1983.
f Gysi and Speigner, 1984, p. 35.
g Gysi and Speigner, 1984, p. 50.
h The percentage concerns the tertiary and quartiary sectors, in 1975. Traffic is included, which in turn is excluded from the percentages of other countries (Boh, 1980, p. 20).
i The percentage includes the tertiary and quartiary sectors in 1972 (Boh, 1980, p. 22).
j Boh, 1980, p. 17.
k Lockwood and Knowles, 1984, pp. 5-6.

Table 5.3. *The percentage proportion of women caring themselves for their children, in two generations**

	Older generation (mothers) Mothers not at all employed when the interviewed person was		Younger generation (their daughters) Cared for the first child, when it was	
	under school age	at school age	0-3 years old	4-6 years old
Soviet Union	18	12	..	..
Poland	40	33	(32-7)a	(30)a
Hungary**	63	..	73	47
Finland	70	59	56	45
GDR	..	..	..	..
Slovenia**	64	64	27	16
France	..	..	..	..
FRG	73	..	(68)b	(92)b (64)b
Norway	93	82	83	79
Sweden**	..	..	52c	
Great Britain	..	..	(70)d	(38)d
Italy**	71	68	62	53
Netherlands	95	95	74	75

*On the basis of the national surveys made for this project. The older generation covers approximately the years of 1920-59. The younger generation covers approximately the years of 1945-80.

The question in the questionnaire concerning the older generation was: 'Did your mother go out to work before you went to school?' and 'Did your mother go out to work when you went to school?' In the case of the younger generation the question was: 'How did you arrange the day care of your first child, when this was 0-3 and 4-6 years old?' Percentages in columns 3 and 4 manifest the proportion of women who have themselves taken care of their first child.

**Samples concern only employed women.

a The lower value is taken from the national survey made for this project (1983-4). The percentage covers those families, who have arranged the day care of the children at home. The higher figure is from 1967. See Piotrowsky, 1969, p. 35.

b 92 per cent is probably too great. According to Microcensus (1976) 32 per cent of the women who had one child aged 0-2 were employed. In the case of a child aged 0-6, 36 per cent of women were employed (Nave-Herz, 1980, Appendix Table 25b). This means that 68 per cent and 64 per cent better correspond to reality than 92 per cent, which was obtained from the survey made for this project.

c Children aged 0-6.

dIn 1980, of women aged 16-59 with 0-4 or 5-9 years old child (Lockwood and Knowles, 1984, p. 4).

Table 5.4. *The percentage rates of women having cared for their first child themselves according to the birth year of the woman**

Mother's birth year	1920-29		1930-39		1940-49		1950-59	
Child's age	0-3	(4-6)	0-3	(4-6)	0-3	(4-6)	0-3	(4-6)
Soviet Union	..	(..)	..	(..)	..	(..)	..	(..)
Poland	..	(..)	..	(..)	..	(..)	..	(..)
Hungary**	63	(51)	69	(47)	86	(47)	..	(..)
Finland	69	(64)	57	(49)	46	(33)	52	(32)
GDR	..	(..)	..	(..)	..	(..)	..	(..)
Slovenia**	41	(24)	27	(19)	13	(5)		
France	..	(..)	..	(..)	..	(..)	..	(..)
FRGa		93b		93b		94b		90b
Norway	95	(94)	78	(72)	79	(65)	77	
Sweden**		75b	..	(..)		53b		26b
Great Britain	..	(..)	..	(..)	..	(..)	..	(..)
Italy**	..	(..)	71	(58)	56	(46)	60	(54)
Netherlands	81	(81)	82	(82)	70	(70)	..	(..)

*On the basis of the national surveys made for this project.
**Samples concern only employed women.
a See note (b) to Table 5.3.
b Children aged 0-6.

The final problem in constructing the patterns is to determine the boundaries of each model. No country represents any pure pattern. In every country there are housewives and employed married women, and the proportions of these groups of women have changed in every country from 1960 to 1980. So the classification of countries according to the patterns may vary within time, as can be seen in Figure 5.1. The final classification of countries based on which pattern they typically adhere to, has been made on the basis of information from 1980.

1. The *housewife pattern* could also be called traditional (Dahlström, 1962, p. 18; Holter, 1973, p. 60; Rapoport's chapter in this book). The criterion for this pattern is simply

that the majority of younger married women are housewives, i.e. more than 60 per cent. According to this kind of definition, the following countries belonged to this pattern:

1960	1970	1980
Netherlands	Netherlands	Netherlands
Norway	Norway	Italy
Italy	Italy	
Sweden		
France		
Great Britain		
FRG		

If we have a look at generational differences, we can see that the housewife pattern was very common among women of the older generation, i.e. born before 1930 (cf. Table 4). Only the Soviet Union is an exception to this rule. Among women born in 1940-9 the pattern was becoming less popular. As can be seen in Figure 1, there was a change in the 1960s and 1970s, when the women's movement made the employment of married women a great public issue. In spite of the wide extent of the change, the housewife pattern is still common in two countries, namely in the Netherlands and in Italy. Italy with its quite large-scale informal work (Sgritta and Saporiti, 1980, pp. 51-2), however, could better be located between this and the following pattern.

2. *Of the moderate sex role pattern* it is typical that married women have a shorter or longer period of interruption from the job. The idea is that women are expected to stay at home, when their children are small. Part-time jobs and other respective solutions, which help women to combine paid work and domestic responsibilities better than full-time work, are also typical of this pattern (Musgrave and Wheeler-Bennett, 1972, p. 95).

The ideology of the moderate pattern began to appear in public debate after the Second World War, especially in the 1950s, but in some countries not until in the 1960s (Clason, Lameijer and Bosman, 1981, p. 41). The view was presented, for example, in Alva Myrdal's and Viola Klein's book *Women's Two Roles* (1968, pp. 12-22), which became popular, at least in the Nordic countries (Jallinoja, 1983, pp. 146-9). Edmund Dahlström called this sex role ideology 'moderate' (Dahlström, 1962, pp. 23-4). Historically, the pattern follows the first-mentioned one. In the moderate sex role pattern the idea that the family continuously needs a woman's full-time participation is disappearing. It is only small children who need a full-time mother. An expression for this kind of solution is that women have 'some sort of career', contrasted to the 'wholly dedicated career women' (Musgrave and Wheeler-Bennett, 1972, p. 93). The countries of the moderate sex role pattern were:

1960	1970	1980
Hungary	Great Britain	France
Finland	Sweden	FRG
	FRG	Sweden
	France	Norway
		Great Britain

On the basis of Figure 5.1, Sweden and Norway could be classified as belonging to the next pattern in 1980, but because of the high proportion (41-52 per cent) of part-time work among females, these countries have still been considered as typically belonging to the group of countries with moderate sex role pattern (cf. Table 5.2).

3. Other conceptual expressions for *the pattern of employed woman* have been 'egalitarian' (Holter, 1973, p. 60) and 'radical' (Dahlström, 1962, p. 23). Women's participation in the labour-force is very high in this pattern (over 70 per cent). Part-time work is atypical of this pattern, and most women do not interrupt their job careers longer than for the period of official maternity leave. The national surveys made for our project revealed that 66-85 per cent of women, who lived in the countries of this pattern, have interrupted their paid work no more than two years (Poland, Hungary, the Soviet Union). In the countries of the moderate or housewife pattern, the percentages are much smaller, 15-32 per cent (the Netherlands and Norway). The countries belonging to this pattern were:

1960	1970	1980
Soviet Union	Soviet Union	Soviet Union
Poland	Poland	Poland
GDR*	GDR	GDR
	Finland	Hungary
	Hungary	Finland

*Data are not available. The GDR has been allocated to this pattern on the basis of information on the proportion of females in the total labour force.

Differences between the countries

The queries about the different patterns discussed above mainly relate to the fact that in some countries the speed of change has been rapid, whereas in other countries it has been relatively slow. In every country, the direction of the change has been the same, from the dominance of the 'housewife pattern' towards the more evident dominance of the 'pattern of employed woman'. To explain variations between countries, the materialist theories have been used as a starting-point. According to them the level of industrialisation, i.e. the modernisation of a society, is closely related to the employment rate of women. The other life sphere, which in these theories is often associated with this issue, consists of indicators of the 'modernity' of family life. In this respect, reproductive strategies and other demographic factors have been thought to be of significance (Tilly and Scott, 1978, p. 103).

The indicators chosen here to measure the level of modernisation of a society and family life are not sufficient, so they do not fully express the complexity of relationships between these three life spheres and their nature. But these indicators have very often been used in research into this kind of problems.

First of all, the 12 countries are classified by the employment rates of women into three groups. The classification was made according to the above-mentioned patterns. Some other indicators measuring the existing sex role practices are also used to widen the picture of this life sphere. These indicators are: the proportion of female students of all university students and the proportion of women in the service sector.

The level of industrialisation is measured simply by the proportion of the non-agricultural sector within the total labour force. In this respect, the countries are classified into two groups: (1) early and advanced industrialised countries and (2) late and rapidly industrialised countries. This indicator is accompanied by an indicator concerning the proportion of the labour force in the service sector, which is generally supposed to be connected with the number of women in the labour force.

Finally, two indicators have been chosen to measure the 'modernity' of family life, namely divorce and fertility rates. Both of them have been understood to relate to the employment rates of women. The relevance of the above-mentioned theories is 'tested' in a very simple way. The countries are classified according to each indicator into two or three groups, depending on how great differences between them there are. In Figure 5.2 solid circles (●) indicate a high degree of 'modernity', while open circles (○) a low degree of 'modernity'. The group (marked by a half-solid circle ◐) between these two poles is used if the aggregate figures give reason for it (the dispersion of an indicator is great).

Table 5.5. The non-agricultural labour force as a percentage of the total labour force, 1950-80*

	1950	1960	1970	1980
Soviet Union	..	..	74	..
Poland	43	57	66	70a
Hungary	53	..	75	78
Finland	54	65	80	89
GDR	74	..	88	..
Slovenia	92	93b	96b	..
France	64	80	87	92
FRG	78	88	92	94
Norway	74	81	88	92
Sweden	79	86	92	94
Great Britain	95	95	..	98
Italy	53	73	81	87
Netherlands	81	89	..	..

**Suomen tilastollinen vuosikirja* 1953, 1965, 1973, 1983 (Statistical Yearbook of Finland)
aIn 1975 (Morawski and Seppänen, 1978, p. 39).
bIn 1965 and 1975 respectively; Boh, 1980, p. 21.

The main conclusion drawn from the two first columns of Figure 5.2 measuring the modernity of women is that the employment rates of women are related to women's general *educational level* as measured by 'females of all university students'. The more generally women are employed, the closer is their educational level to that of men. The employment and education of women then go well hand in hand. The historical comparative analysis, however, reveals that the proportion of females in the total non-agricultural labour force increases earlier than the proportion of females among all students. This means that women tend first to occupy low-level jobs and to venture only later higher-level jobs and education, too.

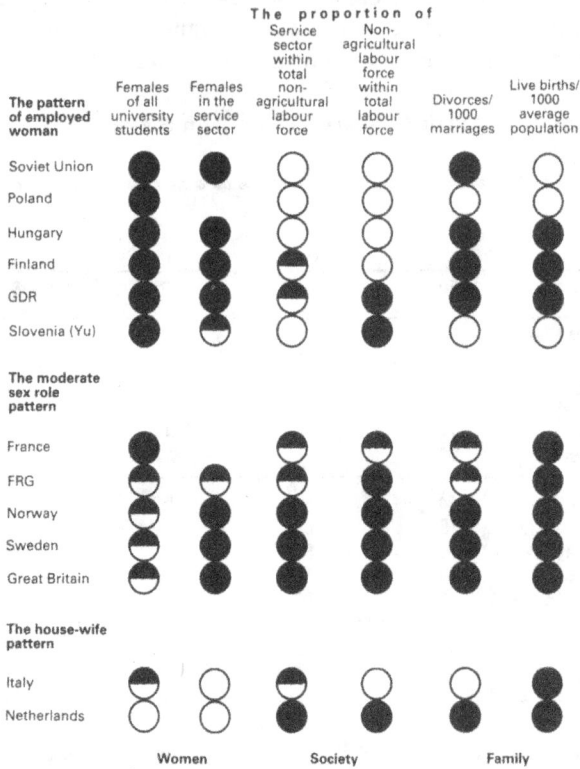

	Females of all university students	Females in the service sector	The proportion of		Divorces/ 1000 marriages	Live births/ 1000 average population
The pattern of employed woman			Service sector within total non-agricultural labour force	Non-agricultural labour force within total labour force		

The moderate sex role pattern

The house-wife pattern

Women   Society   Family

Exact figures and sources as given in Tables 2, 5 and 6

Females of all university level students:
= 50 − 44%;   = 39 − 32%;   = 25%.

Females in service sector:
= 70 − 57%;   = 53 − 51%;   = 43 − 44%.

Service sector of the total non-agricultural labour force:
= 58 − 55%;   = 50 − 43%;   = 38 − 36%.

Non-agricultural labour force within total labour force:
= in 1950 74 − 95%;   = in 1950 43 − 64%
  in 1980 92 − 98%;   in 1980 70 − 92%

Divorces/1000 marriages:
= 509 − 320;   = 265 − 201;   = 165 − 124.

Live births/1000 average population:
= 10.0 − 14.9;   = 16.0 − 19.4

Figure 5.2. Classification of countries according to the 'modernity' of a society, women and the family (1980) (for exact figures and sources see Tables 5.2, 5.5 and 5.6)

112

Table 5.6. *Divorces/1000 marriages and live births/1000 average population around 1980*

	Divorces/1000 marriages[*]	Live births/ 1000 average population[**]
Soviet Union	332[a]	19.0
Poland	125	19.4
Hungary	355	12.5
Finland	320	13.2
GDR	349	14.2
Slovenia[***]	201	14.5
France	254	14.9
FRG	265	10.0
Norway	320	12.4
Sweden	509	11.3
Great Britain	411	13.1
Italy	135[b]	10.9
Netherlands	333	12.5

[*]*Demographic Yearbook 1982.* United Nations, Tables 31 and 32.
[**]Ibid.: Table 4.
[***]In 1983; *Statisticni letopis* (1984).
[a]In 1976 (Kharchev, 1982, p. 39).
[b]In 1978, separated included (Sgritta and Saporiti, 1980, p. 166).

This also supports the view, according to which it was the working-class women who were the first ones among married women to enter the labour force (Shorter, 1977, pp. 255-7). And it was only later that well-educated women tended to be more often employed than the less educated ones, as came out in the national surveys of our project (in Finland, Slovenia, Hungary very clearly, in the Netherlands and Italy less clearly, and in the FRG not at all).

The proportion of women in the service sector coincides with the general employment rates of women, too. But it is important to notice that the advancement of the service sector is not in a positive relation to the employment rates of women (see column 3 in Figure 2). For example, in many socialist countries this sector is not very advanced and in spite of this the participation of women in the labour force is very high. Or in the Netherlands the service sector was very developed already in the 1950s and despite this the employment of women has remained at a low level. This result at least partly conflicts with the interpretations that have been commonly presented. The employment rates of women then do not relate directly to the supply of 'suitable jobs for women' (see Tilly and Scott, 1978, pp. 216 and 230; Haavio-Mannila's chapter on gender segregation in this book).

If we then look at the relationship of the employment of women to the level of *industrialisation* of a society, we can make the following conclusions (column 4 in Figure 2). First of all, it is worth mentioning that there are some significant conflicting results concerning the materialist theories we referred to. The employment rates of women are clearly highest in countries where industrialisation occurred comparatively late, whereas the employment rates of women are moderate or even low in countries where industrialisation began much earlier. The result demonstrates that the influence of industrialisation on women's employment is of an indirect character. In the long run, it increases their participation in the labour force, but how it does this depends on some other factors.

The most important factor, perhaps, is that in the late and rapidly industrialised countries the increased demand for labour was restricted to a particular and quite short period, mainly in the 1960s. The atmosphere in the 1960s began to be favourable for the employment of women. On the other hand, however, in early industrialised countries the demand for labour could be fulfilled by males, which was in line with the earlier prevailing ideal. Thus, the 'ideal of housewife' could be better realised in these countries than in the later industrialised ones. It is then the speed and timing of industrialisation rather than the fact of industrialisation itself which has influenced the employment rates of married women, causing thus differences between the industrialised countries in this way too.

If we now examine how some indicators of *family life* reflect its relationship to the participation of married women in the labour force, the main results are as follows. Family life has changed in every country in the same way. Relatively small changes occurred in the 1950s, either in divorce or in fertility rates. The transition was larger in the 1960s and, in the case of divorce, even greater in the 1970s. Thus these changes accompanied the increase in women's participation in the labour force. But more detailed examinations reveal that the relationship is even here not quite direct.

One of the most important conclusions is that family life is not directly dependent on the prevailing sex role model or vice versa. In countries, where the housewife pattern is still common, the divorce rates can be quite high (column 5) and the fertility rates quite low (column 6 in Figure 2). In this respect, the small size of the family is not unilinearly connected with the pattern of employed women, or vice versa, the housewife pattern with a larger number of children in the family, as is often presumed. This kind of conclusion is evident when using national aggregate figures. But when comparing women with only one child to women with more children, the impact of the number of children is according to the hypothesis. The former women are more generally employed than the latter ones, which emerged very clearly from our national surveys (the Netherlands, Finland, Slovenia very clearly; Italy and Hungary relatively clearly; and FRG not at all).

The results presented here justify the following conclusions. At a very general level the three above-mentioned life spheres are connected to each other. The sex role patterns are accompanied by industrialisation and the modernisation of family life (in this case by an increase in the number of divorces and declining fertility). The relationship is, however, indirect. There are many inter-mediating factors which make the relationship rather complex. Thus there is some reason for saying that women's participation in the labour force and family life have *a relative independence* in relation both to each other and to the rate of industrialisation. That is, the impact of the transition from a less modern to a more modern state varies in these life spheres, depending on many national contexts, which still await closer inquiry.

The impact of ideologies

Here we examine only ideologies which have been formative in the issue of women's participation in the labour force and in that of their relationship to the family. Ideologies are generally understood to have not a decisive role in promoting a change, but rather a role of intermediating character. They may either hasten or detain the change, which was originally caused by some objective force.

Among social movements the *women's movement* has had an important influence on women's participation in the labour force.

The activation of the movement in the 1960s and 1970s was accompanied by an increase in the employment of women. This sort of synchronism suggests that the increase in the participation of married women in the labour force has the character of a movement. The public debate on the issue was not only large scale since the 1960s but also internationally parallel. When a phenomenon is like a social movement, it spreads irrespective of the economic and structural circumstances of a society (Jallinoja, 1983, pp. 25-30; see also Tilly, Tilly and Tilly, 1980, p. 247). It then breaks up obstacles which until recently strongly restricted the employment of married women. But even the meaning of the women's movement and of the public debate inspired by it is not quite unambiguous. The consequences of the women's movement have not been equally strong in each country, which can also be seen in the employment rates of women.

Socialism as an ideology seems to have had the same sort of consequences in women's participation in the labour force as the women's movement. Socialism has favoured the employment of women on the basis of equality. It has also favoured 'social labour' instead of 'private labour'. It seems to be that socialism as an ideology has perhaps been of great significance in the increase of married women's employment, because all socialist countries put into effect the pattern of employed women relatively early. Some modifications of the pattern are also possible, irrespective of the tradition of socialism.

In Hungary, mothers generally take care of their small children (cf. Table 4) because of a long maternity leave. Mothers are allowed to stay at home until the child is 3 years old. The long maternity leave is used in full primarily by female manual workers and least by well-educated women (Sas, 1981, p. 14). In Poland, the recent crisis has created a situation which also, but on another basis, has tended to increase the traditional solutions. The fertility rate has increased and people now emphasise the significance of the family as a life sphere, where they can determine their own life patterns, while possibilities for individual autonomy outside the family have diminished (Haavio-Mannila, Liljeström and Sokolowska, 1985, pp. 88-9).

Religious values are also of some significance in connection with the employment of married women. All European Churches have taken a stand in this issue. The Churches have mainly been on the side of the familistic view, which among other things means that the family is understood as a natural place for married women

(Morgan, 1966; Goody, 1983, pp. 83-182; Mount, 1984, pp. 25-41). In the socialist countries, except in Poland, religion is no longer of great importance. This tendency has supported the high employment rates of married women. Countries where protestantism has had the major position, have experienced a strong secularisation. In this way the influence of religion is no longer so great. In countries where a comparatively large part of the population is Catholic, the role of religion is still of some importance, which supports the maintenance of the housewife patterns in spite of the otherwise strong modernisation process taking place in society.

All above-mentioned ideological tendencies have fostered the employment of married women. It is, however, impossible to clarify the extent to which ideology has maintained an independent position. It is also worthy of reminder that, even in socialist countries, there have been and still are individuals and groups who are on the side of the familistic view. Adherents of this standpoint have not yet united into a movement as in the United States (Berger and Berger, 1984, pp. 84-90). Even there it is too soon to say how far-reaching the consequences of this sort of movement may be. In Europe, the debate associated with the familistic movement has emerged in the question of the employment of mothers with children less than 3 years old. The issue has been discussed in many European countries, but only Finland (1985) and Hungary have put into effect a maternity or parental leave of three years.

Concluding remarks

In the long run, industrialisation or the modernisation of a society in general increases the employment of married women. In the long run, too, the latter is related to the modernisation of family life, in this case to smaller families, and an increase in the number of divorces. The results indicate that the relationships between these spheres are not absolutely direct. In fact, only comparative analyses can help to reveal the complicated nature of the change. This means that it is not only labour-market conditions but many other factors too which influence the speed of the change in married women's participation in the labour force. All these objective and ideological factors work either for or against the labour-force participation of married women.

In spite of the tendency in every country to move in its own particular way from the dominance of the housewife pattern towards the pattern of employed woman, some regularities could be outlined. In Figure 5.3 all countries have been classified according to the dominant pattern in 1960, 1970 and 1980. By following the types of transition, two main distinct groups emerge.

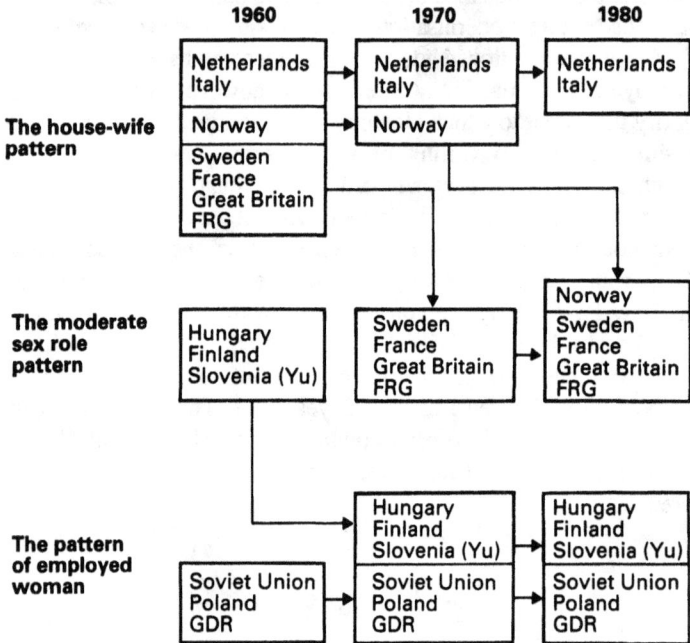

	1960	1970	1980
The house-wife pattern	Netherlands Italy →	Netherlands Italy →	Netherlands Italy
	Norway →	Norway	
	Sweden France Great Britain FRG		
The moderate sex role pattern			Norway
	Hungary Finland Slovenia (Yu)	Sweden France Great Britain FRG	Sweden France Great Britain FRG
The pattern of employed woman		Hungary Finland Slovenia (Yu) →	Hungary Finland Slovenia (Yu)
	Soviet Union Poland GDR →	Soviet Union Poland GDR →	Soviet Union Poland GDR

Figure 5.3. The classification of countries according to the dominant pattern, in 1960, 1970 and 1980 (for sources see Figure 5.1 and Table 5.1)

The first one consists of countries where the housewife pattern was common in 1960 but this pattern was substituted by the moderate sex role pattern after 1970. The core of this group is formed by Sweden, France, Great Britain and the FRG. In 1980, Norway 'joined' the group. These countries are characterised by the following features: early advanced industrialisation (high income level), strong independent women's movements (especially in the 1970s), high or moderate divorce rates and low fertility rates.

All these factors are related, according to many theories, to high employment rates of women. At least to some extent a reverse outcome leads one to look for a factor which has prevented the labour-force participation of married women in spite of otherwise favourable conditions. This factor is suggested to be associated with the attitudes concerning the relationship of women to the family. The effect of this factor could have been the following one. During the early period of industrialisation and urbanisation, the housewife ideal was formed by the middle class. Because of well-advanced industrialisation the middle class could become large and powerful. For this reason it was also possible to retain the culturally significant ideal of the housewife role. This ideal then became a factor which in a relatively independent way could hold back the labour-force participation of married women, irrespective of otherwise favourable conditions for the employment of these women.

In the other group, the situation is to some extent of the opposite kind. The group consists of countries which adopted the pattern of women's employment relatively early. The core of the group is formed by the Soviet Union, Poland and the GDR. In 1970, Hungary, Finland and Slovenia 'joined' the group. These countries are characterised by the following features: late and rapid industrialisation (moderate income level), a poorly expanded service sector, socialism (except Finland), no strong women's movement (except Finland where it is relatively moderate), partly high and partly low divorce rates.

The high employment rates of married women in this group seem to relate most clearly to socialism and late industrialisation. Together they have created both objective and cultural conditions for the rapid increase in married women's participation in the labour force. Although even in these countries at an earlier period the housewife ideal was generally accepted, without a strong and large middle class this could not be formed into a nation-wide ideal. It was thus comparatively easy to abandon in a situation where the demand for labour during the period of rapid industrialisation very much increased.

Riitta Jallinoja

References

Allen, P. (1970): *Free Space. A Perspective on the Small Group in Women's Liberation*. New York

Berger, P. (1979): *Facing up to Modernity. Excursion in Society, Politics, and Religion*. Harmondsworth

Berger, P. and Berger, B. (1984): *The War over the Family. Capturing the Middle Ground*. Harmondsworth

Boh, K. (1980): 'Changes in the Life Patterns of Families in Europe'. National Report from Slovenia (Yugoslavia). Institute of Sociology, University of Ljubljana (Vienna Centre background material)

Burgess, E., Locke, H. and Thomes, M. (1963): *The Family. From Institution to Companionship*. New York

Clason, Ch., Lameijer, I. and Bosman, R. (1981): 'The Family in the Netherlands since 1945'. National Report based on historical, statistical and other data available. Rijks Universiteit Groningen (Vienna Centre background material)

Dahlström, E. (1962): 'Analys av könsrolldebatten (Analysis of the sexual debate)'. In: *Kvinnors liv och arbete* (Women's life and work), Stockholm

Delphy, Ch. (1980): 'The Main Enemy. A Materialist Analysis of Women's Oppression'. *Exploration in Feminism*, No. 3. London

Demographic Yearbook (1982) United Nations, New York

The Economic Role of Women in the ECE Region (1980). United Nations, New York

Eisenstein, Z. (1979): 'Developing a Theory of Capitalist Patriarchy and Socialist Feminism'. In: Eisenstein, Z. (ed.): *Capitalist Patriarchy and the Case for Socialist Feminism*. New York

Engels, F. (1884/1902): *The Origin of the Family, Private Property and the State*. Chicago

Frykman, J. and Löfgren, O. (1979): 'Den kultiverade människan' (The cultural man). Skrifter utgivna av Etnologiska sällskapet i Lund, Lund

Goode, W. (1963): *World Revolution and Family Pattern*. New York

Goody, J. (1983): *The Development of the Family and Marriage in Europe. Past and Present Publications*. Cambridge

Gysi, J. and Speigner, W. (1984): 'Changes in the Life Patterns of Families in Europe'. Volume IV: National Report from the German Democratic Republic. (Vienna Centre background material), Vienna

Haavio-Mannila, E., Liljeström, R. and Sokolowska, M. (1985): 'The State, the Family and the Position of Women in the Nordic Countries and Poland'. In: Risto Alapuro et al. (eds): *Small States in Comparative Perspective*. Norwegian University Press

Holter, H. (1973): *Könsroller och samhällsstruktur* (Sex notes and the structure of society). Stockholm

Jallinoja, R. (1980): 'Miehet ja naiset' (Men and women). In: Valkonen, T. et al.: *Suomalaiset. Yhteiskunnan rakenne teollistumisen aikana* (Firms. The structure of society during industrialisation), Porvoo - Helsinki - Juva

Jallinoja, R. (1983): *Suomalaisen naisasialiikkeen taistelukaudet* (The active periods of the Finnish women's movement). Porvoo - Helsinki - Juva

Jallinoja, R. (1984): 'Perhekäsityksistä perhettä koskeviin ratkaisuihih' (Family views and solutions in family life). In: Haavio-Mannila, E., Jallinoja, R.

Women between Family and Employment

and Strandell, H.: *Perhe, työ ja tunteet. Ristiriitoja ja ratkaisuja* (Family, work and feelings. Conflicts and solutions). Porvoo - Helsinki - Juva

Janssen-Jurreit, M.L. (1982): *Sexism. The Male Monopoly on History & Thought.* London

Kharchev, A.G. (1982): 'Changes in the Family Pattern in the USSR'. National Report (Vienna Centre background material), Vienna

Lapidus, G. (1979): *Women in Soviet Society. Equality, Development and Social Change.* Berkeley

Lockwood, B. and Knowles, W. (1984): 'Women at Work in Great Britain'. In: Marilyn Davidson and Cary Cooper (ed.): *Working Women. An International Survey.* Chichester

Mitchell, J. (1966): 'Women: the Longest Revolution'. *New Left Review,* No. 40, 1966

Morawski, W. and Seppänen, P. (1978): 'Industrialization and Modernization'. In: E. Allardt and Wlodzimierz (ed.): *Social Structure and Change. Finland and Poland. Comparative Perspective.* Warszawa

Morgan, D. (1980): *Social Theory and the Family.* London

Morgan, E. (1966): *The Puritan Family. Religion and Domestic Relations in Seventeenth-century New England.* New York

Mount, F. (1984): *Den samhällsfarliga familjen* (The subversive family). Stockholm

Musgrave, B. and Wheeler-Bennett, F. (eds) (1972): *Women at Work. Combining Family with a Career.* London

Myrdal, A. and Klein, V. (1968): *Women's Two Roles. Home and Work.* London 1956, reprinted 1968

Nave-Herz, R. (1980): 'Changes in the Life Patterns of Families in Europe'. Bericht über die Bundesrepublik Deutschland. (Vienna Centre back-ground material), Vienna

Parsons, T. (1956): 'Family Structure and the Socialization of the Child'. In: Parsons, T. and Bales, R.: *Family Socialization and Interaction Process.* London

Pinchbeck, I. (1969): *Women Workers and the Industrial Revolution 1750-1850.* 1930/reprinted 1969

Piotrowsky, J. (1969): *Family Needs Resulting from an Increased Employment of Married Women: Adequacy of Existing Resources to Meet These Needs.* Warsaw

Reed, E. (1971): *Problems of Women's Liberation, a Marxist Approach.* New York

Rowbotham, Sh. (1976): *Woman's Consciousness, Man's World.* Harmondsworth

Sas, J. (1981): 'Certain Characteristic Features of Socio-economic Development in Hungary'. (Vienna Centre background material), Vienna

Sgritta, G.B. and Saporiti, A. (1980): 'Family, Labour Market and the State in Italy, from 1945 to the present', Rome. (Vienna Centre background material), Vienna

Shorter, E. (1977): *The Making of the Modern Family.* Glasgow

Stone, L. (1979): *The Family, Sex and Marriage in England 1500-1800.* Harmondsworth

Suomen tilastollinen vuosikirja (Statistical yearbook of Finland) 1953, 1965, 1973 and 1983

Statisticni letopis SR Slovenije (Statistical yearbook of Slovenia), Ljubljana, 1984

Tilly, Ch., Tilly, L. and Tilly, R. (1980): *The Rebellious Century 1830-1930.* Cambridge, Mass.

Riitta Jallinoja

Tilly, L. and Scott, J. (1978): *Women, Work & Family.* New York
Winch, R. (1963): *The Modern Family.* New York
Yearbook of Labour Statistics. ILO, Geneva 1975 and 1984

6

Gender Segregation in Paid and Unpaid Work*

Elina Haavio-Mannila

Types of gender segregation

The division of labour between men and women is based partly on biological sex differences but it is also a social and cultural phenomenon: it varies across time and place. R.E. Pahl (1984, p. 14) points out that 'work has to be understood both historically and in context; it has changed in the past, it is changing now, and it will continue to change in the future; above all, work done by members of households is the central process around which society is structured. In different periods and contexts some work becomes of greater significance: women's waged work is of particular importance for ordinary middle-class households... in the 1980s.'

Work in society can be divided in three sectors: *productive, re-productive and organising work.* Productive and reproductive work were earlier carried out mainly at home, and there was not much organising work. In the nineteenth century production was taken over by factories. In the twentieth century the public sector has adopted many reproductive functions. Organising work like planning, administrative and controlling work have increased both in the private sector and in state activities.

The increase in female employment in the recent decades has first and foremost consisted in women moving into service occupations. For example, in 1970 in twelve of the European countries participating in our study the proportion of women in service occupations varied between 37 and 71 per cent, while women made only 7-30 per cent of the production workers. More

*I would like to thank here the Academy of Finland for funding the Finnish survey.

specifically, women were over-represented among office, sales, service and professional workers and under-represented among administrative and managerial workers, production workers, transport equipment operators and labourers, and in most countries also among agricultural and forestry workers, fishermen and hunters (United Nations, 1980, p. 95).

This horizontal division of labour between men and women does not provide a full picture. There is also a status differentiation: men are situated on the upper status levels, while women on the lower ones of the occupational hierarchies. The figure below illustrates these two dimensions of the sex division of labour:

Status of work	Sector of work		
	Production	Organisation	Reproduction
High	Men	Men	Men (Women)
Low	Men	Women	Women

The macro-level gender segregation at work in occupations, industries and jobs (cf. Reskin, 1984) has its parallels at the micro-level of the workplace. The functional gender segregation - men and women doing different sorts of work - often leads to social segregation in daily interaction. This may be problematic for women, who are excluded from informal communication networks which are influential in career advancement.

Functional gender segregation also means in many cases physical separation of men and women. The different environments create separate work cultures which are maintained through symbolic segregation, i.e. belief systems stressing gender differences in proper behaviour and natural abilities (cf. Epstein, 1985, pp. 29-51).

But functional gender segregation does not necessarily mean social segregation. Men and women may perform different tasks in the same workplace, having contact with each other. In this case men and women may be in a *complementary role relationship* with each other in the same way as in the family.

Reasons for and consequences of gender segregation

The continuing pattern of a gender segregated labour market is well documented (e.g. Nordisk Ministerråd, 1985; United Nations, 1980; Bielby and Baron, 1982; Hartman and Reskin, 1983; Reskin, 1984). Attempts to get more women into men's jobs and more men into women's jobs have not been very successful (cf. Liljeström et al., 1978; Fürst, 1985).

Analyses of the reasons for gender segregation at work have focused on whether women choose typically female occupations or are excluded from better-paying male-dominated occupations. The former position assumes that because women's traditional domestic roles required interrupting their careers for childrearing, it is economically advantageous for them to pursue occupations that do not penalise intermittent employment. It has also been assumed that female occupations are easier to combine with family life than traditional men's occupations. According to the other explanation, women often face open discrimination in the labour market, in job assignments and promotion (Reskin, 1984).

The first explanation for gender segregation at work has not been supported by evidence. Paula England (1984, pp. 726-49) has shown that women who spend more time out of the labour force choose traditionally female occupations no more frequently than those who work continuously, and female occupations penalise breaks in employment no less than male occupations do.

The most problematic consequence of the gender-based division of paid work is the low wages of female dominated occupations. This uneven division of pay in male and female dominated occupations, respectively, has led to the feminisation of poverty (cf. Scott, 1984).

Gender segregation in the workplace

Occupational gender segregation in Europe is more common in the West and North than in the East and South. In Eastern Europe integration of men and women is related to women's work in traditional men's occupations, for example in industry; in Southern Europe it is related to men's work in traditional women's occupations, for example in sales and private service work (Haavio-Mannila, 1981, pp. 6-12).

125

Table 6.1. Functional and social gender segregation in paid work (percentages)

Functional segregation

S1	Assen (NL)		Urban Norway		Sweden			Urban Finland		Slovenian cities		Warsaw	
	W	M	W	M	W*	W**	M**	W	M	W	M	W	M
Only own sex	37	43	30	38	44	18	51	40	42	28	48	26	40
Mainly own sex	36	31	32	30	43	34	33	31	32	34	20	44	26
Both men and women	7	7	22	15	9	30	12	13	15	28	24	20	20
Only or mainly other sex	2	3	8	7	-	17	2	6	2	3	5	6	6
Works alone	13	14	7	10	4	1	2	9	9	7	3	4	8
No answer	5	2	1	-				1	-	-	-	-	-
	100	100	100	100	100	100	100	100	100	100	100	100	100
N	59	103	170	205	299	320	266	281	296	183	147	144	178

Social segregation

S2	Assen (NL)		Urban Finland		Slovenian cities		Hungary		Orel		Warsaw	
	W	M	W	M	W	M	W	M	W	M	W	M
Only own sex	16	25	5	7	14	21	6	19	14	7	7	4
Mainly own sex	29	44	21	33	35	20	12	50	35	30	43	51
Both men and women	35	22	65	54	41	42	59	30	33	34	43	39
Only or mainly other sex	17	9	7	6	10	6	22	1	8	11	7	6
No contacts or answer	3	-	2	-	-	11	1	-	10	18	-	-
	100	100	100	100	100	100	100	100	100	100	100	100
N	58	101	281	296	183	147	78	78	..	..	144	178

S1 = Sex of people doing same sort of work at one's workplace; S2 = Sex of people with whom one is in daily contact at work; W = Women; M = Men.
* Caregivers (municipal workers).
** Metal and manufacturing workers.

Our survey on changes in family patterns included two questions about gender segregation in the workplace. One of them refers to *functional segregation*, the other to *social segregation* (Table 6.1).

A large majority (62-87 per cent) of the respondents are doing same sort of work at their workplaces mainly with members of their own gender group. Men's jobs are a little more gender-segregated than women's. This is a result of the larger number of men than women in the labour force. Due to their lesser exposure to working together with the other sex it may be more difficult for men to accept women as equal partners in working life than it is for women to work with men.

Daily contacts at work may include more often people of the other sex who are not sharing the same tasks. From 18 to 69 per cent of the interviewed men and women meet at work mainly persons of their own sex group, that is, are socially segregated from the other sex.

The order of the national samples as to the extent of gender segregation thus varies by type of segregation and gender.

No large systematic differences between the countries in the degree of gender segregation in paid work can be found from our sample data. Functional segregation of men's and women's work is common all over Europe. Social segregation of the sexes in daily contacts at work is not as strict. Many work role sets include both men and women.

Some features of women and their work in gender-segregated and non-segregated workplaces are presented in Table 6.2.

The most striking finding from these data is that the *incomes* of women in gender-segregated work are consistently lower than those of women in non-segregated work. As for age, educational level, employment status and working hours there are no consistent differences, but on the whole our data support the assumption that social segregation at the workplace is connected for women with lower education and employment status than in the case of non-segregated work. Segregated work for women also more often means less flexible and more closely controlled working hours.

Table 6.2. *Characteristics of women and their work in gender-segregated and non-gender-segregated work* (percentages)*

	Assen (NL)		Urban Finland			Hungary		Slovenian cities	
	S	I	S	C	I	S	I	S	I
Age**									
Younger	..	..	51	46	47	48	29	26	40
Middle	..	..	27	25	30	20	42	38	36
Older	..	..	22	29	23	32	29	36	24
			100	100	100	100	100	100	100
Education									
Lower	62	35	59	50	43	4	21	40	28
Middle	33	53	32	44	23	72	68	43	58
Higher	5	12	9	6	34	24	11	17	14
	100	100	100	100	100	100	100	100	100
Employment status									
Worker	..	..	41	24	20	22	71	45	25
Lower status employee	..	..	48	65	30	72	18	36	59
Upper status employee	..	..	11	11	50	4	4	19	16
No answer						2	7		
			100	100	100	100	100	100	100
Income									
Lower	..	..	34	24	14	8	4	52	21
Middle	..	..	54	51	38	64	56	40	64
Higher	..	..	12	25	48	28	40	8	15
			100	100	100	100	100	100	100
Hours of work***									
Shorter	70	35	14	12	19	24	7	..	..
Middle	15	65	29	34	38	54	54	..	..
Longer	15	-	57	54	43	22	39	..	..
	100	100	100	100	100	100	100		
Regular daytime work	..	..	77	77	75	..	..	58	74
Flexible work hours	..	..	25	42	34	..	..	31	46
Close control of working time	..	..	54	35	30	..	..	52	44
N	*21*	*17*	*81*	*159*	*56*	*50*	*28*	*90*	*93*

S=Segregated; I=Integrated; C=Complementary.

* Gender segregation refers in the Hungarian and Dutch samples to functional segregation, in the Yugoslavian to social segregation (cf. Table 6.1). In the Finnish sample *segregated* work means that both the job and contacts at work are mostly with own sex, while *complementary* means that there are daily contacts with members of the other sex even though most people doing the same sort of work are of one's own sex. In *integrated* work men and women share the same kind of work.

** Age groups are in Finland: 25-36, 37-46 and 47-64 years; in Hungary: -40, 41-50 and 51-60 years, and in Slovenia: 25-34, 35-44 and 45-55 years.

*** The categories 'shorter', 'middle', 'longer' mean in Finland: 1-19, 20-39 and 40+ hours, in Assen (Netherlands): 1-19, 20-40 and 41+ hours per week, respectively.

These findings support the assumption that for women it is occupationally disadvantageous to work in gender-segregated workplaces and jobs in both East and West. For men, it seems to be almost better to work only with other men, and not in the same job or workplace as women. This can be seen from the Finnish data. High incomes were received by 74 per cent (N = 109) of men in gender-segregated, 72 per cent (N = 125) in complementary and 66 per cent (N = 47) in integrated work (for definitions see the note to Table 6.2). Thus one can understand men's lack of interest in attempts to equalise men's and women's wages by diminishing gender segregation at work through affirmative action type of policies, or by paying equal wages for work of comparable worth.

Caregiving work and family life

A large part of female-dominated employment consists of helping, attending, serving and caring for other people. Paid caregiving work has increased in the European welfare societies since the 1960s. Much of the paid caregiving work consists of similar tasks to those which housewives, mothers and sisters have always conducted for family members and relatives. The work is often performed for persons who cannot themselves manage the necessities of everyday life: children, the sick, handicapped and elderly (Haavio-Mannila, 1983). This kind of work can be very stressful mentally, and it has been found that burnout, i.e. exhaustion, indifference and cynical attitudes towards clients, as well as absenteeism and dissatisfaction, are all special risks in caregiving occupations (Pines, 1980).

Does the similarity of tasks and of human relations problems to be solved both at work and at home make one more tired and more often cause stress or burnout reactions than other kinds of jobs? Is it easier to have different demands from family and from work? Or does the similarity between paid work and family obligations mean a better fulfilment of the demands of both life spheres? How are the marital relations affected by one of the spouses being engaged in a 'labour of love' for other people?

Paid caregiving is here theoretically defined as provision of services which traditionally have been and are still given by the family to its members. To find an operational definition which unambiguously separates caregiving work from other kind of work is difficult. On the basis of the objective classification of occupations it also turned out that the occupations included in this category were not the same in all countries. Health care, social care and catering work were included everywhere, but in addition teaching was included in the samples from Rome, urban Norway and Slovenia. (In order to examine the validity of the objective classification of occupations as caregiving ones, respondents in Finland and Norway were asked if their work was related to care and attendance. Of the 100 female social, health and catering Finnish workers 64 said that their work is related to care and attendance. Catering, i.e. kitchen-workers and cleaners, least often identified with caring work. On the other hand, 28 of the 92 women subjectively identifying with caring work were not working in social and health care or catering. Many of them were teachers. In Tables 6.3 and 6.4 Finnish caregivers are defined on the basis of their occupation, and not by their subjective definition of their work.)

In the following analysis women caregivers are compared with other working women. Comparison groups differ in the examined countries. In the sample from Rome there are no other groups interviewed with which one could compare caregivers. The Swedish sample includes only metal and manufacturing workers in addition to lower-status caregivers in the public sector. In the Norwegian sample one had to drop the comparison with blue-collar workers, because there were only seven women manual workers in the sample. In the sample from Oldenburg one can compare caregivers with industrial workers. In the Slovenian sample caregivers are compared with both industrial and white-collar workers, and the large sample from Finland allows comparisons with professionals, office workers and industrial workers.

Table 6.3. Women's gender segregation, work motives and the reciprocal influence of family and work (percentages)

	Urban Finland 1	2	3	Oldenburg 4	5	Sweden 6	7	8	Urban Norway 9	10	Slovenian cities 11	12	13
Sex of persons doing same sort of work at one's workplace													
Only or mainly women	39	84	77	77	..	..	87	53	70	53	72	71	52
Both men and women	33	5	7	11	..	..	9	29	21	23	26	19	34
Only or mainly men	18	4	1	6	..	..	-	17	6	10	-	6	2
Works alone or no answer	10	7	15	6	..	..	4	1	3	14	2	4	12
	100	100	100	100			100	100	100	100	100	100	100
Major motive for work													
Interesting work	82	78	73	42	..	..	76	33	76	72	..	..	..
Earnings only	6	9	19	34	..	..	10	34	17	19	..	..	..
Comradeship with workmates	6	10	5	24	..	..	14	33	7	9	..	..	..
No answer	6	3	3										
	100	100	100	100			100	100	100	100			
Agreeing with following statements:													
'I take my job worries home with me'	73	48	42	34	38	14	37	22	43	49	70	53	61
'My family has to suffer because my heart is in my work'	56	30	28	21	..	..	6	10	26	19	21	13	9
'I worry about the children rather often when I am at work' (only those with children)	16	45	52	63	36	20	..	..	12	10	51	53	45
(N)	(51)	(77)	(99)	(93)	(52)	(35)	(299)	(320)	(90)	(69)	(52)	(19)	(76)

1 = Professionals; 2 = Office workers; 3 = Caregivers; 4 = Industrial workers; 5 = Caregivers; 6 = Industrial workers; 7 = Caregivers; 8 = Industrial workers; 9 = Caregivers; 10 = Other white-collar workers; 11 = Caregivers; 12 = Industrial workers; 13 = Other white-collar workers

Before examining the influence of a caregiving occupation on family life, the gender segregation, the quality of work, and the work satisfaction of caregiving women are compared with those of other women in our samples. This is done in order to set a context to the discussion on the spillover problems between caregiving work and the family.

Female-domination in caregiving occupations leads to functional gender segregation at the workplace: 70-86 per cent of persons doing the same sort of work at the workplaces of caregivers are women. In most comparison groups gender segregation is less pro-nounced. Only in Slovenian cities are women industrial workers as segregated as caregiving women (Table 6.3).

Some qualitative aspects of caregiving work can be reported on the basis of the Finnish data. Caregiving work in Finland includes taking responsibility for and serving other people but seldom involves the use of machines. Caregivers have more often than other employed women independent and challenging jobs, which involve decision-making, planning, initiative, responsibility, and the use of various skills. Frequently caregiving work also requires further training. At the same time it is more often mentally and physically stressful, has negative effects on health, and can be exhausting and demanding. However, caregiving work is seen as interesting and varied. It does not bring in lots of money or opportunities for promotion, but one feels that it is appreciated by others (Haavio-Mannila, 1985, pp. 173-88).

Caregiving work seems to give more satisfaction than manufacturing work. Of the Finnish, Norwegian and Swedish caregiver women 73-85 per cent, whereas of the Finnish and Swedish industrial workers only 33-42 per cent chose among three alternatives the following: 'My job is interesting. It gives me not only pay but also a sense of purpose and comradeship'. In the same way as professional and office work, caregiving work also gives social and personal rewards in addition to material benefits. In manufacturing, women quite often work mostly for the earnings or the comradeship with workmates.

The strength of the satisfying and challenging nature of caring work is reflected in the difficulties experienced in escaping from it during leisure time. Caregivers everywhere seem to take their job worries home with them more often than industrial workers, and in the Slovenian sample even more often than other white-collar employees. The differences between caregivers and other whitecollar

workers as to other strains between family and work come out differently in the various samples. Caregivers less often than professionals but more often than industrial workers find that 'my family
has to suffer because my heart is in my work'. On the other hand,
caregivers often worry about their children when they are at work -
about as much as industrial workers, and much more often than
professionals. More than other employees, caregivers seem to
worry both about work when at home and about family when at
work, and this is probably stressful.

Caregivers in Finland get as much social support from their
husbands as other women (Table 6.4). However, the husbands of
caregivers, according to their separately given replies to our questionnaire, state that they do not get as much support and comfort
from their wives as the husbands of women working in other
fields.

Table 6.4. Social support between spouses of married caregivers and other married
women in urban Finland (percentages)

	Profes-sionals	Office workers	Care-givers	Industrial workers
Receives very much support and comfort from the spouse when encountering diffi-culties or problems				
Own replies	43	36	41	41
Replies by husband	48	43	33	40
Receives very much or quite a lot of support from the spouse in issues related to one's work				
Own replies	59	64	66	55
Replies by husband	52	57	40	50
Number of families*	(42)	(56)	(71)	(22)

*Due to technical reasons here the number of industrial workers is smaller than in
other tables.

The explanation of this difference may be that caregiving as a
'labour of love' (Finch and Groves, 1983) may be difficult to ex-

tend in all directions. There may be no caring resources left after an exhausting working day in paid caregiving.

Another explanation to the lower level of emotional care received by the husbands of Finnish caregivers from their wives may be that these husbands have unrealistically high expectations of nurturing and social support at home. The husbands of caregivers may perhaps expect that caregivers in general should be more caring than other women. If this is true, it is understandable that they become frustrated when their wives have less energy left for caring at home than the husbands anticipated when choosing their spouses.

The reciprocal influence of work and family among paid caregivers seems to be problematic in two ways. Firstly, caregivers worry about their paid work at home, and about their family responsibilities at work. It is difficult to combine two overlapping roles, one at work and the other at home. The similarity of the demands of both roles does not provide distance enough for relaxing and holding the two life spheres separate. Secondly, caring resources are not endless. After an exhausting day in helping and serving clients, the caregiver has not much energy left for giving support and comfort to the husband who, in addition, may expect more informal nurturing than an average husband.

Gender segregation in unpaid work at home

In Europe, the division of housework in the family is still segregated by gender even when both spouses are employed. According to time budget studies in 1974-81 in Denmark, Finland, Hungary, Norway, Poland, Switzerland and the United Kingdom, economically active men spend more time in gainful employment than women. Hours worked by women as percentages of those by men vary between 61 in Norway and 88 in Hungary. But an even wider gender gap can be seen in domestic work: men spend only 15-16 hours per week on housework, women 19-33 hours. In Finland women spend 1.9 times as much time on housework as men, in Switzerland 3.8 times; the other four countries fall in between (Niemi, 1983, pp. 16-17).

Very few households in our samples include other persons than members of the nuclear family, i.e. spouses and their children. Only in Rome and in the Russian town Orel are members of the extended family at least physically available to share the house-work in a significant proportion of households.

Differences in the employment rate of the wives and in house-hold structure in the samples limit the value of comparisons. In addition, national variations in the questions asked makes detailed comparisons of the division of domestic work difficult. In Table 6.5 only two categories are used: the task is carried out by (1) wife alone and (2) husband alone.

As an example of gender segregation in domestic work, we first examine the gender division of labour in preparing meals for the family in the total samples studied. From Table 6.5 it emerges that the husband is very seldom the only one to carry out the task of cooking and that the proportion of wives being alone respon-sible for the task of cooking varies between 99 per cent among the oldest couples in Oldenburg to 37 per cent in the Slovenian cities.

From some countries we also have data on the participation of other persons than husband and wife in domestic work (Table 6.6). In Orel 18 per cent, in the other three samples 2-10 per cent of the respondents report that somebody else than the husband or wife prepares food for the household. The higher percentage in Orel is probably due to more relatives living together with the nuclear family than in the other countries.

In addition to cooking, gender differentiation at home is very common on other daily chores, too. Laundry, cleaning, washing the dishes and shopping are mostly done by the wife alone, and very seldom by the husband alone. The task of keeping contact with relatives in Oldenburg (FRG) and the Dutch town Assen is a feminine task; in the other countries it is mostly shared by family members.

Taking care of family finances is the least gender-segregated of the tasks studied. Wives do it most commonly in Oldenburg, hus-bands among caregivers in Rome. In urban Norway and Slovenian cities it is often shared by the family members. Minor repairs at home - which is the only typically male domestic task studied - are seldom conducted by wives alone. As Table 6.5 shows it varies to what degree it is the husband alone who performs this kind of work.

Degree of gender segregation in unpaid work will next be ex-amined separately for traditionally female and male tasks. The tra-ditionally female tasks: cooking, doing the laundry, cleaning, washing the dishes and shopping, are most commonly performed

by the wife alone in the total samples of families studied in Oldenburg in the FRG and Assen in the Netherlands.

Table 6.5. Gender segregation of unpaid domestic work in the family with two spouses present according to replies by the wife (percentages)

Domestic task	About half of wives are employed				Three-fourths of wives are employed				All wives employed	
	1			2	3	4	5	6	7*	8
	Year of marriage 1950	-70	-80							
Cooking										
wife alone	99	80	75	79	50	58	71	53	37	57
husband alone	-	3	6	4	-	1	2	4	1	4
Doing the laundry										
wife alone	99	96	92	91	68	71	76	51	80	71
husband alone	-	-	-	3	1	1	3	5	3	2
Cleaning										
wife alone	80	76	59	71	60	54	49	28	31	44
husband alone	4	2	7	2	-	1	1	5	1	3
Washing up the dishes										
wife alone	75	63	54	33	33	44	49	34	34	51
husband alone	1	3	2	6	1	1	5	5	2	6
Shopping										
wife alone	62	57	41	55	40	35	52	..	25	48
husband alone	4	6	5	5	1	2	7	..	4	12
Keeping contact with relatives										
wife alone	78	59	67	48	17	18	18	24	11	32
husband alone	11	15	4	4	-	4	3	3	1	5
Taking care of family finances										
wife alone	54	37	43	33	17	18	34	36	23	24
husband alone	31	43	29	18	8	25	23	9	10	49
Minor repairs at home										
wife alone	3	2	-	6	13	2	7	9	7	15
husband alone	88	91	93	68	20	31	82	45	67	58
(N)	(69)	(120)	(89)	(131)	(215)	(213)	(195)	(..)	(183)	(300)

Employment of the wives in the interviewed families

1 = Oldenburg; 2 = Assen; 3 = Urban Norway; 4 = Urban Finland; 5 = Warsaw; 6 = Orel; 7 = Slovenian cities; 8 = Caregivers in Rome

*In Slovenia information on the share of the husband was given by husbands them-selves (N = 147).

Table 6.6. *Participation of other persons than husband or wife in domestic work according to replies by the wife (percentages)*

Domestic task	Nether-lands	Urban Norway	Warsaw	Orel	Care-givers in Rome
Cooking	4	2	10	18	6
Doing the laundry	3	1	9	24	12
Cleaning	10	4	21	35	19
Washing up the dishes	32	8	23	35	9
Shopping	2	2	11	..	3
Keeping contacts with relatives	-	1	4	14	1
Taking care of family finances	-	-	3	10	2
Minor repairs at home	6	4	2	15	12
(N)	(132)	(215)	(195)	(..)	(300)

Urban Norway and Finland, Warsaw and caregivers in Rome fall in between, while the Slovenian cities and the Russian town Orel show least gender segregation in traditionally female household tasks. In Orel this is partly explained by other members of the extended family participating in daily housework.

Minor repairs at home, which are traditionally male tasks, are most gender-segregated in Oldenburg and Warsaw. Also in Assen, among caregivers in Rome and in the Slovenian cities the husband alone performs them in most families. Least gender segregation appears in this field in urban Norway. In urban Finland and in Orel these 'male' tasks are relatively often shared by the wife and/or others.

Our surveys thus show that household work is still divided between men and women in a traditional way: women work in the kitchen, men do minor repairs. Of the tasks examined, keeping contact with relatives and taking care of family finances are the ones shared most commonly.

Conclusion

Division of work between men and women outside and inside the family is universal. Occupations, industries and jobs are segregated by gender. There is also a clear differentiation of women's and men's work tasks and social contacts at the workplace level.

In Europe, according to our sample survey data, functional gender segregation at the workplace is more pronounced than social segregation at work. That is, men and women more often are members of the same work role set, have contacts with each other, than perform the same work tasks.

Our results indicate that there is more functional gender segregation in the Netherlands, Finland, and Sweden than in Norway, Poland and Yugoslavia. Social gender segregation at work is more common in the Netherlands and Yugoslavia than in Finland, Hungary, Poland and the Soviet Union.

Women's paid work is to a great extent reproductive work, that is, health and social care, catering and teaching.

The growth in the number of paid caregivers is connected with the expansion of the public sector in European welfare states. Care of children, the sick, the handicapped and the elderly is more and more considered to be the responsibility of the state, not of individuals or families.

Education in helping professions has expanded, a development which has partly undermined some basic human principles in caregiving. Tasks have somewhat arbitrarily been divided between different occupational groups. Caregiving has been transformed from everyday wisdom to scientific knowledge (Liljeström and Jarup, 1983). And this has meant more than just an improvement in the quality of care.

Gender-segregated women's work in caregiving overlaps family life. There seems to be some problems in conducting similar type of work outside and inside the home. Caregivers worry about work at home and about home at work and they are not able to keep them separate in their minds. The qualitative overlapping of paid and unpaid women's work is stressful.

In urban Finland married women working in care-oriented occupations have difficulties in extending their nurturance to family members. Their husbands report that they do not get as much social support and comfort from their wives as the husbands of women doing other kind of work. This may indicate that members of caregivers' families are to some extent deprived of getting a 'normal' amount of informal care from the wife.

In the division of unpaid domestic work between men and women clear cross-national variation was found. Segregation in this connection meant that the wife alone performs daily household chores and the husband alone makes small repairs at home and takes care of family finances. In integrated families spouses share domestic work.

Gender segregation of unpaid domestic work is most common in the samples of those families in which the wives' participation in the labour force varies (i.e. in Assen and Oldenburg) while the least segregated samples were found in Orel and in the Slovenian cities. Urban Norway and Finland, Warsaw and Rome are in between. Our data from Oldenburg - and also from other urban areas - show that younger couples share housework more than the older ones. Thus in the future inequality in the division of labour at home will perhaps diminish.

Gender segregation in paid work is connected in case of women with low education and employment status, close control, inflexibility of working hours, and low pay. Among men it is linked with more positive qualities of work. Thus it is more in the interest of women than of men to fight against functional and social segregation of the sexes at work.

References

Bielby, W.T. and Baron, J.N. (1982): 'A Woman's Place is with Other Women: Sex Segregation in the Workplace'. Department of Sociology, University of California, Santa Barbara (manuscript)

England, P. (1984): 'Wage Appreciation and Depreciation: A Test of Neoclassical Economic Explanations of Occupational Segregation'. *Social Forces*, Vol. 62, March 1984

Epstein, C.F. (1985): 'Ideal Roles and Real Roles or the Fallacy of the Misplaced Dichotomy'. In: *Research in Social Stratification and Mobility*, Vol. 4, Greenwich, Connecticut, JAI Press

Finch, J. and Groves, D. (eds) (1983): *A Labour of Love: Women, Work and Caring*. London, Routledge & Kegan Paul

Fürst, G. (1985): 'Reträtten från mansjobben' (The retreat from male jobs). Monograph from the Department of Sociology, University of Gothenburgh, No. 34

Haavio-Mannila, E. (1981): 'Yhteiskunnan rakennemuutokset ja sukupuolten asema' (Structural changes in society and position of men and women). *AVO-Ammatinvalinta*, Vol. 26, No. 6

Elina Haavio-Mannila

Haavio-Mannila, E. (1983): 'Caregiving in the Welfare State'. *Acta Sociologica*, 26 (1983), 1, pp. 61-82

Haavio-Mannila, E. (1985): 'Caregivers as an Occupational Group'. In: Kasvio, A. and Kaukonen, E. (eds): *Working Life in Transition*. Proceedings of the Finnish-Soviet Seminar. Research Reports 8, Department of Sociology and Social Psychology, University of Tampere

Hartman, H.I. and Reskin, B. (1983): 'Job Segregation: Trends and Prospects'. In: Certos, C.H., Haignere, L. and Steinberg, R.J. (eds): *Occupational Segregation and Its Impact on Working Women*. Albany, Center for Women in Government, SUNY

Liljeström, R. et al. (1978): 'Roles in Transition'. Report on an investigation made for the Advisory Council on Equality between Men and Women. Stockholm

Liljeström, R. and Jarup, B. (1983): 'Vardagsvett och vetenskap i vårdarbete' (Everyday wisdom and science in caring work), *Svenska kommunalarbetarförbundet*, TELAB

Niemi, I. (1983): The 1979 Time Use Study Method. Central Statistical Office of Finland, *Studies* No. 91, Helsinki

Nordisk Ministerråd (1985): *Kvinnans förändrade ställning i samhället-de tudelade arbetsmarknaderna i de nordiske länderna åren 1950-79* (The changed position of women in society - the segregated labour-markets in the Nordic countries 1950-79). Göteborg

Pahl, R.E. (1984): *Divisions of Labour*. Oxford, Basil Blackwell

Pines, A. (1980): *Burnout: From Tedium to Personal Growth*. New York, The Free Press

Reskin, B.F. (1984): 'Sex Segregation in the Workplace'. In: Rix, S. (ed.): *Low Income Women*. Washington, Women's Research and Education Institute

Scott, H. (1984): *Working Your Way to the Bottom - The Feminization of Poverty*. London, Pandora Press

United Nations (1980): *The Economic Role of Women in the ECE Region*. New York, United Nations

7

Psycho-social Dimensions of Paid Work and Family Life

Nevenka Černigoj-Sadar

Introduction

Work and family have been considered as complementary or even compensatory spheres of life, since production, human reproduction and consumption became separated. The family has been treated mainly as the domain of women, privacy and reproduction, while work has been treated mainly as the domain of men, public life and production. Macro-social changes such as the demand for female labour, the spread of egalitarian ideology and more educational opportunities have led to the reconsideration of the above-mentioned dichotomies.

Nowadays the family is still the main locus of a great part of human reproduction. Human reproduction involves activities and work which generate and renew human beings from day to day and from generation to generation. So within a family a great many productive tasks (not only the reproduction of people but also the production of goods and services) are going on but they are not paid for and give less prestige and power than paid work does. Consequently, social activities cannot be divided into distinct spheres of production and reproduction while the distinction between paid and unpaid work remains.

The development trend which indicates that for men and women adulthood today increasingly involves being economically active as well as being a parent (Rapoport and Sierakowski, 1982) is common to all countries in our project (see Riitta Jallinoja's chapter in the present volume). Paid work and family life are becoming parallel life priorities for which people may have different motivations. It is difficult to determine which motive predominates, because the prevailing state ideology, the economic situation of the family and individual motivation are often intertwined. However, both spheres of life are strongly interrelated

141

from a subjective point of view, no matter to what extent paid work and family are formally segregated and evaluated. Subjective experiences reflect as well as influence objective conditions in family and paid work, aspirations and patterns of organisation of everyday life. Men's and women's experiences of the paid work/family interactions may inhibit or enhance their attitudes towards changes of the family patterns.

Studies about the role of men and women in paid work and the family confirm, from a structural point of view, that the family has a constraining influence for women in the sphere of paid work, while paid work strongly limits the men's participation in family life.

'Women's responsibility for mothering and housework undermines their participation in paid labour, as does the family ideology used to justify sex segregation in the labour force and women's subordinate economic position' (Thorne and Yalom, 1982, p. 17). Pleck (1977) speaks about asymmetrically permeable boundaries between work and family roles for both men and women. It is supposed for women that their family role may intrude into their work role whereas for men the work role may intrude into the family role. The most general effect of this one-way permeability of the boundaries between work and family is a sex-segregated labour force: women get low-paid or low-prestige jobs, or jobs that are extensions of their domestic roles. At home, as well, labour is unequally divided among family members; the females being the ones who do the majority of domestic tasks. On the psychological level it leads to distress, lower career aspirations and commitment, as well as lower achievement motivation in women. This paid work/family interaction pattern is reproduced due to the following strongly interrelated factors:

- Norms not any more codified in law but still alive in everyday practice such as 'man is the main breadwinner, woman is the caretaker of family members'.
- Biosocial and cultural factors: the most pertinent among them being different socialisation patterns for boys and girls so that the construction of their social reality is different.
- Economic factors: although the gender differences in financial rewards for paid jobs are becoming smaller, employed women earn less than men even when their education is equal.

At the same time this pattern is enforced by the lag between changes occurring for women in the macro-social world of work and changes in the micro-social world of the family (Rapoport and Rapoport, 1971). Any change in the sex division of work within the family is often perceived as a serious threat to the established form of gender identity (Mackintosh, 1984). Traditional and modern values concerning the social division of labour and realities of everyday life are in conflict. The family members' needs are often competing and the established routine for satisfying them is not taken for granted any more. Therefore new alternative patterns of relationship between paid work and family are being sought.

Analysis of the relationships between paid work and the family

Patterns of interaction between paid work and the family are complex and changing due to singular and interactive effects of broad social, cohort-specific and life-cycle-specific changes and processes of personal development. In analysing these patterns two elements are taken into account: (1) the prevailing directions of the interaction; and (2) the content of the interaction.

Each of these two elements has at least three possible variations:

1. Direction(s) of interaction:
    a. Work (W) has much influence on family (F) and family has little or no influence on work; W $\rightleftharpoons$ F
    b. Work has much influence on family and family has much influence on work; W $\rightleftharpoons$ F
    c. Work has little or no influence on family and family has much influence on work. W $\rightleftharpoons$ F

We can speak about one-way permeability boundaries if the influence goes mainly in one direction, either from work to family or from family to work. If, however, the influences go in both directions, work $\rightarrow$ family and family $\rightarrow$ work respectively, we speak about two-way permeability boundaries.

2. The content of the interaction may have the following effects:
    a. positive,

b. negative,
c. positive and negative.

The influences vary greatly in their content as well as in their effects. For example, paid work may increase the sense of competence in women and improve their skills which is reflected positively in their family life. But on the other hand, it may create conflicts if paid work imposes limitations on the time women can spend with their families or can even lessen their commitment to family members and caregiving tasks.

The model for analysing the patterns of paid work/family interactions is based on the following assumptions.

Any individual is potentially capable of developing multiple links between work and non-work spheres (Champoux, 1980; Kabanoff, 1980) which are the result of his/her endeavour to balance the demands of work and the family, and the support she/he gets from formal and informal groups and institutions. Characteristics of these links are indicators of changes in the allocation and meaning of work/family roles in men and women.

The experienced positive influences of work on family and family on work, respectively, do not mean exclusion of conflicts between the two spheres of life.

In this paper patterns of interaction between work and family will be described, with special attention to the gender differences and the differences among countries. The following subject areas will be covered:

- the interaction of paid work and the family will be analysed from the point of view of social relationships and incentives for work,
- positive and negative influences between paid work and the family will be analysed, as well as
- the division of labour within the family and its psychological effects.

In the analysis empirical data are used from the following countries: Finland, Hungary, Norway, Poland, Soviet Union (women only), Sweden and Yugoslavia (Slovenia). The comparison is made only for full-time employed respondents who have at least one child living at home. It is only in the Swedish sample that 17 per cent to 55 per cent of the men and 3 per cent to 37 per cent of the women in different age groups have no children at home, so this sample is not compared to the others when problems relevant to the presence of children are discussed. Furthermore, not all countries participating in our project could be included in the analysis for the lack of other relevant data.

Specific characteristics of the compared samples and the descriptive level of the analysis limit the scope of generalisation of our results. We can therefore speak only about tendencies in differences and similarities between countries and among various groups of respondents. In consequence of such methodological restrictions the analysis is mostly limited to the identification of the problems rather than their explanation.

Hierarchy of social relations

The priority people give to activities in different spheres of life as well as the motivations for them reveal the meaning of these activities. It was supposed that the importance attached to relationships with workmates and household members may indicate whether paid work or family has priority, at least in the sphere of social relations.

Comparing the results from the Finnish, Hungarian, Polish, Slovenian and Soviet samples, no significant sex differences within the countries are found, while there are significant differences between the countries. As to the importance of social relations, two main groups of respondents may be discerned. Those who give priority to social relations inside the family and those for whom social relations with household members and workmates are equally important. The first group is most numerous in the Finnish sample, the second one in the Soviet sample. Social relations with family members are as important as relations with workmates also for more than half of the respondents in the Slovenian sample and half of the respondents in the Hungarian sample (Table 7.1).

Table 7.1. Importance of social relations (percentages)* 'Which is more important to you, relations with workmates or household members?'

Relations are important with		Countries				
		PL	SL	H	SU	SF
- Workmates						
	Women	1	3	1	2	1
	Men	5	3	1	.	0
- Both equally						
	Women	50	59	45	78	28
	Men	57	56	47	.	21
- Household members						
	Women	49	38	49	20	71
	Men	38	41	47	.	76
(N)	Women	(195)	(183)	(78)	(.)	(156)
	Men	(196)	(147)	(78)	(.)	(187)

*Data for the Swedish and Norwegian samples are not available.
PL - Poland, SL - Slovenia, H - Hungary, SU - the town Orel in the Soviet Union, SF - Finland

Rarely do people give priority to their relationships with workmates only. It seems that specific societal and normative contexts characteristic of each of our samples determine the importance of social relationships because there are no systematic influences of sex, age and education. However, priority given to the relationships with family members is not as explicit in socialist countries as it is in Finland.

Motivation for paid work

Employed people may have different motivations for their jobs. They may be motivated by extrinsic rewards such as money or social prestige and/or by intrinsic rewards, i.e. when the work is interesting and allows self-realisation.

Our data reveal that financial reasons are the most frequent but not the only motivation for paid work. Financial motivation is in most respondents accompanied by at least one expressive or intrinsic motive. When asked whether intrinsic or extrinsic motives have priority, the majority of respondents chose the intrinsic ones. This indicates that paid work gives life a sense of purpose and belonging, or it is perceived as interesting and/or provides an opportunity for the development of human potential. In all countries intrinsic motivation for paid work increases with education. Associated with the educational level are also differences between the sexes, especially in intrinsic motivation. The higher the education, the less are the differences, and vice versa. In people with lower education, intrinsic motivation is also low and sex differences are greater: men have a stronger identification with work than women. However, the influence of age on motivation is variable and no common trend can be revealed in the countries included in the analysis.

The influence of paid work on family life

The examples of positive and negative influences of paid work on family life are presented in Table 7.2.

Work may give satisfaction reflected positively in the family and may also contribute to understanding the spouse's pre-occupations at work. Such positive influences vary greatly among countries. The positive influences are most common among respondents in the Finnish and Slovenian samples, followed by respondents in the Polish, Hungarian and Norwegian samples and quite rare in the Russian sample. Positive influences are systematically determined by demographic and educational factors. In this respect general trends are found common to all countries compared, with only few exceptions. The higher the age and educational level, the more often does paid work give satisfaction which is reflected positively in the family and contributes to the understanding of the spouse's preoccupations at work.

Negative influences of work are mainly shown in lack of attention or time for family members and for household work, which is disturbing for family relations. The frequencies and differences among the countries for negative influences are lower than for the positive ones.

Concerning negative influences, each country has its own specificities. There is no general trend connected with age and education. Negative influences are determined by more factors, especially by those in the work system and the organisational patterns of everyday life. In all countries there are men who leave the household work entirely to their partners, while this is rare for women.

Table 7.2. Influence of work on family life (percentage of positive answers)*

'Did your job(s) ever influence your family life in any of the following ways or is it doing so now?'		Countries					
		PL	SL	H	SU	SF	N
Not enough time for children	Women	32	28	35	7	28	.
	Men	43	40	39	.	31	.
Not paying enough attention to children	Women	34	26	17	9	.	.
	Men	41	38	14	.	.	.
Not enough time for spouse	Women	31	25	30	3	.	.
	Men	44	42	34	.	.	.
Not paying enough attention to spouse	Women	29	25	18	3	39	.
	Men	32	40	23	.	21	.
Not enough time to keep the household going	Women	41	26	11	11	.	.
	Men	30	29	5	.	.	.
Had to leave the household work completely to spouse	Women	5	10	1	2	.	.
	Men	27	35	14	.	.	.
Gave satisfaction reflected positively in family	Women	26	88	36	17	73	39
	Men	31	78	27	.	71	26
Contributed to understanding of spouse's worries at work	Women	.	67	24	5	63	42
	Men	.	66	18	.	53	16
(N)	Women	(195)	(183)	(78)	(.)	(156)	(79)
	Men	(195)	(147)	(78)	(.)	(187)	(99)

*For the abbreviations of countries, see Table 1 + N - Norway.

Women more often than men experience the influence of work on family life as positive whereas paid work has negative influences on family life mostly for men. Differences between the sexes are greater in the case of the negative influences than in that of the positive ones. Empirical results from Slovenia indicate that major differences between the sexes are to be seen in the accumulation of various influences. Among men often both negative and positive influences accumulate in one and the same person, whereas women mostly experience either only positive or only negative influences (Černigoj-Sadar, 1982).

The influence of family on paid work

The family is the source of socio-emotional support to its members and the place where different abilities and skills are learned. This is confirmed also by our empirical results (Table 7.3). Most of our respondents experience the transfer of personal satisfaction, positive social relationships and skills learned in the family to the working situation. The transfer of personal satisfaction is most characteristic for the Slovenian sample, while the transfer of social relations and skills is characteristic of the Norwegian sample. However, such experiences are more often expressed by women than by men. The greatest gender differences are in the transfer of skills, which confirms the hypothesis that most women have jobs which have similarities with their family roles. These are jobs where qualities such as caring for others, dexterity, punctuality and cleanness are required, and are precisely those for which women are qualified through socialisation in the family (Kergoat, 1984).

The family also has negative influences on paid work which are reflected in different limitations and shortcomings such as: limitations in the choice of working place, in social contacts with workmates, in participation in socio-political activities, and the way in which it affects promotion and interferes with concentration at work. Such experiences are mostly found for women but vary among countries. The perception of constraints imposed by the family appears to reflect the prevailing norms and the countries' social policies.

In socialist countries formal socio-political activity is, together with employment, considered most important for achieving gender equality and also for improving one's quality of life. Most rights and benefits are derived from personal employment in the public sector.

Table 7.3. Influence of family on work (percentage of positive answers)*

'Has the fact that you take/ took care of your family ever'		Countries				
		SL	H	SU	SF	N
Limited the choice of	Women	20	23a	.	25	26
working place	Men	5	15a	.	21	12
Reduced working time	Women	4	37b	2	24	36
	Men	2	52b	.	24	14
Interfered with concen-	Women	27	31	.	19	.
tration at work	Men	16	12	.	13	.
Prevented promotion	Women	13	15	2	14	10
at work	Men	3	1	.	4	5
Prevented participation in	Women	23	10	.	13	10
socio-political activities	Men	9	5	.	9	3
Prevented meeting with	Women	22	19	.	16	0
workmates	Men	15	6	.	9	3
Taught you how to take care of other	Women	58	55	.	62	77
people at work	Men	63	51	.	57	60
Learned things which were	Women	54	28	.	63	68
useful in your job	Men	43	26	.	42	53
Given satisfaction reflected	Women	90	27	.	76	74
positively at work	Men	85	33	.	67	74
(N)	Women	(183)	(78)	(.)	(156)	(79)
	Men	(147)	(78)	(.)	(187)	(99)

*For the abbreviations of countries, see Table 1 + N - Norway.
aCare for the family was decisive for the choice of working place.
bCare for the family was decisive for working time.

Women in Slovenia more often than others complained about lack of concentration at work, limitations in political participation and in contacts with workmates, whereas women in Norway and Finland most often mentioned the limits in choice of working place and in working hours. These differences can be explained by the fact that in Slovenia most women are in full-time employment regardless of their family situation, and after they have been at work for some time they experience stress and limitations in social contacts. Limitations imposed by the family in the Scandinavian countries, however, come earlier, in the phase when a woman is in search of employment. By choosing the most convenient job, the one which is adapted to her family situation, she reduces the possible stresses.

Inter-country (Slovenia, Norway, Finland and Hungary) differences in the rank order of influences of the family on work are significant for women but not for men. Thus, it may be concluded that cultural factors and specific life situations in determining the family's influence on work are more important for women than for men.

Patterns of interaction between paid work and the family

Paid work has more negative influences on family for men than for women and the family has more negative influences on paid work for women than for men. Concerning the negative influences this means that the hypothesis of the one-way permeability for paid work/family boundaries being different for men and women is confirmed. Positive psycho-social influences, however, go both ways, i.e. from family to paid work and vice versa. Such experiences are more frequent for women than for men. The differences between sexes are smaller in the positive experiences of paid work/family interactions than in the negative ones. The most general positive experiences of work and family are more or less the same (personal satisfaction) for both sexes, while the negative ones and their sources are different. For women the family is the source of conflict in relation to work, whereas for men paid work is the source of conflict situations in relation to the family.

Employed women are as much motivated for work intrinsically as men while other motives are different. The opportunity to engage in social relationships with other workers is more frequently mentioned by women than by men, while it is just the opposite concerning the opportunity of gaining new skills or knowledge. It is still an open question whether differences between men and women may be attributed to different motivations at the beginning of their professional careers, or whether it is the consequence of adaptation to a social situation in which women do not have the same opportunities as men in the labour market. Empirical studies (Fogarty, Rapoport and Rapoport, 1971; Battagliola, 1984) and comments made by interviewed persons in Slovenia indicate that women are behaviourally, cognitively and emotionally more responsive and adaptive to actual life situations than men. In adapting to different situations they take into account the needs of the family members more often than their own.

In general positive influences were mentioned more often than the negative ones. The reason may be in the individual or social belief 'that it is good to have both paid work and a family'. This, however, does not mean that the tensions between paid work and the family have been avoided (Table 7.4). For women the transfer of family problems to the work situation is greater than for men. The transfer of problems from work to family life goes in the opposite direction, and men are more occupied by work problems at home than women. The greatest gender differences in the reconciliation of work/family demands are in the Hungarian and Polish samples, the smallest is in the Finnish one. Concerning the extensions of work/family tensions for men, there are no systematic differences among the countries with different political systems. However, for women, some work/family tensions are more specific for the samples from the socialist countries than from the capitalist ones. Women in socialist countries experience negative influences from family to working life more often than women in the Scandinavian countries. Employed women in Finland experience more extreme negative influences of paid work in their family life. Most of them give priority to the relationship with family members which places greater emphasis on the quality of family life. At the same time, they are much involved in their work, so it is difficult for them to realise all their family aspirations.

Most anxious about their children while they are at work are women in the Soviet sample, followed by women in the Hungarian and the Slovenian samples. The lowest percentage of worried women is found in Norway. The socialisation of childcare and upbringing does not lower the mental preoccupation of mothers while they are at the workplace. They feel responsible and have to organise their family life no matter who takes care of the children while they are not at home.

Table 7.4. *Tensions between job and family life (percentages of positive answers)**

Statements	Countries						
	PL	SL	H	SU	SF	N	S
'When at home I worry about my job'							
Women	33	61	22	.	49	58	29
Men	8	68	31	.	48	42	18
'I am too tired after day's work to be up to being harmonious and happy with my children'							
Women	37	32	29	30	42	23	28
Men	43	31	36	.	45	54	22
'My family has to suffer because my heart is in my work'							
Women	14	13	4	.	37	38	10
Men	7	21	14	.	50	38	10
'I worry about my children rather often when I am at work on my job'							
Women	66	48	65	80	44	10	28
Men	62	36	46	.	51	26	22
'I cannot improve my position at my job because of all my responsibilities at home'							
Women	33	15	18	16	11	13	9
Men	8	4	3	.	7	6	5
(N) Women	(195)	(183)	(78)	(.)	(156)	(79)	(619)
Men	(195)	(147)	(78)	(.)	(187)	(99)	(266)

*For the abbreviation of countries, see Table 1 + N - Norway, S - Sweden.

Women also experience the accumulation of unbalanced work/ family demands at the working place. It may be hypothesised that there is a great probability that women who worry about their children while being at work will hardly improve their professional position. This may also explain why a relatively low percentage of women perceive the limitations for promotion. They are so much occupied with other problems that they do not even think about it. Differences between sexes concerning promotional constraints are greater within one country than the differences for the same sex among different countries.

Goals and forms of achievement-motivation are more closely tied to social acceptability in women than in men. Therefore the conflict between intellectual and other female roles is common in all compared countries, but is more often expressed in the economically less developed ones.

Some psychological dimensions of the division of household tasks

Sharing household labour among partners varies according to the task to be done. Symmetrical division of labour is most frequent in caring and upbringing of children (24 per cent to 55 per cent). Most couples also co-operate in social contacts with relatives, institutions and in arranging financial matters. According to the answers given by women about cooking, washing dishes and cleaning the house, the symmetrical division of labour is less present in the samples from the socialist countries, especially in Slovenia (13 per cent) and in Orel, Soviet Union (14 per cent), than in the Scandinavian ones (29 per cent to 37 per cent).

The traditional division of labour within the family, with the exception of some tasks, is disappearing slowly. Families with a symmetrical division of labour are still quite rare. Women organise and are responsible for most of the household tasks. One of the possible reasons for such a situation is the different perception of the division of labour in the family. Men perceive help in household tasks as equal division of labour with the partner, while for women it is only occasional help and not a real relief. In spite of it, most family members are satisfied with the existing division of labour (men: 89 per cent to 97 per cent, women: 68 per cent to 89 per cent). The most dissatisfied with the existing division of labour are women in the Soviet sample. Half of them want it to be changed, while in the Hungarian sample only 9 per cent have such aspirations. In the socialist countries possibilities for change are seen in the transformation of relations among family members, that is, in a more equal redistribution of tasks. All other solutions such as paid help, transfer of some household tasks to private or public services, part-time jobs or even giving up the job are rarely thought about.

However, the question arises to whom does a more symmetrical division of labour bring what advantage or disadvantage? The Slovenian and Finnish samples were used to give at least a tentative answer to this problem. Each sample was divided in three groups according to the extent of the symmetrical division of some household tasks. In the first group there was no task sharing, while in the third, two or more tasks were shared among partners. The three groups were compared concerning the influence of family on paid work.

For women a more symmetrical division of household tasks increases the positive influences of family on paid work, and decreases the negative ones. For Finnish men the tendency is towards an increase of negative influences of family on work with a more symmetrical division of household tasks. On the contrary, in Slovenia there are no significant differences among those men who share the household tasks with the partner and those who do not. The positive influence of a more symmetrical division of household tasks for women is obvious while for men the results are ambiguous.

Conclusion

To understand the relations between gender, production and reproduction, it is necessary to take into account the interplay of the proclaimed social norms, the actual practice and the individual life experiences. Though the results of many studies, including ours, show considerable sex segregation and antagonisms, it should be pointed out that what is usually thought of as discrimination, is not always perceived as negative by women. Although their position is supposed to be inferior, most women seem to underline more positive experiences than negative ones. Paid work and family are as rewarding for women as for men, sometimes even more for women. Among the most frequently mentioned influences of paid work on family and vice versa are personal satisfaction and learning of better social relationships. This is reported by both men and women in all compared countries.

The experienced positive influence of paid work on family and/or vice versa does not mean that there are no conflicts between these two spheres. Positive relations imply also more engagement in family and paid work and in turn more confrontations with existing social, economic and individual limitations. Cultural, historical and economic factors determine which life sphere will be the source of conflicts.

Concerning the relations between paid work and the family some quite general patterns emerge. The source of conflicts for women is the family, whereas for men it is paid work. The content of the conflict reflects the kinds of options and manoeuvrability, the social system and the actual practice offered to men and women. For example, for Scandinavian women the constraints deriving from the family already appear in the phase of seeking employment, while for the Hungarian and Slovenian women problems emerge at the workplace itself.

Women in socialist countries are mostly full-time employed no matter what their family situation is. The range of options is limited and gives little space for flexibility. This may be among the reasons that they experience more problems at their workplaces than the women in Scandinavian samples. As far as negative experiences related to paid work and family are concerned, there are less differences among men than among women in the different countries. This means that different political and cultural systems confront women with a greater variety of life experiences than men. However, psycho-social mechanisms of paid work/family interactions are more similar among women in the different countries than between men and women in the same country. The relationships between paid work and the family are influenced by age and education. This especially applies to the negative influences, but no general trend can be found for the countries compared.

While in personal experience work and family are strongly interwoven, on the institutional level paid work and the family exist as two separated sub-systems. That is why the same sphere of life can at the same time be the source of conflicts as well as the source of affirmation and identity.

The family is as important for men as it is for women and paid work is as important for women as it is for men, no matter who is playing the dominant role in either sphere of life. Integrity of the primary group and positive social relations are decisive for women in resolving everyday problems. Women play the key role in the spheres that seem meaningful to them, where they are hidden, but powerful decision makers. Their expectations and aspirations are adjusted to their real-life situations. However, the struggle to balance responsibilities and work to be done for others with the development of one's own capacities remains unresolved. Socialist and capitalist systems of social stratification are based on the notion that certain activity clusters are more important than others. In both systems paid work has priority over unpaid work. Social institutions established to help the family do in fact support formal separation of the production and reproduction spheres, that is, the separation of family life and the economic institutions of society. That may be one of the main sources of conflicting demands. As long as these basic structural and ideological elements of the existing social relations do not change, partial changes in each sphere of life will not have positive long-term effects. In the context of paid work/family relations, constraints deriving from the family for women are just the one side of the same coin whose reverse shows constraints deriving from paid work for men. Therefore, institutionalised help to the family and the redistribution of domestic tasks cannot have the expected effects. Empirical data indicate that, for example, a more symmetrical division of labour in the family is not necessarily connected with more satisfaction in family members. Also a tendency is indicated that a more symmetrical division of domestic tasks leads to a re-allocation of the work/family tensions as regards the male partners.

To conclude, we can say that relevant changes in the allocation and meaning of work/family roles have occurred, but more as a result of demands imposed by the actual life situations than as a process of 'joint optimisation' of the collaboration of different social groups (Fogarty, Rapoport and Rapoport, 1971, p. 492). Both employed men and women experience conflicts, but these are of a different type and so are ways of resolving them. Consequently, the conspicuous gap between idealised images of equality and practice remain.

References

Battagliola, F. (1984): 'Employés et employées. Trajectoires professionnelles et familiales'. In: *Le sexe du travail*. Presses universitaires de Grenoble

Champoux, J.E. (1980): *The Multidimensional Nature of the Relationship between Work and Nonwork.* University of New Mexico

Černigoj-Sadar, N. (1982): 'Relationship between Work and Family'. Paper presented at 20th Congress of Applied Psychology, Edinburgh

Fogarty, M.P., Rapoport, R. and Rapoport, R.N. (1971): *Sex, Career and Family.* George Allen & Unwin, London

Kabanoff, B. (1980): 'Work and Nonwork: a Review of Models, Methods and Findings'. *Psychological Bulletin*, Vol. 88, No. 1

Kergoat, D. (1984): 'Les rapports sociaux de sexe: un nouveau question pour la sociologie'. Paper presented at the Seminar 'Il sesso del lavoro' Salerno, December 1984

Mackintosh, M. (1984): 'Gender and Economics'. In: Young, K. Wolkowitz, C., McCullagh, R. (eds): *Of Marriage and the Market*. Routledge & Kegan Paul, London

Pleck, J.H. (1977): 'The Work/Family Role System'. *Social Problems*, Vol. 24, 1977

Rapoport, R. and Rapoport, R.N. (1971): *Dual-Career Families*. London, Penguin

Rapoport, R. and Sierakowski, M. (1982): *Recent Social Trends in Family and Work in Britain*. Institute for Family and Environmental Research, London

Thorne, B. and Yalom, M. (1982): *Rethinking Family*. Longman, London

8

Tensions between Paid Working Hours and Family Life*

Rosemarie Nave-Herz

Introduction

The examination of the interrelationships between the world of work and family life - or more exactly between paid and unpaid work - must also take into account external circumstances. One of these is the time factor, which is the subject of the present paper.

The amount of time available for unpaid work depends on the time spent on paid work, because in Europe the upper limits of working hours are legally determined and because 'time' is not a dimension that can be arbitrarily expanded. The lack of personal choice about the distribution of time between occupation and family can cause tension between the two spheres. In many Western European countries it is possible to choose between different occupational time-blocks (e.g. part time and full time). However, because of the economic losses involved, this does not lead to any true alternative for the majority of employed persons. The fact that during the last few years workers everywhere in Europe have demanded a redistribution of time, giving more to the family and less to paid work, proves that a conflict does exist here.

Within the new women's movement in particular the need for cuts in working hours has been argued. This demand is based on the possibility of easing the individual combination of occupational and family duties for working fathers and mothers and particularly for single working parents. In public discussion it is also argued that shorter working hours would increase the likelihood of men participating more in domestic work. Such a view assumes that a redistribution of time will always be used for

*I would like to express my thanks to the VW Stiftung for its financial support provided for the West German part of this study.

the benefit of domestic work. However, a general cut in working hours could also have the effect of providing more time of leisure, voluntary work or work for the 'black labour market'.

Unfortunately this chapter cannot cover all the implications of a redistribution of time. I will concentrate only on the interdependence between the length of working hours of one spouse and the extent of his/her participation in domestic work.

First I will examine the question of the existence of a relationship between the length of paid working hours of men outside the house and their participation in domestic work. Second, whether the amount of paid working hours of women influences the extent to which their spouses participate in domestic work. I want to test the 'time available' hypothesis, which claims that the extent to which a spouse takes over family activities depends on the amount of time he devotes to paid work.

In investigations based on this assumption, only women were considered and the samples were differentiated according to employment/unemployment and the number of children. They proved that employed women are helped by their husbands in their domestic duties more than women not in paid work, but nevertheless the various specific burdens and responsibilities divided between the sexes are maintained (cf. Blood and Wolfe, 1960; Fogarty, Rapoport and Rapoport, 1971; Rapoport and Rapoport, 1983; Glatzer and Zapf, 1977, pp. 126-9; Hunt, 1980; Condran and Bode, 1982, p. 422; Geerken and Gove, 1983; Müller-Andritzky, 1984, p. 278; Collins, 1985, p. 72; Portner, 1983; Davidson and Cooper, 1984). The results concerning the differentiation according to the presence or absence of children and according to the number of children are contradictory. So Campbell (1970, p. 72) and Farkas (1976, pp. 473-84) discovered that husbands in families with children help more readily. Perrucci et al. (1978, pp. 53-66), however, did not find any correlation between the number of children and the husband's assistance. A Swiss research project, in which 600 couples were interviewed, reveals that husbands withdraw from domestic assistance as soon as they have children, even if their wives are employed (Ryffel-Gericke, 1983, p. 106).

The question whether husbands would help more if their weekly and extra-familial working hours are shortened was not taken into consideration. I am going to deal with this question below.

Within one country it is only to a limited extent possible to show a correlation between the length of extra-domestic working time and intra-familial distribution of work. It is so because a national comparison - for instance between men with 'normal' working hours and men who either work overtime at the moment or who are compelled to do short-time work - might reveal distortions caused by the short-term nature of this practice.

Because the range of the weekly working hours is different among the European countries, an intercultural comparison would present a first provisional picture. At least there would be no need to follow this question if the assumed interrelations showed no correlation, since then the length of working time would have to be disregarded as an independent variable. With this 'rough' method, more detailed statements are not possible.

Furthermore it must also be tested whether the length of women's working hours plays a part in the intra-familial distribution of work and whether this factor influences the subjectively perceived burden of employment. For this purpose, the data from some countries can be sub-divided into full-time and part-time working women, in order to compare interculturally the national results. But first the varying proportion of part-time working women in Europe will be shown as well as the differences in attitudes towards part-time work in Western and Eastern European countries.

Finally the effects of shift-work on families will be examined and then the statements of women on shift-work in contrast to women working regular hours will be analysed, comparing the cultures concerned.

The limitation to these working-hour models results from the data acquired from the national research. Even with the restriction of the analysis to these models, there is information about only a few countries available; it was the Dutch, the Norwegian and West German research which differentiated between full-time and part-time employment of women, and the Norwegian, West German and Italian research which differentiated between shift and regular work.

Rosemarie Nave-Herz

Differences between countries in working hours per week and in their intra-familial distribution of labour

The weekly working hours (for non-agricultural activities) in the single countries given in the International Yearbook of Labour for 1983 vary from 34 to 46 hours: 34 hours in Belgium; 36 hours in Sweden and Norway; 39 hours in Spain, Italy and France; 40 hours in Hungary, Ireland, the Netherlands, the Federal Republic of Germany and Finland; 41 hours in the USSR and Great Britain; 43 3/4 hours in the German Democratic Republic and 46 hours in Yugoslavia (International Labour Organization, 1984, p. 527).

This information not only shows considerable differences between the countries, but also that higher and lower working hours do not directly depend upon certain economic and political systems.

If we now compare the intra-familial distribution of labour of the individual countries it is obvious that the 'time available' hypothesis cannot be maintained: namely the countries with more working hours partly show a division of labour more egalitarian than in those with less working hours (e.g. Finland versus Norway; USSR versus Yugoslavia) and differences between countries with the same amount of working hours can also be shown (e.g. the Federal Republic of Germany and Hungary; see also Lupri, 1983).

However, the following facts are interesting: if we put the domestic activities, performed by both the wives and the husbands, in a positional order, nearly the same sequence can be recognised.

The categories 'contacts with relatives' and 'contacts with institutions' show the highest values in nearly every country. This means that the connection between the (small) family system and the external systems is rarely left to one partner.

If we compare the activities at the lowest position that is the activities that are least often mentioned as being performed not only by the wife but also by the husband, the correlation is surprising, too: everywhere 'laundry' and 'domestic repairs' show the lowest values, quite independently of the amount of time taken by paid work. In the last section of this paper we are going to give some possible explanations for the empirical findings described here.

The influence of part-time and full-time work on family life

Part-time work is a regular form of employment which differs from normal working time only by being shorter (Commission of the European Communities, 1984, p. 20). It is not limited to half-time work but refers to a level of working hours which is different from full-time work. Essentially part-time work is practised by women everywhere in Europe and especially by married mothers with family duties. But from this it cannot be concluded that many women have a choice between part-time and full-time employment. This is neither true in the Eastern European countries (except certain groups of mothers in the GDR) nor in the Western European states. Since here for many women a real choice is out of question because of the current situation in the labour market or due to the financial situation of their families.

In different European countries the amount of part-time work varies enormously: from 0 to more than 50 per cent of all female employees. Part-time work is particularly widespread for women in Norway and the Netherlands (52 per cent), in Denmark (50 per cent), in Sweden and Great Britain (46 per cent). In Italy its proportion is small (7 per cent) (Labour Force Sample Survey, 1979, p. 33) and in Eastern Europe it hardly exists (with the exception of the GDR where a law stipulates that part-time work without a reduction in earnings is possible for mothers with at least two dependent children under 16; in addition they are also entitled to a day per month for housework; see Ruhl and Weisse, 1982, p. 47). However, in the GDR part-time work is debated, too, and it is not encouraged by the government, just like in the other Eastern European countries, where the economic and ideological importance of full-time employment for everyone is emphasised.

In Western Europe views on part-time employment vary in the different social groups, from radical refusal to strong acceptance and intense demand for a solution of problems concerning both the labour market and the family. These arguments are not specific to particular countries, rather to particular social groups.

Space limitations do not allow here the discussion of the arguments of each group; however, it should be emphasised that in all countries - although with different intensity (e.g. in Sweden more than in Norway) - most trade-union groups are opposed to part-time work, although not all members of the trade-union organisations do so. The following reasons are mentioned:

163

increase of labour intensity, disadvantages concerning wages and taxes, less social security, less integration into the work, fewer opportunities for further training, division into two employee groups and so on. The refusal of part-time work is often combined with the demand for shortening the working hours in general.

Part-time work is supported by different Western European governments (e.g. of the FRG; see Epping and Menter, 1977), particularly with the hope of a reduction in unemployment. However, in both Western and Eastern European countries supporters and demanders of part-time jobs are predominantly women, especially mothers, no matter whether they already work part-time, full-time or not at all. They consider part-time jobs either as a release from their heavy double burden or as their only opportunity to participate in the labour process (Brüning, 1982, p. 195; Commission of the European Communities, 1984, p. 21).

However, there are also certain groups of women in all countries, mostly feminists, who see in part-time work the creation or the stabilisation of sex inequality. In their opinion the better compatibility between employment and family life means in reality disadvantageous conditions on the labour market and an inadequate old-age pension, and furthermore the reinforcement of the traditional distribution of tasks in the family sector (cf. Hoff, 1982).

Some empirical data from our study prove this assertion. However, it must be emphasised that the following statements should be treated with caution, because of the regional and quantitative limits of the three examinations (the West German, the Dutch and the Norwegian). These show, namely, that part-time working women are supported even less by their husbands or other members of the family in the domestic activities than full-time working women are. At first the reason for this seems to be that this group of women spend less time on their job - in contrast to what was shown in the preceding section - and so the 'time-available' hypothesis seems to be confirmed. I will return to this in the last section.

If one looks at the kind of activities more closely, one can see that primarily routine work is left more often to the part-time working women than to the full-time working ones, for example in the case of the preparation of meals; in Norway about 25 per cent, in the Netherlands about 72 per cent, in the FRG about 14 per cent more part-time than full-time working women are doing this activity. And similarly regarding the laundry these figures are higher in Norway by about 21 per cent, in the Netherlands about 4 per cent, in the FRG about 5 per cent. Only repair jobs are performed more often by husbands with part-time working wives than by husbands with full-time employed wives.

If you create again a ranking order for each of the three nations corresponding to the quantitative dimensions of each domestic activity, which are just as well carried out by the wife as by the husband, and if one differentiates between full-time and part-time working women, one can clearly see, too, that daily repetitive routine work is more often done by part-time than by full-time working women. The cleaning of the home, dish washing and cooking move to a lower position on the list of activities done by both partners. In all three countries the washing of clothes has the lowest position.

However, it is interesting to see which activities showed no change in their rank order: the category 'contact with public authorities' remains in the top position in the Netherlands and Norway, and in the middle position in the FRG. This means that people with different working hours react with the least flexibility on these activities.

The empirical data of the research in Oldenburg (FRG) was subjected to multiple regression analyses in order to answer in depth the question of how the intra-familial distribution of labour depends on the working hours. The result of the analysis supported the 'time available' hypothesis: the greater the participation of the wife in the employment system, the less is her participation in domestic routine work. In contrast to this, looking at the administrative and similar activities (e.g. correspondence with authorities, financial transactions, organisation of holidays, shopping) there seems to be no difference: no matter how many children there are and of what size the household is, no matter whether the women work part-time, full-time or only some hours a day, the execution of these activities does not differ. However, by differentiating not according to the working hours of the wives but to those of the husbands, it becomes evident that not the wives' but the husbands' lack of time is of importance. The longer the working hours of the husbands are, the less do they take over administrative and similar tasks.

Summarising the statements of this chapter referring to the 'time available' hypothesis so far, we can say that the empirical results suggest that the hypothesis seems to be true for the execution of daily routine work, rather than for administrative and similar activities.

However, the part-time working women do not seem to be satisfied with this distribution of domestic labour at all, at least the number of satisfied women among them is lower than among full-time working women. The differences in Norway are 12 per cent, in the Netherlands 8 per cent and in the FRG 4 per cent. But the available information cannot explain the high rate of dissatisfaction; for this, the reasons for part-time work would be necessary. However, one could assume that these women's desire for compatibility between work and family activities turn out to be different from what they originally imagined, because it is only them - and not other family members - who are expected to balance their job and household requirements. Further, they might realise that the legitimation for the demand of a redistribution of domestic work is weakened by the fact that they are only part-time employed.

Even though part-time working women are more often dissatisfied with the intra-familial distribution of labour, they rarely see their family life burdened by their employment. This may be concluded from the answers obtained in each of the three investigations.

Besides, the Norwegian research explains that the women who are temporarily less burdened by their job refuse all statements referring to matrimonial conflicts much more strongly than full-time working women, with the exception of discussions concerning alcohol consumption. It must be remarked that alcohol serves as a means to reduce tension with regard to irrational conflicts.

Altogether the present data suggest that part-time working women complain less of difficulties in the balance between their employment and family duties, but they must do more routine work, and the number of women who are dissatisfied with the distribution of labour is higher among part-time working than among full-time working women. In this respect both arguments - for and against part-time work - apply to these women: part-time work, namely, is indeed the only way of participating in employment for many mothers, and for them it seems to be a form of work which allows a combination of employment and family activities; at the same time, however, it serves to maintain traditional family roles and therefore demands adaptation only from women, which leads to a stabilisation of sex inequality.

This ambiguous position, in which part-time working women have to live, namely neither keeping the traditional position of a 'housewife only', nor full integration into employment, becomes thus quite evident.

Shift-work and its influence on family life

There are many studies concerning the effects of shift-work on family life, e.g. on the socialisation of children, especially on their achievements at school, on the family's behaviour during leisure time, on marriage, or about the burden of domestic work for shift-working women. They all point more or less to negative consequences for the shift-worker and the family, which increase with certain forms of shift-work (e.g. alternating shifts) or if both spouses have this kind of job (Tasto, 1978; Cervinika et al., 1979; Werner et al., 1980).

In the scope of our investigation, data on such transfer effects are available from the Norwegian, the Italian and the West German research. They support the results achieved by other studies and also go further into their background.

Studies about the domestic assistance of husbands have shown that shift-working women who work every night are supported the most by their husbands; our results confirm this trend. They also show that shift-working women are relieved of their domestic duties more often than other women, full-time working women with regular working hours included. If one differentiates routine domestic tasks from non-regular and administrative work here again, it becomes obvious that husbands take more part in the former activities. In contrast to this, all other categories (e.g. 'contacts with relatives', 'with public authorities', 'mechanical activities') do not show this uniform trend. Thus domestic routine work proved to be more flexible again.

In spite of the women's relief from domestic routine work there are fewer shift-working wives who are satisfied with the given distribution of labour than other wives, even fewer than among the part-time working wives: in the Norwegian study their proportion is about 10 per cent and in the West German study about 15 per cent less; we have no data from Italy on this question. The available data suggest that satisfaction with the intra-familial distribution of labour is not influenced by a comparison with the situation of other women, it rather seems to depend on one's own demand for an egalitarian distribution of labour.

Furthermore, if we compare feelings of a subjective burden - caused by shift-work - we get contradictory results from the three investigations: in Norway and Italy shift-work causes more tension than other forms of work with regard to family life; in contrast to this, West German shift-working wives do not see their family life burdened by their employment, however, they see their career hindered by their family (Nauck, 1985, p. 95). These national differences may possibly find their explanation in the reasons for the acceptance of shift-work; but unfortunately the research does not provide any information about this. Other studies carried out in various countries have shown that different motives lead to shift-work: for many women the motive is the desire for a combination of being employed and having a family. Therefore shift- and night-work seem to be a 'transition stage' for certain phases or situations of the family. For other women better wages play a role in undertaking shift-work (Rohmann, 1984), namely at the time when they have to secure their family financially with their employment. Above all, this concerns women who are single parents. An overwhelming reason stated by men is better wages (Eisenblätter, 1970, p. 587).

Finally I would like to emphasise: if the 'time available' hypothesis seems to find a certain support among shift-working wives, a reason may be that they are away from home during the time when their husbands stay there. Clearly, in empirical investigations married partners should not only be asked about their personal responsibility for domestic activities, but also synchronous studies of their time-budget should be made, which might possibly reveal the different causes of the intra-familial distribution of labour.

Summary and final consideration

As stated at the beginning, working hours do influence family life in so far as it depends on their length how much time within the whole time-budget is available for familial domestic and leisure time activities. Accordingly, the 'time available' hypothesis proceeds from the intra-familial division of labour, which depends on the married partner's participation in the employment system and furthermore on the length of the working time.

The analysis proved that the 'time available' hypothesis cannot be maintained at this general level, because it does not seem to apply to both sexes to the same extent. Therefore no correlation was found between the length of working time of any country and the degree of men's participation in family activities.

In contrast, women's working time seems to play a certain part in their relief from domestic tasks, because the likelihood of higher participation by men increases with full-time and shift-working women but not with part-time working women. And this is independent of nationality. The connection between intra-familial distribution of labour and shift-work by women allows the assumption that the fact of the wife's absence from home while the husband is there 'forces' changes in traditional patterns - a circumstance which does not exist for part-time working women. ·

The intercultural comparison of domestic activities, for which mostly both partners are responsible, proves that such activities which link the family system and the outside-sysem (e.g. contact to authorities/relatives and so on) take the first place nearly everywhere. In a system-theoretical view we can call them 'the system-overlapping activities'.

Another result was that the husbands stick to the system-overlapping activities, irrespective of their wives' time-budget; that is, they react the least flexibly in the field of working hours and forms. On the other hand, some daily routine tasks, i.e. the 'system-internal' activities, are allocated more flexibly, depending on the wives' time-budget.

Activities called 'system-internal' are those which refer directly to the reproduction of the family system (cooking, cleaning, laundry, mending clothes, etc.); of course, this theoretical division between system-internal and system-overlapping activities does not postulate that the first do not have any system-overlapping effects. This differentiation of terms was only chosen for heuristic reasons.

Furthermore, looking at system-internal activities more closely one can see that the 'time available' hypothesis does not apply to all activities to the same extent. Partners with a different 'time-budget' react least flexibly to those activities which are most seldom a joint responsibility for both of them in each examined country. In other words, the strongly gender-specific activities are redistributed to a smaller extent than other domestic routine work, even if one partner has a tight time-budget. More specifically, in all countries researched domestic repair work is left to the husband, the laundry mostly to the wife (independently of the temporal burden of employment). And this applies even where the laundry is done by machines, that is, where it is hardly comparable with its old, traditional forms. Even if technology has changed domestic work, husbands hardly show any stronger interest. The continuation of the influence of traditions on the intra-familial distribution of labour is clear everywhere in Europe, irrespective of the economic and political system. All theoretical concepts explaining the intra-familial distribution of labour - and also the 'time available' hypothesis - are limited in their validity as long as they do not succeed to include the historical-cultural factor as an independent variable in their explanations.

References

Becker, G.S. (ed.) (1981): *A Treatise on the Family.* London

Blood, R.O. and Wolfe, D.M. (1960): *Husbands and Wives.* London

Brüning, D.P. (1982): *Teilzeitbeschäftigung und Leistungsfähigkeit des öffentlichen Dienstes.* München

Campbell, F. (1970): 'Family Growth and Variation in Family Role Structure'. *Journal of Marriage and the Family,* vol. 32, No. 1 (February)

Cervinika et al. (1979): *Gesundheitliche und soziale Aspekte der Schichtarbeit.* Institut für Gesellschaftspolitik, Wien

Collins, R. (1985): 'Horses for Courses - Ideology and the Division of Domestic Labour'. In: Close, P. and Collins, R. (eds); *Family and Economy in Modern Society.* London

Commission of the European Communities (1984): *Women and Men of Europe in 1983.* Brussels

Condran, J.G. and Bode, J.G. (1982): 'Rush of Man, Working Wives and Family Division of Labor, Middletown 1980'. *Journal of Marriage and the Family,* vol. 44, No. 2 (May)

Davidson, M.J. and Cooper, C.L. (1984): *Working Women - An International Survey.* New York

Eisenblätter, O. (1970): 'Zur Arbeit der Frau im Dreischichtsystem'. In: *Arbeit und Arbeitsrecht*

Epping, R. and Menter, G. (1977): *Teilzeitarbeit bei Beamtinnen.* Schriftenreihe des BMJFG

Farkas, G. (1976): 'Education, Wages Rates, and the Division of Labour between Husband and Wife'. *Journal of Marriage and the Family,* vol. 38, No. 3 (August)

Fogarty, M., Rapoport, R. and Rapoport, R.N. (1971): *Sex, Career and the Family.* London

Geerken, M. and Gove, W. (1983): *At Home and at Work - The Family Allocation of Labour.* Beverly Hills

Paid Working Hours and Family Life

Glatzer, W. and Zapf, W. (ed.) (1977): *Lebensqualitäten in der Bundesrepublik.* Frankfurt

Hoff, A. (1982): 'Warum sind die Gewerkschaften gegen flexible Arbeitszeitregelungen?' In: Offe, C. et al. (eds): *Arbeitszeitpolitik.* Frankfurt

Hunt, P. (1980): *Gender and Class Consciousness.* London

International Labour Organization (1984): *Yearbook of Labour Statistics.* Genf *Labour Force Sample Survey 1979.* Luxemburg, 1981

Lupri, E. (ed.) (1983): *The Changing Position of Women in Family and Society.* Leiden

Müller-Andritzky, M. (1984): 'Arbeitsteilung im Haushalt - empirische Befunde'. In: *Hauswirtschaftliche Wissenschaft,* Vol. 32, No. 5 (October)

Nauck, B. (1985): *Ressourcen, Aufgabenallokation und familiäre Spannungen im Familienzyklus, Abschlußbericht - Teil II,* Oldenburg

Perrucci, C.C., Potter, H.R. and Rhoads, D.L. (1978): 'Determinants of Male Family-Role Performance'. *Psychology of Women Quarterly*

Portner, J. (1983): 'Work and Family - Achieving a Balance'. In: McCubbin, H.J. and Figleg, C.R. (eds): *Stress and the Family.* New York

Rapoport, R. and Rapoport, R.N. (1983): *Work and the Family.* Melbourne

Rohmann, R. (1984): *Frauen und Schichtarbeit.* Institut Frau und Gesellschaft, Hannover

Ruhl, H. and Weisse, H. (1982): *Sozialpolitische Maßnahmen - konkret für jeden.* 2nd edition, Berlin

Ryffel-Gericke, Ch. (1983): *Männer in Familie und Beruf - eine empirische Untersuchung zur Situation Schweizer Ehemänner.* Diessenhofen

Tasto, D.L. (1978): *Health Consequences of Shiftwork.* Meulo Park/Cal.

Werner, E. et al. (1980): *Schichtarbeit als Langzeiteinfluß auf betriebliche, private und soziale Bezüge.* Opladen

9

The Impact of Marriage and Children on the Division of Gender Roles

Andrée Michel

Anthropological and historical research indicate that though the division of work between sexes in the family characterises almost all human societies, it does not necessarily imply economic inequality between the spouses. In fact, research has shown that in barter economy, in which paid work was non-existent, the wife's contribution to the resources of the family was considered as important and valuable as the husband's since both were equally needed for the family's survival (for the developing countries see Skar, 1981; for Europe, Segalen, 1980).

The beginning of capitalism and the increase of monetary exchanges in Europe in the fourteenth century appeared simultaneously with a new division of work in the family and the new pattern of the conjugal family. In this pattern, the husband was declared the head and the breadwinner of the family because of his monetary income as a petty trader, manufacturer or craftsman, whilst his wife, who was carrying out an unpaid job in the backyard of her husband's shop as well as performing all the unpaid domestic chores, was considered as a 'non-working housewife'. The legitimation of this unequal economic status was reinforced when European states imposed family laws which subordinated the wife to the husband, recognising him as the head of the family and the manager of the family wealth. Furthermore, theologians, authors and philosophers praised this new division of roles in their writings and teachings. So, in spite of many protests from women through the centuries, this family model has survived until now. In the middle of the twentieth century it found its most impressive sociological legitimation in Talcott Parsons's theory.

In Parsons's theory, while the social system tends to specialise and differentiate its various functions, the nuclear family is a sub-system which follows the same path towards specialisation and differentiation. The specialisation of the masculine and feminine roles is required for the maintenance of the family sub-system and provides a basis for the socialisation of children and their integration into larger society (Parsons, 1954). To be the bread-winner of the family is the main role for an adult man in society, whilst the wife is the main performer of household chores and childcare. This structure is needed for the adequate functioning of the family group. Parsons's theory is supported by the findings of Robert Bales and Morris Zelditch, who show that a small social group cannot be integrated without the performance of the instru-mental roles and the expressive roles by two different persons. So, if in the family the husband fulfils the instrumental role of bread-winner, the wife is the person who should fulfil the expressive role or the role of 'the socio-metric star' (Zelditch, 1955).

Parsons's theory of the nuclear family was tested with data drawn from empirical research on sex roles in the family and the adequacy of the sex role division for the functioning of the family group. In the United States, for instance, Murray Straus found that when American families are solving a problem with children, the father was exerting both the instrumental and expressive roles more often than the wife (Straus, 1967), which indicates that the instrumental and the expressive roles are not incompatible and are not two opposite poles on the same socio-psychological dimension (Slater, 1961). In France, A. Michel tested Parsons's theory with data collected on a representative sample of urban families. She found that the less differentiated the gender roles in French urban families are, the better are the agreement, understanding and communication between the couple, the wife's satisfaction, and the more often the couple succeeds in fulfilling their plans for family life concerning the number of children, their education and the equipment of the household (Michel, 1971).

Parsons's theory also states that there can be an exception to the traditional gender role division if the wife is working outside, but this work should be marginalised and not in competition with the breadwinner role of the husband, in order to maintain the good functioning of the nuclear family (Parsons, 1954). This aspect of Parsons's theory is not confirmed by the results of the Vienna Centre research group. For instance, Elina Haavio-Mannila shows that 'low incomes of women are not producing love or happiness in marriage ... According to Finnish data ... men are more in love ... with wives having a high employment status and income (both absolutely and in comparison with the husband) than with low status and poorly paid wives' (Haavio-Mannila, 1985). In the same perspective Rosemarie Nave-Herz found (see her chapter in the present volume) that in West Germany, the Netherlands and Norway, women with part-time occupation must do routine work more often, and the number of women who are dissatisfied with the distribution of labour is higher among part-time working than among full-time employed women. When all these data are compared, they indicate the same trend: the family in which gender roles are strictly specialised and differentiated is not the best integrated family model for husbands as well as for wives.

Furthermore, this traditional family model is detrimental to the economic independence of women and their equality with men in the access to economic resources. In 1980, the United Nations revealed that examination of world statistics showed that women are performing two-thirds of the total number of hours worked (paid and unpaid work), earn only one-third of the total world income and own only 1 per cent of the total private property of land, which in the developing countries is still the main means for production (Women, 1980). Therefore it can be said that the traditional division of gender roles is not only detrimental to the satisfaction of the spouses and to family integration, but it also confers an unfair status on women in societal life since they are deprived of equal access to economic resources while they work longer hours (for paid and unpaid work) than men.

The purpose of this chapter will be modest: starting from the division of gender roles in paid and unpaid work in the different European countries, we intend to show the respective influence of marriage and children on this traditional gender role division. Our two hypotheses are that marriage (the legal bond between spouses) on the one hand and children on the other are reinforcing the traditional gender-role division between spouses.

To test these two hypotheses, we will use primarily the quantitative data collected in Europe by the research group of the Vienna Centre, taken either from census material or from surveys conducted on large samples. Therefore the data used will not interfere with but will complement other data resulting from surveys with more limited and specific samples (as for instance those concerning caregivers).

Traditional division of gender roles related to unpaid work

Unpaid work can be measured either by the number of hours devoted to it or by its monetary value. For instance, in the US (Oli, 1976) and in Canada (Proulx, 1978), the value of unpaid work is estimated to be from 35 to 40 per cent of the total Gross National Product (GNP). In France it is estimated to amount to half of the Gross Domestic Product (GDP).

Table 9.1. Time (hours and minutes) spent on unpaid work by men and women in some European countries*

	Men		Women		Year
	non-working	working	non-working	working	
			per day		
Finland		1:49		3:39	1979
France**	2:04	1:04	6:06	4:00	1974
Hungary					1972
managers		1:01		3:06	
skilled		1:06		4:05	
Poland					1976
employees		2:50		4:57	
Norway	2:01		5:08		
Yugoslavia		0:33	7:09	4:23	1965
			per week		
Great Britain		9:09	45:05	35:03[a]	1973
				23:01[b]	
Slovenia		33:00		57:07	1984
USSR***6		16:00		30:14	

*Unless otherwise stated, it was the National Reports and other background materials of the project that were used as a source.
**National Institute of Statistics, men and women under 65.
***Karpoukine and Kouznetsova quoted by Helene Yvert-Jalu in "Les femmmes et l'emploi en Union Soviétique", *Revue d'études comparatives est-ouest*, 1984, No. 4.
[a]Part-time; [b]Full-time.

In this section, we will limit our investigation concerning the quantitative aspect of unpaid work to the number of hours spent on it by men and women, and to the impact of marriage and children upon the traditional division of gender roles. Table 9.1 shows that in each European country investigated, the number of hours spent on unpaid work is always higher for women than for men, whatever the occupational status of men and women, or the method of time-budget calculation (per week or per day) are. This number is four or five times higher when women are not employed (France and Great Britain) or three times higher when they are employed (Great Britain).

Table 9.2. Time (hours and minutes) spent on unpaid work by marital status and presence of children in Finland and France (per day)

Country	Men		Women		Year
Finland					
unmarried*	0:59		1:18		1984
married with no child*	2:08		4:03		1984
married with child*	2:18		5:15		1984
France					
no child**	1:21	6a		3:55b	1974
with children**	1:30	7:55a		4:58b	1974

*Niemi, I., Kiiski, S. and Liikkanen, M.: *Use of Time in Finland,* Central Statistical Office of Finland, Helsinki, 1981.
**National Institute of Statistics, men and women under 65.
aUnemployed; bEmployed.

Table 9.2 gives data for Finland and France, two countries in which time-budget information could be cross-tabulated either for marital status or for the presence of children in the family.

In Finland, marriage increases the time spent on unpaid work by one hour for men and by three hours for women, which indicates that marriage increases the traditional division of gender roles in the couple; furthermore, married men with children increase the time they spend on unpaid work by ten minutes in comparison with married men with no children, whilst the corresponding increase is one hour and 12 minutes for married women. So the two hypotheses are verified in Finland.

In France, data are not available to compare single and married men and women as far as unpaid work is concerned. Therefore the first hypothesis cannot be tested. With the presence of children, French men increase the time spent on unpaid work by nine minutes per day whilst women increase their time by two hours if they are not employed or one hour if they are employed. So the second hypothesis is also verified in France.

Traditional division of gender roles related to paid work

In the following sections, we will test the two hypotheses according to which the traditional division of gender roles related to paid work is reinforced by marriage and children. Since in the traditional division of gender roles, legitimated by Talcott Parsons and Morris Zelditch, the husband is the official breadwinner and the wife plays the expressive role by performing domestic activities (unpaid work), it can be expected that in spite of social changes which moved more and more women into the labour market, there are still structural obstacles to the full integration of women as equal partners with men in paid work. In fact, statistics show that activity rates of men and women are not equal, that women are employed in part-time work more often than men and that they earn lower salaries or wages.

Women's participation in the labour force

According to Blood and Wolfe's theory, paid work is a 'resource' which increases the potential for bargaining for a better status in marital life (Blood and Wolfe, 1960). Since the traditional division of gender roles ascribes to wives a subordinate status in relation to the husband, it can be expected that the social system, which is also patriarchal, will create obstacles to the full participation and commitment of women to the labour market. In fact, in spite of great changes in the traditional division of gender roles concerning paid work (as it is shown in Hildur Ve's chapter), the activity rates of women are lower than those of men. The activity rates of men and women in European countries make it possible to calculate the percentage of men and women outside the labour force.

Table 9.3 shows that there is still a gender gap between percentages of men and women outside the labour force: in each country there are more women than men outside the labour force, which means that European women are more often than men obliged to rely on someone else for meeting their basic economic needs and are deprived of financial autonomy. In her chapter Riita Jallinoja presents a theory about the differences in gender gap concerning paid work in European countries. Here the concern is to test the two hypotheses according to which marriage and children reinforce the traditional gender gap as far as paid work is concerned.

Table 9.3 also shows that in Great Britain where the personal marital status of women is controlled, married women are three times more likely than single women to be outside the labour force (35 per cent and 8 per cent respectively). The negative impact of marriage on the activity rate of married women does not appear in Norway as far as the access to paid work is concerned. So the first hypothesis concerning the impact of marriage on women's activity rates is verified for Great Britain but not for Norway.

Table 9.3. Percentage of men and women outside the labour force in some European countries*

	Men	all	Women married	single	Year
Denmark	24		52		1979
Finland	26		43		1979
France	31		44		1981
GDR	0	10			1981
Great Britain**	3	20	62		1971
		31[a]	35[a]	8[a]	1984
Italy	46	76			1978
Netherlands	31	72			1979
Norway	26		54		1979
Poland	12	27			1978
Slovenia (Yugoslavia)	15	28			1984
Sweden	26		57		1979
USSR	13	18			1970

*Unless otherwise stated, it was the National Reports and other background material of the project that were used as a source.
**People from 25 to 34.
[a]Martin, J. and Roberts, C.: *Women and Employment. A Lifetime Perspective*, Department of Employment, Office of Population Censuses and Surveys, London, 1984.

Table 9.4 indicates that the second hypothesis is verified: in each European country where there are children in the family, the percentage of women outside the labour force is higher than in couples with no child. Furthermore the higher the number of children, the higher the number of women staying outside the labour force.

Table 9.4. Percentage of women outside the labour force, by number of children in some European countries*

	No child	1	2	3	4 and more	Year
	Number of children					
France**	26		36	63		1982
Great Britain***	19	39	45	52	58	1984
Italy (Lombardy)	55	66	72			1979
Poland	31	36	39	43	50	1970

*Unless otherwise stated, it was the National Reports and other background material of the project that were used as a source.
**National Institute of Statistics, women between 25 and 55.
***Martin, J. and Roberts, C.: *Women and Employment. A Lifetime Perspective.* Department of Employment, Office of Population Censuses and Surveys, London, 1984.

European data are not sufficient to demonstrate the incompatibility between marriage and women's participation in the labour force in each country, whilst there is empirical evidence (see Table 9.4) that the presence of children increases the percentage of women staying outside the labour force, whereas it does not affect the percentage of men staying outside. This indicates that with the number of children, the traditional division of gender role concerning paid work is reinforced. That is, the second hypothesis is verified.

Women's part-time work

Working part-time does not provide an opportunity for full integration in the labour market, since research carried out in France, the Federal Republic of Germany, England and the United States has shown that part-time work is associated with low occupational status, low wages, low protection by social security and low participation in paid holidays (Jallade, 1984). Therefore it is not surprising that part-time work is associated with women's participation in the labour force and not with that of men.

Table 9.5. Percentage of men and women working part-time (out of 100 'working' people of each sex) in some European countries*

	Tertiary sector men	Tertiary sector women	Industry men	Industry women	Year
Belgium**	1.8	18.6	0.5	6.5	1981
Denmark**	8.8	49.8	2.3	32.8	1980
FRG**	1.6	30.6	0.5	22.6	1981
Finland	4.3	17.0			1979
France**	2.6	17.8	0.9	7.6	1981
Great Britain**	5.5	46.9	1.6	26.4	1981
Italy**	1.6	6.8	1.8	4.7	1981
Netherlands**	13.6	51.6	4.1	34.5	1981
Norway	10.0	52.3			1980
Sweden	6.9	46.3			1980

*Unless otherwise stated, it was the National Reports and other background material of the project that were used as a source.
**EEC: 30 jours d'Europe, No. 310, mai 1984.

Table 9.6. Percentage of men and women working part-time, by marital status in Great Britain and the Netherlands

	Men	all	Women married	single	Year
Great Britain*	5.5	28	33	3	1984
Netherlands**			57	11	1975

*Martin, J. and Roberts, C.: Women and Employment. A Lifetime Perspective, Department of Employment, Office of Population Censuses and Surveys, London, 1984.
**It was the Dutch National Report that served as a source.

Table 9.5 shows that whereas - in the tertiary sector - the highest percentage of men working part-time is 13.6 per cent (Dutch datum) the percentage for women working part-time rises from 46 to 52 per cent (data from Denmark, Great Britain, the Netherlands, Norway, Sweden). In other European countries (Belgium, Finland, Federal Republic of Germany and France) the rating of women working part-time in the tertiary sector is about 20 per cent. In the industrial sector, the discrepancy between men and women is as high as in the tertiary sector. The highest percentage of men working part-time in industry is 4 per cent (in the Netherlands), whereas it is about a third of all women working in industry in the Netherlands and Denmark, and about a quarter in Great Britain and in the Federal Republic of Germany.

Table 9.6 shows that there are five times as many women working part-time among married women as among single women in the Netherlands, and ten times as many in Great Britain.

The first hypothesis is verified as far as part-time employment is concerned: marriage reinforces the traditional division of gender roles, which implies that the breadwinner role is the husband's main responsibility, while this role is marginal for wives.

Table 9.7. Percentage of women working part-time, by number of children in Great Britain, Italy and Norway*

| | Number of children | | | | |
	No child	1	2	3 and more	Year
Great Britain**	20	35[a]			1984
Italy (Lombardy)	37	41	49	59	1979
Norway	44	54	64	68	1975

*Unless otherwise stated, it was the National Reports and other background material of the project that were used as a source.
**Martin, J. and Roberts, C.: *Women and Employment. A Lifetime Perspective*, Department of Employment, Office of Population Censuses and Surveys, London, 1984.
[a]One child or more.

Table 9.7 shows the situation when women are employed in paid work: the higher the number of children, the higher the percentage of women working part-time. For instance, in Great Britain, while only 20 per cent of the women with no children work part-time, the percentage is 35 per cent for married women with children. In Italy and in Norway, 59 to 68 per cent of the women with 3 children or more work part-time, while the percentages are 36 per cent in Italy and 44 per cent in Norway for married women with no children.

So, the second hypothesis is verified: the presence of children in the family reinforces the traditional division of gender roles and maintains women in a marginal status in the labour force.

Women's occupational status

To earn a living for the family is the main responsibility of the husband, head of the family and official breadwinner in the traditional division of gender roles. So when women are employed, they are usually discriminated against as far as wages are concerned, even if they are performing the same job as men. 'Equal pay for equal work' or 'equal pay for work of equal value' are the two main demands of women who are discriminated against in the labour market.

Table 9.8 shows that in ten European countries in which data are available for the comparison of hourly salaries earned by men and women working in the same sphere of activity, women earn less than men. In six out of the ten European countries, the hourly salary earned by women is 30 per cent lower than the men's salaries, while it is from 10 to 20 per cent lower in the other countries (Italy, Denmark, Sweden).

Table 9.8. Percentage of male average hourly salary gained by women in the same sphere of activity in some European countries*

	Percentage	Year
Denmark**	85.7	1981
FRG**	72.8	1981
Finland**	72.4	
France**	79.5	1981
Great Britain**	70	1981
Hungary		
skilled	71	1974
semi-skilled	72	1974
unskilled	76.3	1974
Italy**	84.8	1981
Netherlands**	72.6	1981
Sweden	92	1979

*Unless otherwise stated, it was the National Reports and other background material of the project that were used as a source.
**EEC: *30 jours d'Europe*, No. 310, mai 1984.

Lack of data in the National Reports of this project concerning European women's wages according to their marital status and the number of children does not make it possible to test the hypothesis of the reinforcement of gender gap concerning wages in consequence of marriage and the presence of children. However, everywhere in Europe occupational status is strongly correlated with the salary level: generally the higher the occupational status, the higher the salary. Therefore the first hypothesis will be tested with data concerning the impact of marriage upon the occupational status of men and women, since these data exist for the United States and for France. In the United States, Paul Glick (1975) notes that the higher the occupational grade of women, the higher the number of unmarried women. In France, while the percentage of unmarried men decreases with high occupational status, the opposite is true for women: the higher the occupational status of women, the higher the percentage of unmarried women. Statistics show that the percentages of unmarried women is 11 per cent among female semi-skilled or unskilled blue-collar workers, 16 per cent among skilled blue-collar workers, 17 per cent among female clerks, 23 per cent among women in middle management and 27 per cent among women in high management (Roussel, 1975; Singly, 1982). In other words, most men cannot improve their occupational status without the domestic help of their wives, while most women cannot improve their occupational status if they are married and overloaded with domestic tasks. Occupational achievement and marriage tend to be incompatible for women, while it is just the opposite for men. However, there are no data available to test the second hypothesis.

The leisure time of women

Leisure time is not only passive relaxation or time spent for personal hobbies. It can also be spent on social activity, personal development or continuing education, since integration into the labour market today requires more often than in the past better education and adjustment to new technology. The traditional division of gender roles implies a domestic overload on women in the family and low involvement of husbands in this work. Therefore women usually spend fewer hours than men on leisure as is shown in Table 9.9, whatever their occupational status (unemployed or employed) or their work commitment (part time or full time). The single exception concerns English housewives who gain in leisure time what they lose in economic autonomy.

The first hypothesis is that the number of hours spent on leisure decreases more for women than for men with marriage, and therefore the gender gap is reinforced. Table 9.10 shows that the hypothesis is verified: in Finland, for instance, married men without children have three hours less of leisure than unmarried men, while married women with children have five hours less leisure than single women without children - which indicates that the gender gap increases between spouses with children as far as leisure time is concerned. It also means that the chances for married women to improve their occupational status by attending courses for continuing education are smaller than for married men.

*Table 9.9. Time (hours and minutes) for leisure by sex in some European countries**

	Men		Women		Year
	un-employed	employed	un-employed	employed	
			per day		
France**	6:02	3:09	4:03	2:09	1974
GDR	6:32			5:08	1977
Poland	4:52			3:30	1976
			per week		
Great Britain***	31:07		44:04	31:02[a] 25:07[b]	

*Unless otherwise stated, it was the National Reports and other background material of the project that were used as a source.
**National Institute of Statistics, men and women under 65.
***People from 30 to 39.
[a]Part-time.
[b]Full-time.

The second hypothesis says that the number of children reinforces the traditional division of gender role as far as leisure is concerned. Since childcare and related domestic work are the main duties of women in the traditional division of gender roles, and since childcare is time-consuming, it can be expected that with the presence of children at home the gap between husbands and wives will increase as regards leisure time. Table 9.10 verifies this hypothesis. In France, where data are available for comparison, unmarried and married men spend about four hours per day on leisure, whatever the number of children, while women with children reduce their leisure time per day by 20 minutes when compared to women with no children. This means that the gap between the leisure time of spouses increases with the presence of children: when there are no children, the difference of leisure time between spouses is 56 minutes per day in favour of men; with children at home, the difference is 72 minutes.

Table 9.10. Time (hours and minutes) for leisure by marital status and number of children in Finland and France

		Men		Women		Year
		without child	with	without	with child	
			per day			
France*		3:53	3.52	2:57	2:40	1974
			per week			
Finland**						1981
	single	47:00		43:00		
	married	44:00	37:00	38:00	33:00	

*National Institute of Statistics, men and women under 65.
**Niemi, I., Kiiski, S. and Liikkanen, M.: *Use of Time in Finland*, Central Statistical Office of Finland, Helsinki, 1981.

In Finland, the presence of children at home reduces leisure time for both husbands and wives, although each week husbands with children have four additional hours for leisure compared to women with children.

In the Soviet Union, statistics indicate that 'the higher the number of children, the less often women continue their education' (Sikhan, 1984). In 1976, while 28 per cent among women without children continued their education, the percentage was 13 per cent for women with one child, 9 per cent with two children, 7 per cent with three children and 0.6 per cent with four children (Sikhan, 1984).

European data indicate that marriage and children reduce the leisure time more for women than for men.

Conclusion

There is a contradiction in contemporary European families which, according to Edmund Dahlström, has its roots in the patriarchal heritage and the ideal of gender equalisation and gender liberation of the enlightenment, liberalism and socialism. Feminism has renewed this ideal which is opposed by the strong coalition of patriarchy and capitalist or socialist bureaucracy. In fact it can be said that capitalist and socialist bureaucracies are closely interwoven with patriarchy. Bureaucracies stratify society according to social classes, while the patriarchal system stratifies it by sex. European data indicate that social and economic unequal status between the sexes are reinforced when women marry or have children at home, particularly when they want to enter into the labour force with an equal status.

However, the data reveal that the marital status of women is an obstacle to women's access to the labour market less often than the presence of children in their family. For instance, in Norway, married women without children have the same opportunity to enter the labour market as unmarried women without children. But with the presence of children, they are less likely to work full time and to be integrated in the labour market as full participants and not as marginalised workers. In England, housewives spend more time in leisure than men, in spite of their domestic overload. However, with marriage they are far less likely to enter the labour market and to work full time for a full promotion.

If, in some European countries, marriage is no more a factor of reinforcement of the traditional division of gender roles concerning the labour market, it is because women have succeeded in overcoming obstacles in access to paid work. On the opposite side, women have not yet succeeded in overcoming obstacles when the presence of children at home prevents them from entering the labour force, or to have access to promotion at work.

One may conclude that 'because both the sexual division of labour and male domination are so long standing, it will be very difficult to eradicate them and impossible to eradicate the latter without the former. The two are now so inextricably intertwined that it is necessary to eradicate sexual divisions in the labour force in order to end male domination' (Hartmann, 1976). The division of gender role should be abolished not only in paid work but also in unpaid work, i.e. in the family. In her chapter, Hildur Ve will show that women have made a considerable effort to reduce the traditional division of gender roles by entering paid work, and that it will now be the duty of men to take a greater part in 'unpaid work' in the family. One can expect that 'if non-ruling class men are to be free, they will have to recognize their co-option by patriarchal capitalism and relinquish their patriarchal benefits. If women are to be free, they must fight against both patriarchal power and the capitalist organization of society' (Hartmann, 1976).

References

Blood, R. and Wolfe, D. (1960): *Husbands and Wives*. Glencoe (Ill.), The Free Press

Glick, P. (1975): 'A Demographer Looks at American Families'. *Journal of Marriage and the Family*, February 1975, Vol. 37, No. 1

Haavio-Mannila, E. (1985): 'Development and Consequences of Reiss' Wheel Theory of Love'. Paper presented at the National Council on family relations annual conference in Dallas, Texas, November 1985

Hartmann, H. (1976): 'Capitalism, Patriarchy and Job Segregation by Sex'. In: Blaxall, M. and Reagab, B. (eds): *Woman and the Work Place*. Chicago and London, The University of Chicago Press

Jallade, J.-P. (ed.) (1984): *L'Europe à temps partiel*. Paris, Economica

Michel, A. (1971): 'Rôles masculins et féminins dans la famille - Examen de la théorie classique'. *Informations en sciences sociales*, Paris, UNESCO, 10(1) pp. 113-35

Oli, H. (1976): 'The Value of Household Services. A Survey of Empirical Estimates'. *The Review of Income and Wealth*, June 1976, No. 2

Parsons, T. (1954): *Essays in Sociological Theory Pure and Applied*. Glencoe (Ill.), The Free Press

Proulx, M. (1978): *Cinq millions de femmes. Une étude de la femme canadienne au foyer*. Ottawa, Conseil consultatif de la situation de la femme, juin 1978

Roussel, L. (1975): *Le mariage dans la société française*. Paris, Presses universitaires de France

Segalen, M. (1980): *Mari et femme dans la société paysanne*. Paris, Flammarion

Sikhan, N. (1984): 'Le travail des femmes dans les conditions du socialisme', cité par H. Yvert-Jalu in 'Les femmes et l'emploi en Union Soviétique'. *Revue d'études comparatives est-ouest*, déc. 1984, Vol. 15, No. 4

Singly, F. de (1982): 'Mariage, dot scolaire et position sociale'. *Economie et Statistique*, mars 1982, No. 42

Skar, S. (1981): 'Andean Women and the Concept of Space-Time'. In: Ardener, Sh. (ed.): *Women and Space, Ground Rules and Social Maps*. London, Croom Helm, pp. 35-49

Slater, Ph. (1961): 'Parental Role Differentiation'. *American Journal of Sociology*, Vol. LXVII, Nov. 1961

Straus, M. (1967): 'The Influence of Sex of Child and Social Class on Instrumental and Expressive Family Roles in a Laboratory Setting'. *Sociology and Social Research* (Los Angeles, Cal.) No. 52

'Women 1980', *Newsletter 1980*, No. 3; U.N. Division for Economic and Social Information, New York

Zelditch, M. (1955): 'Role Differentiation in the Nuclear Family. A Comparative Study'. In: Parsons, T. and Bales, R. (eds): *Family, Socialization and Interaction Process*. Glencoe (Ill.), The Free Press

Part Three

Reproduction and Caring

10

Historical Changes in the Family's Reproductive Patterns*

Angelo Saporiti

Introduction: the focus of the chapter

Although more implicitly than expressly, and using different yardsticks, the National Reports (1981, 1982, 1984) of the research 'Changes in the Life Patterns of Families in Europe' all bear witness to a declining birth rate as one of the most important changes during recent decades all over Europe. Far from being exclusively a demographic phenomenon, declining birth rate has deep and far-reaching implications, particularly at the familial level, as the major activity within the family is the rearing of children. Indeed, the number of children to be brought up is certainly not the least important change that has affected family life in post-World War II Europe, and as such it deserves careful examination.

Starting from this general assumption, this chapter concentrates on changes in the family's reproductive patterns. As the declining birth rate is not at all a new phenomenon, and since both the National Reports and the empirical studies produced in this book give only scanty and indirect information about our subject, and do not allow us to probe today's relationships between recent changes in family life and reproductive behaviour, our analysis is mainly historical in character, being an attempt to elucidate the major social factors which account for the declining birth rate in a century-long perspective. Moreover, we shall try to suggest at the end of the chapter a framework for the study of reproductive

*This study is part of a wider research carried out by the author on a grant of the Italian Consiglio Nazionale delle Ricerche.

behaviour at both the familial and the individual levels in contemporary Europe. For this end, we shall also take note of some suggestions which emerge from both the National Reports and some of the chapters of this book, and which are in accordance with our argument.

The demographic background

'Non contents d'avoir cessé d'allaiter leur enfants, les femmes cessent d'en vouloir faire'. Just after the middle of the eighteenth century, J.J. Rousseau with these few words in *Emile* grasped a demographic process then just beginning and geographically limited, but that would have soon affected most of Europe: *the fertility transition.*

From a long-term perspective, the extent and the diffusion of the European fertility decline is by now well supported by documentary evidence (Tables 10.1 and 10.2).

Table 10.1. Historical trend in crude birth rate (per 1000 population), selected countries of Europe (five-year averages)

	SF	N	S	F	D	GB (d)	H	NL	I	YU	SU	PL
1778-1782	41.3	31.5	34.6	31.7	40.3	-	-	-	-	-	-	-
			(b)	(c)								
1828-1832	36.9	31.7	32.6	29.9	35.2	31.7	41.8	34.9	38.0	40.5	50.4	-
						(e)	(f)	(g)	(h)	(i)	(k)	
1878-1872	36.2	31.0	29.6	24.9	37.9	34.4	43.7	35.7	36.7	41.7	49.6	39.8
										(j)		(m)
1928-1932	21.5	16.9	15.2	17.8	17.1	16.1	24.8	22.7	25.5	33.6	44.3	31.0
											(l)	
1978-1982	13.3	12.6	11.4	14.4	9.8	12.9	14.1	12.5	11.6	17.0	18.5	19.3
	(a)			(a)	(n)	(a)				(a)	(a)	

SF = Finland; N = Norway; S = Sweden; F = France; D = Germany; GB = United Kingdom; H = Hungary; NL = Netherlands; I = Italy; YU = Yugoslavia; SU = Soviet Union; PL = Poland.
(a) 1978-1981; (b) 1803-1807; (c) 1818-1822; (d) England and Wales; (e) 1838-1842; (f) 1862; (g) 1840-1842; (h) 1862; (i) Serbia, 1862; (j) Serbia; (k) 1861-1862; (l) 1923; (m) 1906-1910; (n) West Germany.
Sources: Mitchell, B.R.: *European Historical Statistics 1750-1970*, Sijthoff & Noordhoff, Alphen aan den Rijn, Netherlands, 1978, Table A3; *Demographic Yearbook*, United Nations, New York, 1978-1982; Glass, D.V. and Grebenik, E.: 'World Population from 1800 to 1950', in *The Cambridge Economic History of Europe*. Vol. VI: The Industrial Revolution and After, Cambridge University Press, Chapter 2, Table 9.

Table 10.2. *Historical trend in total fertility rate (cohorts), selected countries of Europe*

	SF	N	S	F	D	GB	H	NL	I	YU	PL
1836-1845	4.83	4.48	4.38	3.39	-	4.87	-	5.06	-	-	-
	(a)										
1856-1865	4.83	4.22	3.96	3.04	5.02	3.93	-	4.64	5.67	-	-
	(b)				(b)				(c)		
1876-1885	4.08	3.47	3.21	2.38	3.41	2.79	-	3.82	5.13	-	-
	(d)				(d)				(e)		
1896-1905	2.58	2.09	1.90	2.14	2.08	1.96	2.79	2.86	3.14	4.17	-
	(f)				(f)		(g)			(h)	
1916-1925	2.63	2.23	2.05	2.48	1.91	2.05	2.13	2.91	2.36	3.29	2.95
	(i)				(j)		(k)			(l)	(m)
1936-1945	2.05	2.41	2.01	2.45	2.07	2.28	1.92	2.19	2.14	2.40	2.27
	(n)				(o)		(p)			(q)	(q)

For the countries' symbols see Table 10.1.
(a) 1837-1845; (b) 1857-1865; (c) 1856-1860 and 1861-1865 average; (d) 1877-1885; (e) 1876-1880 and 1881-1885 average; (f) 1897-1805; (g) 1895-1899 and 1901-1906 average; (h) 1898-1902 and 1903-1907 average; (i) 1917-1925; (j) 1915-1920 and 1920-1925 average; (k) 1916-1921 and 1921-1926 average; (l) 1917-1921; (m) 1920; (n) 1937-1945; (o) 1936-1940; (p) 1936-1941; (q) 1939-1940.
Sources: Festy, P.: *La fécondité des pays occidentaux de 1870 à 1970* INED, Travaux et Documents, Cahier no 85, Paris, 1979, different tables for SF, N, S, F, D, GB, NL, I; Blayo, C. and Festy, P.: 'La fécondité à l'est et à l'ouest de l'Europe', *Population*, vol. 30, no 4-5, juillet-octobre 1975,

Table 10.3. *Recent trend in crude birth rate (per 1000 population), selected countries of Europe (three year averages)*

	SF	N	S	F	D (b)	GB	H	NL	I	YU	SU	PL
1939-1941	21.1	15.7	15.4	13.8	19.5	14.3	19.5	20.6	22.7	26.9	35.1	25.1
										(c)	(d)	(f)
1949-1951	24.5	19.0	16.5	20.3	16.2	16.0	20.6	22.9	19.5	29.1	26.7	30.4
					(a)						(e)	
1959-1961	18.6	17.4	13.9	18.1	17.6	17.1	14.6	21.2	19.2	23.2	24.6	22.7
					(a)							
1969-1971	13.9	17.0	13.8	16.8	13.6	16.2	14.7	18.8	17.0	18.3	17.4	16.7
					(a)							
1979-1981	13.2	12.7	11.5	14.6	9.9	13.1	14.1	12.6	11.3	16.9	18.4	19.3
					(a)							

For the countries' symbols see Table 10.1. (a) West Germany; (b) England and Wales; (c) 1937-1939; (d) 1938-1940; (e) 1950-1952; (f) 1936-1938.
Source: *Demographic Yearbook*, United Nations, New York, 1971, 1979-1981; Mitchel, B.R.: op. cit., see Table 10.1.

Likewise its continuous decreasing trend over the last fifty years is well documented even if we take into account the short-term fluctuations[1] (see Tables 10.3 and 10.4).

Table 10.4. Recent trend in total fertility rate (periods), selected countries of Europe

Periods	SF	N	S	F	D	GB	H	NL	I	YU	SU	PL
1931-1935	2.40	1.91	1.77	2.16	1.84	1.79	2.16	2.73	3.06	-	-	-
1941-1945	2.60	2.21	2.35	2.11	1.90	1.98	2.48	2.88	2.56 (b)	-	-	-
1951-1955	2.98	2.64	2.23	2.72	2.09	2.19	2.71	3.04	2.30	3.36 (f)	-	3.64
1961-1965	2.58	2.93	2.33	2.84	2.49	2.83	1.84	3.15	2.50	2.68 (f)	2.46 (d)	2.67
1971-1975	1.62	2.25	1.89	2.24	1.63	2.06	2.10	1.98	2.31	2.30 (f)	2.43	2.25
1976-1980	1.67 (a)	1.68 (a)	1.65	1.87	1.42 (f)	1.78	2.13 (a)	1.59	1.65	2.20 (c)	2.34 (e)	2.19 (a)

For the countries' symbols see Table 10.1.
(a) 1976-1979; (b) 1940-1945; (c) 1976-1978; (d) 1965; (e) 1977-1978; (f) West Germany.
Sources: Festy, P., see Table 10.2; Calot, G. and Blayo, C.: *Recent Course of Fertility in Non-communist European Countries*, INED, Paris, 1981; Blayo, C. and Festy, P., see Table 10.2; Biraben, J.-N.: 'Données statistiques', *Population*, vol. 30, nos. 4-5, juillet-octobre 1975; Bourgeois-Pichat, J.: 'Recent Demographic Change in Western Europe: An Assessment', *Population and Development Review*, vol. 7, no. 1, March 1981.

Leaving aside comments on the quantitative aspects of the fertility course over the past two centuries, we can show that from the point of view of population history, fertility decline is one of the two elements - the other being a similar decrease in mortality - of that radical change in the European demographic phase which marked the passage from the ancient régime to modern society, and to which specialists refer as the *demographic transition*. Briefly stated, it is the passage from a demographic pattern characterised by high birth and death rates to a pattern, marked first by a slump in death rates and the persistence of high birth rates (or a slight decrease at the most), then by a slump in the latter as well.

It was F.W. Notenstein (1945) who first brought this characteristic demographic trend before the scientific audience. Afterwards it was reproposed and developed by many scholars, and it still stands as a reference for describing the demographic evolution of economically advanced societies. Nevertheless, as so often is the case with empirical generalisations, it is more an ideal construction than a precise reconstruction of the actual historical course of European demographic evolution. As it has been recently stated, 'some fundamental relations postulated by the theory of the demographic transition seemed to be contradicted at many points in the historical record of the demographic behaviour of European countries for which data were available' (Organski et al., 1984, p. 25). It has been ascertained, for example, that it is not true that the decline of mortality has always and everywhere preceded the decline of fertility, or that the latter slumped immediately after the mortality decline (see e.g. Schofield, 1976, pp. 1057-8; Wrigley and Schofield, 1981; World Bank, 1984). It is also true that fertility has not always followed a continuous decreasing course: it has rather followed a whole series of oscillations. Likewise, it must be remembered that it began in different times in Europe: historical experience and available data show that it affected France relatively early (Henry, 1965; Bourgeois-Pichat, 1965) and then North-Western Europe, the Southern countries, and only recently Eastern Europe.

Demographic 'facts' as 'signs'

Even if accepting the latter modifications it remains true that the European fertility decline is a demographic 'fact'. But observation and recording of demographic facts only show us, at the most, phenomena in their purest state, but do not necessarily provide their understanding. Since every population lives in its own historically determined 'space' (Schofield, 1976, p. 1053), taking into account only demographic variables tells us nothing about the 'nature' of the recorded phenomena, nor about mechanisms which govern their dynamics. To this end 'we need not be concerned with the internal variables of the demographic system of population, but with the external ones and their impact on both the structure and the dynamics of this system' (Mackensen, 1982, p. 253).

It does not mean that demographic facts are devoid of interest. Indeed, they can be considered as indicators, as signs revealing inner tendencies that concern society as a whole (Ariès, 1980, p. 654; Caldwell, 1981, p. 24). From this point of view the course of the fertility decline in Europe is the unmistakable sign of a radical change in the *reproductive models* of the population. It is traceable to contingent factors in its short-term fluctuations and to complex phenomena of social, economic and cultural changes in its secular trend.

From a historical perspective what interests us the most is the long-term change in reproductive behaviour. It is still not at all clear though what the relationships between fertility decline and social change are. What is usually referred to as the 'theory' of demographic transition is still essentially a descriptive scheme more than a proper theory capable of systematically clarifying the causal mechanisms of the transition from high to low fertility (see Demeny, 1968; Mackensen, 1982; Federici, 1984).

The difficulty in answering the two fundamental questions about fertility transition in Europe is not surprising: to which factors can this overturning in reproductive behaviour be historically ascribed and what are the factors that not only determine its persistence but also its accentuation in contemporary Europe?

Such difficulty is even greater since the task of explanation may be faced at three different levels. Indeed, following Mackensen (1982, pp. 262-5), fertility may be analysed firstly at a *macro-level* using national empirical aggregations; secondly, at the so-called *meso-level*, which involves resorting to particular homogeneous sections of the population. Lastly, it can be analysed at a *micro-level*, resorting to single units such as individuals, couples, and families.

This brief reference to the subject as well as the purport of this paper in the frame of the research presented in this book, are enough to justify the restricted aims and the limits of the analysis given below. By surveying the huge amount of material accumulated on the subject, we shall try to integrate the three above-mentioned levels of analysis to show what seems to be a more interesting interpretation of fertility decline in Europe on the one hand, and to emphasise the probable determining factors of reproductive behaviour of today's population on the other.

An outline of the fertility transition theory

Conventional wisdom suggests the existence of some constants associated with fertility decline. Usually they go under substantially equivalent terms such as 'modernisation', 'development' or 'industrialisation', and include the transition from a rural-agricultural society to an urban-industrial one, the development of the political system (Organski et al., 1984), the secularisation of society, social mobility, mass-schooling, the surfacing of a new system of values and other social processes. Even though the correlation between fertility decline and all these social changes is far from being unambiguous, there is no doubt that wherever it has taken place, the modernisation process has brought about radical changes in the reproductive behaviour of the population. This relationship, however, risks being a useless distraction if it remains at the highest level of abstraction and is not supported by genuine and specific explanatory hypotheses; indeed, the modernisation process can explain all and nothing at the same time, and fertility decline may become synonymous of modernisation instead of being explained.

As to the abstraction of the relationship, it has to be stressed that all scholars agree in considering it only as a synthetic way of expressing the basic line of fertility decline. As some of them have shown (Knodel and van de Walle, 1979; Coale and Watkins, 1985), the transition from high to low fertility took place under a wide variety of socio-economic, institutional, cultural and demographic conditions. The only factor common to most European countries is the period in which the fertility decline took on a more significant rhythm, that is the decades from 1880 to 1910 (Knodel and van de Walle, 1979, p. 235). There exists, nevertheless, a general explanation of fertility decline, according to which, at a given moment of European history a causal process began, so that changes in the reproductive structure of the society brought about another set of individual and social changes from which a system of values favourable to low fertility would have then emerged. Such a new system of values, furthermore, was in turn supported and reinforced by progress in knowledge about, and access to, contraceptive methods.

It still has to be discovered, though, which specific characteristic of the modernisation process played a crucial role in timing the fertility transition: was it the new organisation of production, the better hygienic conditions and the associated mortality decline, the improvement in the standard of living, the secularisation of society, mass-schooling, urbanisation, contraception, or what else?

The discrepancies between such a general explanation and the historical experience have led G. Hawthorn (1982, p. 284) to a conclusion that leaves two possibilities open: either there is not a sole explanation for all cases in which there was a fertility decline or there is a factor not yet discovered (or not yet conceptualised) that may act as a general explanatory factor. Leaving aside the first of the two hypotheses, as its discussion would lead us too far, we can say that to our knowledge such a general factor has in part been conceptualised, even if it still has to undergo further elaboration. Let us see briefly what it is all about.

Even if variously formulated, the thesis according to which fertility decline is the result of a massive change from *uncontrolled* to *controlled* fertility is widespread and agreed upon (Tilly, 1978, p. 42). Ariès (1980, p. 646), for example, writes of an extraordinary change from a situation characterised by 'automatic unplanned behaviour and resigned surrender to impulse and destiny' to one in which procreation is 'governed by the methods of rational and scientific organization, a sort of biological Taylorism'. E.A. Wrigley (1978, p. 152) opposes an 'unconscious rationality exercised by individuals following the norms set for them by the society in which they live' to 'a conscious rationality characteristic of couples in industrial society where family limitations are widespread'.

Now, to get the best from this thesis we first must get rid of two common misunderstandings: that in traditional, pre-modern societies fertility was left exclusively to strictly biological and demographic factors, and that it was a result of 'irrational' behaviour. As to the first point, it is enough to say that as a matter of fact all societies - past or present, elementary or complex - have generated some form of social control in order to limit so-called 'natural fertility'.[2] On the other hand, the foregoing thesis cannot be stated as an opposition between the two identities: uncontrolled fertility = irrationality, and controlled fertility = rationality. Firstly because, as we have already stressed, there is no such a thing as utterly uncontrolled fertility behaviour; but above all because rationality in fertility matters - as well as in all kind of matters - should always be valued and assessed with regard to the 'social space' within which reproductive behaviour is enacted.

Opposing uncontrolled to controlled fertility could therefore be misleading, unless the opposition is properly meant as a change in the source of control of the reproductive behaviour. As Wrigley himself clarifies (1978, p. 148), 'when the demographic transition occurred it did not take the form of a move from a situation in which fertility was uncontrolled to one in which it was reduced by the exercise of prudential restraint... The key change was from a system of control through social institutions to one in which the private choice of individual couples played a major part in governing the fertility rate'. Nor should it be meant that in pre-modern societies individual behaviour was mechanically pre-determined at a societal level. The concept of a social control of fertility means rather that in traditional societies reproductive behaviour was backed by a whole set of 'properties', all favourable to high fertility, that ranged from 'religious doctrine to moral codes, law, education, community customs, marriage habits and family organization' (Notenstein, 1945, p. 39). Only later on, the modernisation process and the growth of a 'population increasingly freed from older taboos and increasingly willing to solve its problems rather than accept them' (Notenstein, 1945, p. 41) would have rendered nearly useless all those 'properties'. In other words, according to such an interpretation, fertility decline would have been due to the growth of individuals through becoming no more *tradition directed* but *inner directed*, as Riesman (1953) puts it.

But even if we accept this interpretation of the opposition between uncontrolled and controlled fertility, it still has to be explained why it should correspond to the high/low fertility dichotomy. As to the subject, a reason frequently produced to explain the high fertility rates in pre-modern societies is the high infant and child mortality characterising them. Actually, even though many scholars attribute a causal priority to mortality (see e.g. Wrigley, 1978; Tilly, Scott and Cohen, 1980, p. 425; Ariès, 1965 and 1980; Stone, 1977), others point out that the observed relationship between mortality and fertility may have the causal ordering reversed (Knodel and van de Walle, 1979, p. 231). So it still remains to explain why 'tradition' encourages high fertility whilst 'modernisation' is conducive to low fertility, and through which specific mechanisms we have moved from one kind of behaviour to the other.

Reproductive behaviour as 'family strategy'

To achieve our aim of explanation, we must move from the macro- to the micro- and meso-analysis. Many reasons could be quoted to justify that, but two of them are determinant. The first one, common and taken for granted, is that the family is the *locus* institutionally set for biological reproduction of mankind in practically all societies.[3] There is no need to warrant the assertion according to which the effort to explain the fertility course must necessarily have as its reference point the family and its historical ups and downs; at most, as Caldwell puts it (1981, p. 21), 'a correct theory of high stable fertility and of fertility decline will be essentially a theory of social and family change'. But in order to do that we also need to take into account the meso-social level of analysis.

Referring to what Anderson (1980) has stated for more general purposes, it can be observed that it is one thing to maintain the plausibility of certain social changes, and another to single out and prove their impact on attitudes and behaviour of individuals and families. In our context it means that it is necessary 'to bridge the gap between the logically consistent determinants of population structure and population dynamics on the one hand..., and the concept of structure and function of the family as the basic unit within the process of population on the other' (Mackensen, 1982, p. 258).

Now, if we assume that the family is a social structure endowed with its own autonomy and capable of producing, or at least influencing, social change, and not a passive recipient of that change,[4] then for a partial covering of that gap it requires the use of the concept of *family strategy*.

Following Bourdieu (1976), by family strategies we mean all those 'practices' that the family utilises for decision making in order to guarantee its continuity and maintain/better its position in society. Even though they recur according to statistically observable regularities within homogeneous sections of the population, these practices are not in conformity with fixed, formal, and explicit rules. On the contrary, they are the 'product of habits, meaning the practical mastery of a small number of implicit principles that have spawned an infinite number of practices and follow their own pattern' (Bourdieu, 1976, p. 141). As such, family strategies represent differentiated solutions elaborated and enacted to face different needs in conformity with the numerous limits imposed by both the external environment and the family unit itself. They can be solutions concerning the inheritance of family property, socialisation, educational and marital choices, the actual composition of the family, or the participation of its members in the labour market or in migration movements. They are also solutions concerning the reproductive behaviour of the couple. Whatever they are, all these solutions must not be taken separately: as Bourdieu reminds us (1976, p. 141), each of them represents only one of the many elements 'in the entire system of biological, cultural and social reproduction by which every group endeavours to pass on to the next generation the full measure of power and privilege it has itself inherited'.

Of course it is for empirical research to detect which particular solutions are adopted depending on the different needs that families have to satisfy. Here the concept of family strategy has been introduced only because it facilitates comprehension of the actual impact of social change on attitudes and behaviour in fertility matters; on the other hand, as its analysis requires the explicit statement of the 'principles which lead to observable regularities or patterns of behaviour among households' (Tilly, 1979, p. 138), it allows us to tie micro-social behaviour to collective behaviour.[5]

Family, modes of production and fertility

Within the framework thus far described, the process demanding most attention is the impact of changes in modes of production on fertility strategies, that is the impact of transition from agricultural, artisan and cottage-industry based on familial and labour-intensive modes of production to a capitalistic one based on a free and monetised labour market.

Social historians have underlined the consequences of this deep change for the reproductive behaviour of the family; demographers and sociologists too have not neglected the subject. But attempts to interpret fertility transition in connection with the evolution of productive and familial structures are still scanty. The one that deserves most attention is Caldwell's *wealth flow theory*, according to which 'fertility is high or low as a result of economic benefit to individuals, couples or families in its being so. Whether high or low fertility is economically rational is determined by social conditions: primarily by the direction of inter-generational wealth flow' (Caldwell, 1982b, p. 152), that is, by the direction of material and non-material resources (work, money, goods, services, guarantees, affective and emotional support) that are passed on within the family from one generation to another. More specifically, according to Caldwell the high fertility of traditional societies is ascribable to the domestic or familial mode of production characterising them, where the resources passing from the younger generations to the elder ones are greater than those going in the opposite direction. The net wealth flow is upward, hence the convenience for the elder generations to adopt high fertility strategies.[6]

It is, however, necessary to clarify and stress two aspects of such a thesis, which reminds us of well-known and consolidated opinions on the economic value of children in traditional societies (Bulatao, 1982; Caldwell, 1983; Fawcett, 1983). First of all, such a strategy can only be put into practice in a society that supports and legitimises familial production at the superstructural level, that is, in a society whose cultural code gives priority to families rather than individuals, and that is sufficiently monolithic to be able to control deviating behaviour easily. Secondly, it must be a society in which the power to make decisions concerning *production and reproduction* lies in the hands of older male generations. As we shall see later, this last point is significant in understanding the mechanisms of fertility transition. At the moment, suffice it to remark that the *raison d'être* and the social legitimation of the economic rationality of high fertility strategies rest on what Caldwell (1981) calls the 'cultural superstructure' of the familial mode of production, and on its coinciding with the general superstructure of traditional society: a society highly segmented by age, sex, marital status and relationships.[7]

As to the conditions that determine fertility decline, according to Caldwell a high fertility level is no longer justified when elder generations have to invest in the younger ones more than they can receive. That could occur only in case of passing from the domestic mode of production to the capitalistic one: 'the real reproductive divide lies between modes of production based largely on net-works of relatives and those in which the individuals may sell their labour to complete strangers' (Caldwell, 1982a), that is those in which elder generations no longer control the placement of family members on the labour market and consumption. In other words, breaking the older male generation's monopoly of control on reproductive and productive matters associated with transition to the capitalist mode of production, involves such changes in the economic relationships within the family that determine a reversal in the net wealth flow and make high fertility strategies uneconomical.

But a change in the mode of production is only a necessary condition for the reversal in the inter-generational wealth flow. Indeed, it could also be the case that 'lack of synchronization in the evolution to greater sophistication of the economic, political and cultural subsystems' (Lesthaeghe, 1980, p. 534) makes traditional societies' superstructure continue to be almost unchanged and to exercise its controlling power even in changing productive conditions. The lag between changes in productive structure and superstructure would allow what Caldwell calls *familial morality* to carry on practising its prerogatives, therefore preventing the ultimate reversing of the net wealth flow: 'until the transition of morality has taken place, the direction of the wealth flow is not likely to reverse' (Caldwell, 1981, p. 12).

Here is the most interesting and questioned point of Caldwell's theory: although he considers the reversal in the wealth flow to be a change that can be reached only when the economy of the nuclear family has been largely isolated from that of the extended kin network, he maintains that such a change arises from a change in the *emotional* balance of the family (Caldwell, 1982a, pp. 152, 346; 1982b, p. 175). In other words, the economic nucleation of the modern family would be a result of a similar nucleation of the affective relationships within the family. As V.N. Thadani (1978, p. 471) says, this means that 'the radical change in parent-child relationships is identified as the "primary factor" in the mergence of the nucleated family, in the reversal of intergenerational wealth flow from parent to children, and in decline of fertility'.

Although some scholars do not agree on this point, it appears, nevertheless, to find support and integration in other research trends in the family field, especially in the so-called *sentiment approach* developed by many historians.[8] That which Caldwell refers to as 'emotional nucleation' of the family can in fact be considered as the outcome of many processes more or less parallel in time, but all converging in their consequences at the familial level: the detachment of the family unit from the surrounding community and the critical change 'from distance, deference and patriarchy' to what Stone (1977, p. 4) has called 'affective individualism'; the growing of 'family's awareness of itself as a precious emotional unit that must be protected by privacy and isolation from outside intrusion' (Shorter, 1975, p. 227); the 'romantic revolution' that radically changed the way of choosing the partner and the intensifying of the emotional and equalitarian aspects of conjugal relationships; the discovery of maternal love and the importance attached to parents' involvement with their infants; the coming of a *sacralised* conception of children's life[9] and of a new world built around them (Plumb, 1975). To sum up, that 'veritable revolution in sensibility, a revolution as important as the French Revolution or the Industrial Revolution' (Ariès, 1980, p. 645) which from Ariès (1965) onwards we have learned to call 'the discovery of childhood', and which produced a 'child-oriented society' in which 'affectivity became centered on family and children ... [and in which] the parent's chief psychological and material investment consisted in helping the children to get ahead' (Ariès, 1980, pp. 645-6).

All these changes within the family were of course parallelled, supported and fostered by wider and converging changes at the societal level. Since it is impossible to go into details, here it is enough to recall that they were changes which led to the arrival of what Macpherson (1982) has called 'possessive individualism'; to the formation of a society in which a 'strong communal system and a fairly monolithic cultural code ... [is substituted] by alterations and diversifications of the moral code in the direction of greater tolerance for individual choices' (Lesthaeghe, 1980, p. 543). There were structural changes too: urbanisation, the increase in social mobility, and above all mass-schooling,[10] just to mention a few. What is more, however, all these transformations would not have asserted themselves if they had not been in compliance with the moral dictates of the new capitalist mode of production: a morality which emphasises 'initiative, individualism and self-reliance to an extent that would have been abhorrent to the traditional family and against the interests of its more powerful members', and promotes 'a respect for work, rather than the dominant attitude found in familial production which gives primacy to respecting and observing the hierarchies of intrafamilial relationships with regard to work' (Caldwell, 1981, p. 11).

As to their impact on family reproductive strategies, all these changes have had two fundamental consequences. An erosion of decisional power of the elder male generations on fertility matters on the one hand, and what has been called the *transition in the value of children* (Bulatao, 1982) on the other. This latter one consists of two essential components: a decrease of upward material wealth flow, and an increase of downward wealth flow, both material and emotional. Both adverse to high fertility, these two elements were such that 'in the end children become an economic burden, and with the emotional flow directed towards them, a large number of them become an emotional burden, too' (Caldwell, 1981, p. 26). A high fertility strategy was no longer rewarding to maintain and did not improve family standing; other and more expensive strategies imposed themselves for this purpose - particularly the socialising and educational ones - and they were compatible only with a low-profile reproductive strategy.

Women's situation and low fertility in contemporary Western societies

If we accept Caldwell's ultimate statement (1981, p. 24) that 'high fertility was not uneconomical in the traditional family engaged in familial production, while it is uneconomical in contemporary societies with a dominant non-familial labour market', it is now time to wonder whether the continuous decline of fertility up to now is ascribable to the same factors that had triggered it off in the past or whether other factors acquired more importance in pushing fertility to lower levels later on.

On this subject Ariès (1980, p. 649) says that 'the decline in the birth rate that began at the end of the eighteenth century and continued until the 1930s was unleashed by an enormous sentimental and financial investment in the child. I see the current decrease as being, on the contrary, provoked by exactly the opposite attitudes. The under-40 generation is leading us into a new epoch, one in which the child occupies a smaller place, to say the least'. This feeling is in compliance with some recent studies on childhood in contemporary societies (see e.g. Postman, 1982). Furthermore, as Ariès himself says, it would show that identical results have been produced by different causes. Nevertheless, he does not say why child-oriented society has been superseded; on the contrary, he seems to reject what many point out as the most important cause of low fertility level in contemporary Western societies: women's emancipation and their place in present society.

We have already stressed the importance of the ending of the older male monopoly of power on production and reproduction, caused by a new mode of production that moves the focus of productive decisions outside the family. We must now underline that the full development of capitalistic 'morality' has more and more eroded the decisional power of older males in fertility matters. The demand of the new capitalist mode of production for adult wage labour, including female labour, and the general process of women's emancipation have in fact brought forth a massive female presence in the labour market, and consequently also an increasing autonomy for women, both economic and psychological.[11] Maybe it is not rash to say that the change from uncontrolled to controlled fertility means that fertility is now not only a strictly family matter, but also mainly a matter of the individual woman's choice.

If the theories we elaborate represent attempts to rationalise the already ongoing social processes, it is not by chance that with the more recent developments in fertility studies 'we have increasingly abandoned the concept of a homogeneous, coherent society, we came closer and closer to an explanatory model in which ... [reproductive] decisions are not seen as primarily determined by social tradition or regulation: the individual, on the contrary, appears as an autonomous personality making decisions, and these can be explained only by pointing to individual features' (Mackensen, 1982, p. 257).[12]

The most immediate reference is to explanatory models like Easterline's or the *new home economic* ones, which have mostly been developed in the framework of the neo-classical economic theory, and which stress the importance of the woman's extra-domestic work (see e.g. Easterlin, 1968; Becker, 1960; Mincer, 1963; Silber, 1981; Schultz, 1974). But it seems more promising to resort to a more typical sociological approach such as the one recently developed by Oppong (1980; 1983) and Federici (1982; 1984). Rather than considering only the link between women's extra-domestic work and their reproductive choices, it extends this link to the whole range of roles that women enact both in the family and in the productive sphere of society because of what has been called their *double presence* (Balbo, 1978).

Among the numerous advantages it offers, such an approach allows us to face, at a more specific level, a matter already considered. Granted that present fertility levels may in part be explained in terms of the growing autonomy of women, again the question we meet in opposing 'tradition' to 'modernisation' arises: why does women's liberation lead to fertility decrease? Is it a linear extension of the effects of the general modernisation process? Or is the relationship between women's emancipation and fertility not a linear one at all, involving instead all those contradictions which have characterised fertility transition up to its stabilisation at a low level.

As to these questions, here and now we can only formulate a hypothesis and suggest a perspective of analysis which, even if indirectly and from a very general point of view, is also suggested by the rich but scattered material included in the National Reports. Briefly, the hypothesis, which follows from Caldwell's, is that the reversal in the inter-generational wealth flow which makes high-fertility *family strategies* uneconomical may have similar effects at the level of *women's reproductive strategies*. That is, it may be that the balance of advantages that a woman receives from her children (economic, social, and psychological) and the resources she invests in them (in terms of direct costs, both material and emotional, and of the so-called *opportunity costs*) is nowadays more and more to her disadvantage. Now, we believe this hypothesis can only be fully developed and checked by following a sociological perspective which assumes the status of women as the primary explanatory variable. Only this approach will help us both to understand the mechanisms that contribute to determining the downward direction of wealth flow at the level of woman/children relationships and to point out the contradiction and the non-deterministic character of the wealth flow with regard to women's reproductive choices.

Here we can only mention this approach, starting from Federici's double differentiation between predominantly 'internal' feminine roles (maternal, conjugal and domestic), 'external' (occupational and community roles) and 'mixed' ones (kin and individual roles) on the one hand, and between 'traditional' roles (maternal, conjugal, domestic, and kin roles) and 'non-traditional' ones (occupational, community, and individual roles) on the other (Federici, 1984, pp. 128 ff).

The mechanism through which a woman's social condition, thus defined, exerts its influence on her reproductive choices follows from the incompatibility of, or at least from the conflict between, the set roles. More precisely, according to Federici (1984, pp. 129-30), the more non-traditional roles 'spread, the more they clash with "internal" roles, or at least with their more traditional conception, owing to reasons of objective (time budget) and subjective (attitudes) incompatibility'. But such a conflict, which comes out in several National Reports,[13] does not necessarily lead to fertility decrease. Indeed, if it is quite correct to hypothesise that the growing importance of non-traditional roles has negative effects on reproductive choices, it still remains that the very same roles give women more freedom and power in fertility decisions, pregnancy included if that is what she desires.

At any rate, the actual reproductive outcomes that follow from the contradictions of women's present situation depend on the specific circumstances of family life, on the values that both partners attach to maternity and paternity, and perhaps even more on a complex set of factors which lead again to the wider social context. As a matter of fact, it must be stressed that the making of the welfare state in industrially advanced societies has been characterised by the growth of a legal system favourable to the family and by an infrastructure network that, though reducing the conflict between traditional and non-traditional roles, may have contradictory consequences on women's reproductive choices.[14] Indeed, the existence of a legislation and of an infrastructure network that protect maternity may have positive effects on fertility, allowing women to reduce to a minimum the downward wealth flow and to maintain their external and non-traditional roles at the same time. But other infrastructures and other legislative measures - especially those concerning the spreading of contraception and abortion - may have negative effects on fertility; that is, women may maintain and improve their social and productive standing, eliminating the downward wealth flow completely.

Conclusions

From the previous analysis two general conclusions follow. First of all it has been ascertained that during the last two centuries European reproductive patterns have radically changed both quantitatively and qualitatively. But unlike the quantitative change, the qualitative one cannot be assimilated with a straight-line evolution. Indeed, it is true that reproductive choices have been made more and more by individuals, but that does not mean that society has ceased exerting its control over them. Rather, the 'space' in which the relevant social units (individuals, couples, and families) decide and enact their choices about fertility has changed, and so have the forms of social control on reproduction. The traditional space, wherein this control has been exerted through an appropriation of female and child labour resources 'by those who, by virtue of age and descent, form the ruling group in an asymmetric structure and exchange system' (Lesthaeghe, 1980,

p. 530) has been substituted by a 'modern space' with a more diffuse and anonymous control structure, which, however, is not necessarily less conditioning or effective.

If it is true that 'a profound, hidden, but intense relationship exists between the long term pattern of the birth rate and attitudes towards the child' (Ariès, 1980, p. 649), and that the 'space' wherein we live is also made up of 'meanings', one may conclude that perhaps fertility decline is the sign of a decline of the ultimate or sacred 'meaning' we attribute to life in favour of more utilitarian or profane 'meanings' (see also Simons, 1982, p. 142).

The second conclusion concerns the necessity to entrust empirical research to check all the assertions appearing in this paper more as hypotheses than as verified propositions, especially as regards fertility determinants in contemporary societies. Such research should be closely tied to the analysis of the relationships between family, market, and the state. Furthermore, only comparative research such as the one co-ordinated by the Vienna Centre may offer some elements to support the recent interpretation by Hawthorn (1982, pp. 294-5) of the present uniformity of fertility levels in practically all Europe: 'fertility has become detached from variations in material conditions and dependent instead on an unprecedentedly tight and common norm. Pre-industrial families make choices in environments in which it often seems that objectively there are very few choices to make. Late industrial families make progressively fewer choices in an environment in which it seems that objectively there are very many to make.'

Notes

1. All the National Reports (1981, 1982, 1984) offer information about the course of fertility during the past 50 years and show the well-known trend: an increase during the years immediately after the Second World War lasting more or less until the mid-sixties, followed by a resumption of the long-term decline which seems to have reached its minimum value in the early eighties. Since, however, this information is not homogeneous either from a demographic or from a historical point of view, and since we are interested in the decline of fertility in a historical perspective, we preferred to use a more complete and homogeneous historical series for the construction of Tables 10.1 to 10.4.

2. 'Natural fertility' means the 'fertility of a human population that makes no deliberate efforts to limit births' (Henry, 1953, p. 135). The mechanisms of fertility control go from the observance of a long postpartum taboo on sexual intercourse to infanticide, from abstinence from intercourse to a particular marriage pattern such

Angelo Saporiti

as the one typical of pre-modern Europe characterised by a relatively later marriage for both males and females, many people permanently unmarried, and many households containing unmarried people (Hajnal, 1965). On the social control of fertility in traditional societies see, amongst the many, N.B. Ryder (1967), E.A. Wrigley (1978), J.C. Caldwell (1982b) and, above all, R. Lesthaeghe (1980).

3. Besides the many variations which have taken place in the past, the phenomenon of illegitimate birth is probably bound to have increasingly more importance in present-day society, as indicated by the information reported by several countries in their National Reports (Finland, France, Great Britain, Sweden). This does not, however, take away any validity from the assumption which will guide our analysis in the following.

4. As, for example, T.K. Hareven (1971) and B. and P.L. Berger (1983) maintain, even if with different arguments and purposes. On this point see also E. Dahlström in this volume.

5. On the concept of family strategies see, besides the previously quoted M. Anderson (1980, particularly Chapter 4), P. Bourdieu (1976) and L.A. Tilly (1979), J. Goody (1973), L. K. Berkner and F. F. Mendels (1978), G. H. Helder (1978), E.A. Wrigley (1978) and G.B. Sgritta (1987).

6. Caldwell has elaborated and developed his theory in many works. When writing about the mode of domestic production, he refers firstly to the mode of production in peasant societies of the Third World. However, as clearly expressed in some of his works (1981; 1982b, p. 179), his theory is also valid for those societies in which, beside a predominant agricultural sector, sectors of artisan and commercial economic activities are present, consequently also for the Europe which we usually define as 'traditional' or 'pre-modern', or even 'pre-capitalistic'. As for the mode of domestic or familial production, see, among others, M. Sahlins (1972) and J. Siskind (1978). For some analysis of fertility decline analogous in some respect to Caldwell's, see L.A. Tilly and J. W. Scott (1978) and N.B. Ryder (1967).

7. On this point see the essay, which we find illuminating, by R. Lesthaeghe (1980) and the one by N. Crook (1978). Furthermore, it is clear that here we refer in particular to that society which is often defined as 'patriarchal society'; for some characteristics of this see E. Dahlström and R. Liljeström (1982).

8. Besides those quoted in the text, see also J.L. Flandrin (1976) and R. Trumbach (1978). One should bear in mind, of course, the criticism directed at this approach, about which see D. Hunt (1970), V.N. Thadani (1978), M. Anderson (1980), L.A. Tilly, J. W. Scott and M. Cohen (1980) and L. A. Pollock (1983).

9. This expression is used by V.A. Zelizer (1981) for an extra-European context (the U.S.) but we think it is suitable for our case as well.

10. In reality, some authors consider the effect of mass-schooling as decisive, if not as a basic explanatory variable, at least as a variable timing the transition from high to low fertility: see again J.C. Caldwell (1980) and W. Minge-Kalman (1978).

11. Although all the National Reports rightly underline the increasing importance of female labour after the Second World War, one must remember - as clearly comes out of these same Reports - that the increase in female labour force has not always or everywhere followed a linear movement, nor has it affected all economic sectors or occupational categories in a uniform way. However, what we are more interested in pointing out is the fact that the more or less generalised entry of women into the labour force has not only been due to strictly economic necessities, but has also been the result of a broader process of emancipation which has affected all aspects of female life. Suggestions in this direction can be found in all the National Reports, and particularly in those from the Netherlands, Sweden

210

and France, in which e.g. A. Michel talks about a 'silent revolution of women'. Another and perhaps more interesting indication of this process of women's emancipation is offered by the fact that often the increase in women's employment has affected in particular married women - see, for example, the National Reports from Finland and Norway, signalling a break with tradition which assigns an exclusively domestic role to married women.

12. In relation to these last statements see, e.g., the conclusions of R. Jallinoja and E. Haavio-Mannila in the Finnish report, where they talk about a 'tendency of privatization [which in part expresses] the rise of individualization or subjectivity' (National Reports, Finland, 1981, p. 49). Also in agreement with the statements of R. Mackensen is the idea of 'conscious childlessness' which C. Clason writes about in her report on the Netherlands (National Reports, the Netherlands, 1984, p. 47).

13. In her report on Slovenia, K. Boh writes that 'women are expected to establish a continuity between the family and employment, required to find ways by which they can fulfil both their family and their work obligations. Naturally this results in a permanent conflict between responsibilities at work and the duties of a wife and mother. As a result, women usually try to effect a compromise by choosing jobs which leave them with enough time and energy for their household tasks' [National Reports, Yugoslavia (Slovenia), 1984, p. 14]. A similar conclusion is reached by G.B. Sgritta and A. Saporiti in their report about Italy (National Reports, Italy, 1982), where they closely examine the empirical literature on female labour and family constraints. Again, R. Jallinoja (in this volume) explicitly states that the family causes a life career different from that of men. Women are moving back and forth between the family and employment.

14. Since space limitations do not permit us to explicate this point, for a comparative picture of the evolution of family policies in the countries represented in this volume we again refer to the National Reports.

References

Anderson, M. (1980): *Approaches to the History of the Western Family 1500-1914.* Macmillan/The Economic History Society, London

Ariès, P. (1965): *Centuries of Childhood. A Social History of Family Life.* Viking, N.Y.

Ariès, P. (1980): 'Two Successive Motivations for the Declining Birth Rate in West'. *Population and Development Review*, Vol. 6, No. 4, December 1980, pp. 645-50

Balbo, L. (1978): "La doppia presenza" (Double présence). *Inchiesta*, 32, 1978, pp. 2-6

Becker, G.S. (1960): *An Economic Analysis of Fertility in Demographic and Economic Change in Developed Countries.* Princeton University Press, Princeton

Berger, B. and Berger, P.L. (1983): *The War over the Family. Capturing the Middle Ground.* Anchor Press/Doubleday, Garden City, N.Y.

Berkner, L.K. and Mendels, F.F. (1978): 'Inheritance Systems, Family Structure and Demographic Patterns in Western Europe'. In: Tilly, C. (ed.): *Historical Studies of Changing Fertility.* Princeton University Press, Princeton

Angelo Saporiti

Bourdieu, P. (1976): 'Marriage Strategies as Strategies of Social Reproduction'. In: Foster, R. and Ranum, O. (eds): *Family and Society. Selection from the Annales: Economie, Sociétés, Civilisations*. Johns Hopkins University Press, Baltimore

Bourgeois-Pichat, J. (1965): 'The General Development of the Population of France since the Eighteenth Century'. In: Glass, D.V. and Eversley, D.E.C. (eds): *Population in History: Essays in Historical Demography*. E. Arnold, London

Bulatao, R.A. (1982): 'The Transition in the Value of Children and the Fertility Transition'. In: Hohn, C. and Mackensen, R. (eds): *Determinants of Fertility Trend Theories Re-examined*. Ordina Ed., Liège

Bulatao, R.A. and Lee, R.D. (eds) (1983): *Determinants of Fertility in Developing Countries*. Academic Press, N.Y., 2 vols

Caldwell, J.C. (1980): 'Mass Education as a Determinant of the Timing of Fertility Decline'. *Population and Development Review*, Vol. 6, No. 2, June 1980, pp. 225-56

Caldwell, J.C. (1981): 'The Mechanisms of Demographic Change in Historical Perspective'. *Population Studies*, Vol. 35, No. 2, pp. 5-27

Caldwell, J.C. (1982a): *Theory of Fertility Decline*. Academic Press, N.Y.

Caldwell, J.C. (1982b): 'The Wealth Flow Theory of Fertility Decline'. In: Hohn, C. and Mackensen, R. (eds): *Determinants of Fertility Trend Theories Re-examined*. Ordina Ed., Liège

Caldwell, J.C. (1983): 'Direct Economic Costs and Benefits of Children'. In: Bulatao, R.A. and Lee, R.D. (eds): *Determinants of Fertility in Developing Countries*. Academic Press, N.Y., Vol. 1

Coale, A. and Watkins, S. (eds) (1985): *The Decline of Fertility in Europe*. Princeton University Press, Princeton

Crook, N. (1978): 'On Social Norms and Fertility Decline'. *The Journal of Development Studies*, Vol. 14, No. 4, July 1978, pp. 198-210

Dahlström, E. and Liljeström, R. (1982): *Working-class Women and Human Reproduction*. Forskningsrapport, No. 70, Report from the Department of Sociology, University of Gothenburg

Demeny, P. (1968): 'Early Fertility Decline in Austria-Hungary: A Lesson in Demographic Transition'. *Daedalus*, Spring 1968

Easterlin, R.A. (1968): *Population Labour Force and Long Swing in Economic Growth*. National Bureau of Economic Research, N.Y.

Fawcett, J.T. (1983): 'Perceptions of the Value of the Children: Satisfaction and Costs'. In: Bulatao, R.A. and Lee, R.D. (eds): *Determinants of Fertility in Developing Countries*. Academic Press, N.Y.

Federici, N. (1982): 'Effects of Social Policies on Women's Role and the Demographic Consequences in Developed Countries'. *International Population Conference*, Manila 1982, vol. III

Federici, N. (1984): *Procreazione, famiglia, lavoro della donna* (Procreation, family and women's work). Loescher, Torino

Flandrin, J.L. (1976): *Familles, parenté, maison, sexualité dans l'ancienne société*. Hachette, Paris

Glass, D.V. and Eversley, D.E.C. (eds) (1965): *Population in History: Essays in Historical Demography*. E. Arnold, London

Goody, J. (1973): 'Strategies of Heirship'. *Comparative Studies in Society and History*, 15, pp. 3-20

Historical Changes in Family Reproduction

Hajnal, J. (1965): 'European Marriage Patterns in Perspective'. In: Glass, D.V. and Eversley, D.E.C. (eds): *Population in History: Essays in Historical Demography*. E. Arnold, London

Hareven, T.K. (1971): 'The History of the Family as an Interdisciplinary Field'. *Journal of Interdisciplinary History*, Vol. II, No. 2, pp. 315-27

Hawthorn, G. (1982): 'The Paradox of the Modern: Determinants of Fertility in Northern and Western Europe since 1950'. In: Hohn, C. and Mackensen, R. (eds): *Determinants of Fertility Trend Theories Re-examined*. Ordina Ed., Liège

Helder, G.H.Jr. (1978): 'Family History and the Life Course'. In: Hareven, R. (eds): *Transitions. The Family and the Life Course in Historical Perspective*. Academic Press, N.Y.

Henry, L. (1953): 'Fondements théoriques des mesures de la fécondité naturelle'. *Revue de l'Institut International de Statistique*, 21, pp. 132-252

Henry, L. (1965): 'The Population of France in the Eighteenth Century'. In: Glass, D.V. and Eversley, D.E.C. (eds): *Population in History: Essays in Historical Demography*. E. Arnold, London

Hohn, C. and Mackensen, R. (eds) (1982): *Determinants of Fertility Trend Theories Re-examined*. Ordina Ed., Liège

Hunt, D. (1970): *Parents and Children in History. The Psychology of Family Life in Early Modern France*. Basic Books, N.Y.

Knodel, J. and Walle, E. van de (1979): 'Lessons from the Past: Policy Implications of Historical Fertility Studies'. *Population and Development Review*, Vol. 5, No. 2, June 1979, pp. 217-245

Lesthaeghe, R. (1980): 'On the Social Control of Human Reproduction'. *Population and Development Review*, Vol. 6, No. 4, December 1980, pp. 527-48

Mackensen, R. (1982): 'Social Change and Reproductive Behaviour - on Continuous Transition'. In: Hohn, C. and Mackensen, R. (eds): *Determinants of Fertility Trend Theories Re-examined*. Ordina Ed., Liège

Macpherson, C.B. (1982): *The Political Theory of Possessive Individualism: Hobbes to Locke*. Oxford University Press, Oxford

Mincer, J. (1963): 'Monetary Price, Opportunity Costs and Income Effect'. In: *Measurement in Economics*. Stanford University Press, Stanford

Minge-Kalman, W. (1978): 'The Industrial Revolution and the European Family: The Institutionalization of "Childhood" as a Market for Family Labor'. *Comparative Studies in Society and History*, Vol. 20, pp. 454-68

National Reports. 'Changes in the Life Patterns of Families in Europe'. (Vienna Centre background material), 1981, 1982, 1984, 3 vols

Notenstein, W. (1945): 'Population. The Long View'. In: Schultz, E. (ed.): *Food for the World*. Chicago University Press, Chicago

Oppong, C. (1980): 'A Synopsis of Seven Roles and Status of Women. An Outline of a Conceptual and Methodological Approach'. *World Employment Programme Research*, Working Paper No. 94, ILO, September 1980

Oppong, C. (1983): 'Women's Roles, Opportunity Costs, and Fertility'. In: Bulatao, R.A. and Lee, R.D. (eds): *Determinants of Fertility in Developing Countries*. Academic Press, N.Y., Vol. 1

Organski, A.F.K. et al. (1984): *Births, Deaths, and Taxes. The Demographic and Political Transition*. University of Chicago Press, Chicago

Plumb, J.H. (1975): 'The New World of Children in Eighteenth-Century England'. *Past and Present*, No. 65, May 1975, pp. 64-95

Angelo Saporiti

Pollock, L.A. (1983): *Forgotten Children. Parent-Child Relations from 1500 to 1900*. Cambridge University Press, Cambridge

Postman, N. (1982): *The Disappearance of Childhood*. Delacort Press, N.Y.

Riesman, D. (1953): *The Lonely Crowd*. Doubleday Anchor Books, N.Y.

Ryder, N.B. (1967): 'The Character of Modern Fertility'. *The Annales of the American Academy*, CCLXIX, 27

Sahlins, M. (1972): *Stone Age Economics*. Aldine-Atherton, Chicago

Schofield, R. (1976): 'La popolazione preindustriale e il suo spazio economico' (The pre-industrial population and its economic space). *Quaderni Storici*, Vol. 33, settembre-dicembre, pp. 1053-72

Schultz, T.W. (ed.) (1974): *Economics of the Family. Marriage, Children and Human Capital*. University of Chicago Press, Chicago, 1973, reprinted 1974

Sgritta, G.B. (1987): 'Strategie familiari e infanzia: dall'analisi istituzionale all'analisi delle condotte strategiche nelle ricerche sociali sulla famiglia italiana' (Family strategy and childhood: from institutional analysis to management strategy in social research on Italian families). In: *Atti del Convegno su 'Strategie familiari e vita quotidiana'* (Contributions to the Conference on 'Family strategies and daily life'), Bologna 15-16 giugno 1984

Sgritta, G.B. and Saporiti, A. (1980): *Family, Labour Market and the State in Italy from 1945 to the Present*. Scuola di Perfezionamento in Sociologia e Ricerca Sociale, Facoltà di Scienze Statistiche Demografiche e Attualiali, Università di Roma, Roma

Shorter, E. (1975): *The Making of the Modern Family*. Basic Books, N.Y.

Silber, J. (1981): 'La théorie économique des ménages et l'étude des phénomènes démographiques'. *Population*, 3

Simons, J. (1982): 'Reproductive Behaviour as Religious Practice'. In: Hohn, C. and Mackensen, R. (eds): *Determinants of Fertility Trend Theories Reexamined*. Ordina Ed., Liège

Siskind, J. (1978): 'Kinship and Modes of Production'. *American Anthropologist*, 80, pp. 860-72

Stone, L. (1977): *The Family, Sex and Marriage in England 1500-1800*. Harper & Row, N.Y.

Thadani, V.N. (1978): 'The Logic of Sentiment: The Family and Social Change'. *Population and Development Review*, Vol. 4, No. 3, September 1978, pp. 457-99

Tilly, C. (1978): 'The Historical Study of Vital Process'. In: Tilly, C. (ed.): *Historical Studies of Changing Fertility*. Princeton University Press, Princeton

Tilly, L.A. (1979): 'Individual Lives and Family Strategies in the French Proletariat'. *Journal of Family History*, Vol. 4, No. 2, Summer 1979, pp. 137-52

Tilly, L.A. and Scott, J.W. (1978): *Women, Work and Family*. Holt, Rinehart & Winston, N.Y.

Tilly, L.A., Scott, J.W. and Cohen, M. (1980): 'Women's Work and European Fertility Patterns'. In: Rotberg, R.I. and Rabb, T.K. (eds): *Marriage and Fertility. Studies in Interdisciplinary History*. Princeton University Press, Princeton

Trumbach, R. (1978): *The Rise of the Egalitarian Family. Aristocratic Kinship and Domestic Relations in Eighteenth-Century England.* Academic Press, N.Y.

World Bank (The) (1984): *World Development Report 1984.* Oxford University Press, N.Y.

Wrigley, E.A. (1978): 'Fertility Strategy for the Individual and the Group'. In: Tilly, C. (ed.): *Historical Studies of Changing Fertility.* Princeton University Press, Princeton

Wrigley, E.A. and Schofield, R. (1981): *The Population History of England, 1541-1871: A Reconstruction.* Harvard University Press, Cambridge, Mass.

Zelizer, V.A. (1981): 'The Price and Value of Children: The Case of Children's Insurance'. *American Journal of Sociology,* Vol. 86, No. 5, pp. 1036-56

11

Caring*

Kari Waerness

Caring, personal service and caregiving work

Caring, helping and serving are important aspects of family life. As a consequence of the division of labour between the sexes, the expectations of care and service and the responsibility for the physical and emotional well-being of the family members, are laid mainly on the female members of the family. Caring and serving are to a high degree defined as housework and motherly care. In addition, a great part of women's paid work in modern society consists in serving, helping and caring for others. To get a better understanding of the changes in the caring functions of the family and the division of labour between the family and the welfare institutions outside the family, we have to reach a better understanding of the concept of 'caring', and differentiate between types of activities which are all named 'caring' or 'caring activities'.

Caring is not something which can be neatly defined by the conceptual categories of the social sciences. These categories were fashioned for new social relations in nineteenth-century capitalism, a time when the organisation of caring went through fundamental changes. As until recently women have been almost invisible in social science, this may explain why the leading social theorists do not give us any sophisticated understanding of relations in the sphere of reproduction, with the result that many of the social sciences in diverse ways obscure changes in the

*I would like to thank here the Norwegian Research Council for Science and Humanities for financing the Norwegian part of the research project.

organisation of caring and the underlying system of gender division of labour on which these new patterns were based.

Not only in the social sciences, but also in moral philosophy, caring has received no attention except as an outcome of ethical behaviour (Noddings, 1984, pp. 1-6). The approach to moral problems through law and principles which dominate in moral philosophy does not seem to provide adequate models for getting a thorough understanding of the moral problems in the context of caring. To 'solve' or rather to 'cope with' such problems requires a mode of thinking that is contextual and narrative rather than formal and abstract (Waerness, 1984), and that is rooted in relatedness, receptivity and responsiveness (Noddings, 1984). Perhaps it can be argued that a tension between the morality of rights and the morality of caring in the way Thomas Aquinas expressed it - 'justice untempered with mercy is brutality and mercy uncontrolled by justice is the mother of dissolution' (quoted in Schumacher, 1980, p. 142) - is part of the human condition. Even if that may be true, there is good reason to assume that the change in the division of labour between the sexes and the growth of the welfare institutions outside the family have made this tension both stronger and more visible. As long as most of the caring takes place in the private sphere and the traditional gender division of labour is accepted, this tension can be seen as kept in some kind of balance.

The reason for this is that the traditional sex-role norms have required women to give priority to the morality of caring and to fulfilling the immediate needs of their family members, while the morality of right has been mainly considered a male concern in the public sphere. When the division of responsibility and labour in reproduction between the family and the state becomes ambiguous and women claim the same citizen rights as men, caring becomes visible as a social problem and thereby a central issue in the social sciences.

As the conceptual and theoretical tools from a sociological tradition are inadequate for the analysis of caring, we use a general definition as a starting point. In broad terms caring is a concept encompassing that range of human experiences which has to do with feeling concern for and taking charge of the well-being of others in a person-to-person setting. This definition tells us that caring is about activities as well as feelings. 'Feeling concern' and 'taking charge' have both practical and psychological implications. Graham (1983) argues, after Rousseau, that caring is experienced as 'a labour of love'.

We often choose the expression 'to care' to convey a sense of the bonds which tie us to other people in a wide variety of social relationships. In our private lives, we 'care *about*' our spouses, our children, our parents, our friends, sometimes our neighbours and even occasional chance encounters; and we 'care *for*' dependants as well as for family members who might as well care for themselves. In our professional lives we are expected to 'care about' colleagues and to 'care for' clients or patients. 'Caring for' and 'caring about' are not mutually exclusive categories, nor are they identical. 'Caring about' someone, in the sense of feeling affection for him/her, is based on feelings of affinity. Caring *for* someone, in the sense of servicing his or her needs, may have little or nothing to do with caring *about* someone. The basis for the provision of the services of caring may be based primarily on other modes of obligation; the carer may be paid for her services, or provide the service because she feels generally compassionate for all people in need or feels subject to social norms about the nature of relationship with close kin and the particular services socially expected of her in those particular relationships. 'Caring about' someone as an emotion *per se* does not necessarily have implications for how people spend their time - except that they might want to spend it together (Ungerson, 1983).

In contrast, caring *for* a person, or as Parker (1981) has recently renamed it, 'tending a person', consumes time, often in such a way that the carer is unable to combine tending with other time-consuming activities and may even become too exhausted to use her remaining time as she may wish. This means that caring for someone at times exceeds the carer's capacity in such a way that she is no longer able to care about the cared for, in the sense of feeling affection for him or her.

The responsibility for caring in the sense of tending, is still ascribed on the basis of sex. What this means is that even if both men and women are expected to care *about* their family, only women are expected to give priority to the caring role over all others.

Those who need care are, firstly, various categories of dependents; children, the sick, the handicapped and the frail elderly. But, in addition, adult, healthy people need to be cared for by others in a variety of situations. Feeling worn out, dejected, tired, depressed - these are fairly common circumstances in which what we need from others is 'to care for us'. In such situations we may feel that we have a right to be cared for and that there should be others who feel that it is their duty or desire to honour this right. Most often we expect this feeling of obligation or desire from persons to whom we are attached through the ties of family, love or friendship. In principle caring for healthy adults might be based on equal give-and-take relationships between people who have personal ties to each other and on their mutual exchange of help, support and kindness. When we say that people 'care for each other', we have this kind of emotional and practical reciprocity in mind. However, since caring tends to be performed predominantly by women, much of their caring for ablebodied adults (husbands, older children and other adult family members) does not imply this kind of reciprocity, and should therefore rather be defined as *personal service* than as caring proper. In such caring relations the cared-for's dependency on the caregiver is not openly recognised. On the contrary, in the case of wives caring for their husbands, it is the caregiver's dependency on the cared-for which mainly characterises the relation. This means that the provision of personal services by wives is taken for granted and often may be more a question of what they are 'forced' to do as the result of their subordinate position in the family than of what they want to do as a result of their concern for their husbands' well-being.

When providing help and services to dependants, the nature of the relationship is very different. It is, firstly, non-reciprocal not only in practice but also by definition. The carer and the cared for might 'care about each other', but not 'for each other' on an egalitarian basis. There can be no symmetrical exchange of help or favours in these relations. Secondly, whereas in the provision of personal services, as mentioned above, the provider is subordinate to the receiver, in the provision of care for dependants, the receivers are subordinate to the providers; they are dependent on the willingness of someone else to care for them.

Whether we analyse caring as 'labour' or as 'love', it seems highly important to make a theoretical distinction between:

1. caring for dependants,
2. caring for superiors,
3. caring in symmetrical relations.

Both in emotional and practical terms, it can be assumed that these different categories of caring relations give rise to different problems as the family structure changes and women's employment outside home increases.

Caring for dependants, i.e. those members of society who by normal social standards are unable to take care of themselves, is the main focus of concern in social policy. Caring for these groups in modern society today is a common task of the family and different social service organisations. Besides, the caring function of the family is no longer assumed to be maintained only or even mainly on the grounds of institutionalised bonds between family members. Instead, greater importance is attached to the emotional bonds. Caring for family members or close kin, has become more a question of caring *about* them than of doing what traditional norms prescribe. This means that the sharing of labour and responsibility between the family and the state in caring for the dependants has become very ambiguous, at the same time as the caring capacity of the family decreases as a result of women's increasing employment outside the home.

Caring for dependants on a consistent and reliable basis we will define here as *caregiving work* whether it is paid or not, and whether it takes place in the private sphere or not. In the following, we will analyse how caregiving patterns of children and elderly family members vary between countries. In addition we will analyse the support and advice given in different problem situations by the family, the informal social networks and the public service system. One important focus in these analyses will be the gender difference in giving and receiving care and how this difference eventually is about to change.

Caregiving work: a model

As long as a great part of society's production was organised within family households, most women could combine caregiving work with active participation in production. When home and workplace became separated both geographically and economically, it became difficult for women to fulfil their traditional care obligations in the family without restricting their participation in the labour market. A relatively low rate of female employment therefore has been one condition for *most* caregiving work being organised as unpaid family work (Sundstrøm, 1980). However, even if women's and especially married women's participation in the labour market has steadily increased in most European countries in the last decades, many studies have documented that most of the caring, not only for children, but also for most other groups of dependants, is still unpaid female family work (Moroney, 1976; Sundstrøm, 1980; Waerness, 1978). This is *one* reason why the sociological description of the growth of the public caregiving services as 'an emptying of the functions of the family' is very inadequate from the women's perspective and needs to be re-examined and qualified. In order to do this, we have to take a closer look at the different institutional settings where caregiving work is performed. A model dividing this work according to two dimensions, important for a better understanding of some of the problems related to the organisation of caring in modern society, is presented in the scheme below.

	Caregiving work	
Life-sphere	Unpaid	Paid
Private	Childcare, care of the sick, the handicapped, and the frail elderly in the home	Caring for dependants in the home by house-maids, childminders, etc.
Public	Help from neighbours in childcare, illness, etc.	Public homehelp and home nursing services
	Help from voluntary workers in charity organisations, self-help groups and mutual aid organisations	Institutional care; day care institutions, crèche or kindergartens, old people's homes, hospitals, etc.

The dimension private/public is not a clear-cut dichotomy. It is a dimension referring to how particularistic the caregiver is allowed to be in her distribution of help and support. 'Public' has a connotation of 'in the sight of everyone', but 'who' and 'how many' is meant by 'everyone' varies. Neighbours have to consider what kind and how much help is 'decent' without breaking the local community's norms for neighbourliness. The caregiving work of voluntary workers and employees in the public sphere is prescribed both by bureaucratic rules and professional norms.

The difference between paid and unpaid caregiving is not always so clear-cut either. Sometimes close relatives are engaged as homehelpers by public social services and both home helpers and other employees in the public social services find it at times necessary to give help and support to clients outside official working hours and to perform tasks which strictly speaking do not belong to their work (Waerness, 1982; Viklund, 1981; Liljeström and Øzgalda, 1980).

It seems reasonable to assume that in the post-war period caregiving work in the private and public spheres has changed in opposite directions in a sense. The shrinking size of the family household contrasts with the public care system becoming more specialised. This means that for the individual dependant there are fewer caregivers in the private sphere to give personal help and support, and at the same time the public care services have become more fragmentary and impersonalised. Besides, many of the social services have not first and foremost replaced informal caregiving, but instead gradually changed content, as an increasing number of professional educators, advisors and consultants have invaded the private sphere. Informal resources also very often have to be mobilised to make use of existing social services. Partly the growth in public care services therefore has increased the necessary time family members have to spend on dealing with bureaucratic organisations and members of the caring professions.

Most studies on community care in modern society show that the social basis of caregiving work provided to a degree which might obviate the need of public care, is *kinship*. The bulk of help is given by close female relatives, a point which seldom is clearly stated. Our next strongest basis of social involvement seems to be that of moral communities associated with churches, friendship nets, voluntary organisations and certain kinds of occupations. When closely examined, the traditional neighbourhoods, highly localised and strongly caring within the confines of quite tightly defined relationships, usually prove to be either kinship networks or networks rooted in religion, occupation or ethnicity (Abrams, 1980). The kind of help and services exchanged between people on the basis of neighbourhood can be assumed to be irregular, not so demanding and be based on norms of reciprocity. More regular and demanding help will most probably be paid, as when neighbours become engaged as childminders. This 'hidden labour market' is, however, important for social integration in many urban neighbourhoods, as it strengthens the bonds between people who otherwise have little contact with each other (Gullestad, 1981).

With the economic recession, in the 1980s we have witnessed an intensification of the debate on the role of voluntary organisations in social services. Even if voluntary organisations that operate on a charitable basis are not so widely accepted, the growth of organisations operating mainly on a self-help or mutual aid basis, nowadays seems to be welcomed by the government authorities in both Eastern and Western countries.

Changes in the care of children

With the modernisation of society, childcare becomes a 'scientific' phenomenon. The ascribed 'natural inclination' of women was no longer assumed to be sufficient for them to become 'good mothers'. In addition, they ought to acquire *some* formal knowledge based on science. They had to be educated and advised by professional 'experts'. This 'scientification' meant that women became subordinated to a new kind of male authority - the authority of scientific knowledge. On the other hand, the emergence of this new kind of authority meant a decline of the authority of the husband/father. As Donzelot (1979, p. 58) points out: 'If the hygienist norms pertaining to the rearing, labour and education of children were able to take effect, this was because they offered children, and correlatively women, the possibility of increased autonomy in opposition to patriarchal authority.'

There have been two important arguments in favour of public childcare facilities: one has been the objective of furthering female employment and the other has been the belief in the advantage of a professional approach to socialisation and education. Today we find that the proportion of children in kindergarten is very high in some countries where employment rates for women are low and vice versa. We also find a short supply of institutional care for children under three, and many kindergartens operate at inconvenient times in relation to normal working hours.[1] These facts may indicate that the belief in professional childcare has been a more effective force in providing public childcare services than the regard for women's employment.

The 'scientific' and professional norms for good childcare have differed between countries and have changed with time. In the post-war period, changes have been very rapid and both experts and lay people have heavily disagreed on what was good for children. With more and more mothers working outside the home and the maids and nannies of earlier times disappearing, more children had to be placed in childcare outside the family. This precipitated in many countries a raging controversy both among experts and lay people with regard to whether or not placement of infants in different kinds of private and public care settings is detrimental to the development of children - a controversy which is still not settled.

From our research we can conclude that the preference for, or acceptance of, professional care for children over the age of 3 is very high both in the East and in the West. For the smaller children, however, the picture is more varied. In the Eastern countries where childcare allowance is available for a period after the end of maternity leave, the pattern of interrupting work for some time has increased, especially among women with less education and in manual jobs.[2] The differences between women in different socio-economic groups may be due both to the fact that the allowance compared to the wages is relatively higher for those on low incomes and to the fear of mothers working in more professional jobs of falling behind in skills. That women in lower positions also experience more difficulty in reconciling work and family life due to more fixed working hours also seems to be important.

From our surveys it comes out that without regard to the proportion of women who have had to leave the labour force for some period in order to take care of children, most of them claim that they stayed at home because they wanted to, not because there were no other alternatives.[3] One interpretation of this finding is that women still give such high priority to the norms arising from the morality of caring that in retrospect it seems self-evident for most of them that they should want to do what these norms prescribe. It seems, however, reasonable to expect in the future more dissatisfaction among women having to follow this pattern of interruption in their labour force participation. Even if the countries where childcare allowances give some economic compensation to women following this pattern, the rising educational level among women means that staying at home for many of them will imply relatively more loss of income and falling behind in knowledge and skills. With increasing education we can also expect that claims based on the morality of rights will come into greater conflict with the traditional female ideal of self-sacrifice and care.[4] The childcare allowance namely does not solve the problems of isolation, which seems to be one of the most negative aspects of the housewife role in modern society with the nuclearised family household as the dominant pattern (Oakley, 1974; Lopata, 1971; Holter et al., 1967).

Without regard to the supply of institutional care, our surveys show that close relatives still are of very great importance for the care of children in urban families in Europe today. The grandparents, and especially the grandmothers are the most important informal helpers in childcare. It varies very much between countries to what degree grandparents give regular care to grandchildren during the day time and how this kind of help is about to change.[5] But grandparents everywhere seem to be the most frequent helpers when young parents need someone to look after their children occasionally.[6] Both the differences in the employment rate of grandmothers and mothers and in the nuclearisation of the family households are probably important factors in explaining the differences between the importance of grandparents as *regular* helpers in childcare. As for the relative importance of grandparents as occasional childcarers, it seems to be somewhat greater for the younger parents than it is for the middle aged and the elderly.[7] In Scandinavia, where the nuclearisation of the family households is most developed, the great majority of grandparents in our surveys report that they in some way or another take part in the care of their grandchildren.[8] As the younger grandparents report this to be true as often as the older ones, there is no sign of a decreasing contact between grandparents and grandchildren, even if the content and meaning of this help and care may be about to change.

In most of Europe the increasing integration of women in the labour market is still dependent to a greater or lesser extent on whether they have the home as their main or only working place; so they not always attain all the rights which are connected to full-time, full-life participation in the labour market. No European country seems to cope with the problem of realising greater equality between the sexes as regards economic welfare and self-realisation, without worsening the children's situation regarding their need for growing up in a stable and intimate milieu. In addition, on the part of the public authorities, there is growing concern with how to make people better parents.

In many research reports, it is stated that parents nowadays feel they are alone in their task of childrearing and highly insecure about their competence as parents.[9] The privacy and isolation of the nuclear family is seen as a reason for this, and in many countries proposals have been made for some kind of 'parental education' as a compensation for the loss of the experiences and to help mothers (parents) to get through by being more closely connected to the extended family and the local community. On the other hand, it is an open question to what degree the growth in health, education and welfare services contributes to the undermining of parents' confidence in their ability to provide for their children's needs as Lasch (1977) claims when he writes about the 'proletarianisation of parenthood'. The problem is how to organise 'parents' education' in such a way that this service does not reinforce parents' dependency on professional judgements (Wanger, 1981). Organising childcare arrangements which emphasise child development and parents' participation, at least in the Western countries, tend to attract more middle-class than working-class parents.[10] As a basis for the further development of public childcare facilities, this ideology therefore may lead to strengthening the educational and cultural differences between children from different socio-economic groups. And, at least in the short run, women's general wish for a greater involvement in activities outside the family also conflicts with this new ideology of public childcare. Today's emphasis on more community care as the basis for the public social services, not only in the field of childcare but also in relation to the care of the sick and disabled, may strengthen the tendency of professional caregivers working rather as advisors and consultants, leaving still more of the practical caregiving tasks to the female members of the family. So far our surveys have shown no tendency to an increase in men's caregiving to an extent which could modify the impression of 'more community care', leading to more demand on women's time.

Caring for the elderly

In sociology as well as in the public debate it is still argued that the care of the old and disabled in modern society is *taken* over or *given* to the state, even though there are general research reports from different European countries documenting that even in the states with the most developed public care system most of the dependent adults still live in their homes and are cared for by family members. This caregiving is mainly women's family work, and the most important caregivers are the older wives. Research from different countries shows that marriage is an important protection against institutionalisation in disablement and old age, especially for men. Both due to the usual age difference between husbands and wives and due to the fact that caregiving is traditionally women's work, marriage functions as a caregiving institution first and foremost for men. The great majority of the elderly in need for public care are women, most of them widows, and many without children. The institutionalisation rates of the old differ much among countries (Sundstrøm, 1980; Shanas et al., 1968). Many societies also have laws levying on the family, in practice on women, the duty of caring for the infirm and the aged. In most Western countries the family is, however, no longer viewed as responsible for the financial support of the aged. But especially outside the realm of financial support, the dividing line for the transfer of the responsibility from the family to the state is unclear, and there appears to be an element of ambivalence expressed in law, policy, programmes and practices (Moroney, 1976; Sundstrøm, 1980). The family seems still to be expected to provide the basic support to dependent adults in a moral sense. Even if the principle of public responsibility exists, how society and the state actually relate to the family is ambiguous (Waerness, 1982).

Most social theories have hitherto evaluated the long-term historical trends in the situation of the elderly as a deterioration relative to the situation of other age groups. This deterioration is very often connected to the loss of the multi-generational or extended family household, assumed to be a consequence of industrialisation and urbanisation. The amount of help and care between the generations has further been assumed to decrease as the nuclearisation of the family households has increased.

Historical studies from the recent years have shown a greatly varying picture of the household organisation in traditional Europe. Laslett (1983) divides pre-industrial Europe into four geographical regions under the titles 'West', 'West/Central or Middle', 'Mediterranean' and 'East', and shows that there was very great variation in the household structure between these regions. In the West, neo-localism - i.e. the tendency of the newly married couple to set up their own household - was very strong, and the proportion of multi-generational households very low. In the Central or Middle region, the tendency of neo-localism was not so strong, but still the usual pattern, while in the Mediterranean countries it was unusual and in the East almost never occurred.

Only in the Mediterranean area and in the East was the proportion of multi-generational households high and the proportion of single-person households low or absent.

The fact that many elderly people in Central Europe in the pre-industrial period (more than in England) lived in large households was not primarily due to more adult children living in the household, but to a larger number of persons living in the family as servants and inmates. The reduction of the size of the household of the elderly in the industrial era is therefore in Western and Central Europe mainly to be explained by the reduction in the number of servants and inmates (Mitterauer and Sieder, 1982).

The differences we find in our surveys in regard to the existence of multi-generational households are in accordance with the differences in pre-industrial time, even though now most of the households are everywhere nuclearised (see Table 11.1).

In addition, setting up one's own household *before* marrying or cohabitating represents a new important trend in the Western countries. The rapid growth of single-person household in the younger age groups during the last decades is an indication of this. This new trend may in the longer run lead to important changes in the division of household labour between the sexes and maybe also in caring for children. Rossi (1985) assumes that the result can be a greater equality in household work as young men get more experience in running their own household. On the other hand she fears that this new trend will weaken the willingness to care for children, as living alone as a young adult means that one does not learn to show consideration to other people in everyday life in the way which is necessary to be good parents. So far we have no empirical studies to confirm or invalidate Rossi's assumptions.

On the other hand, sociological studies from different Western countries have provided ample evidence that the desire of the generations in the family to have separate households may be combined with strong inter-generational family ties (Rosenmayr and Kockies, 1965; Shanas et al. 1968). Higher incomes and social security benefits like pensions accompany more independent living. The hypothesis that what Rosenmayr and Kockies (1965) called 'intimacy at a distance' corresponds to the wishes of both the younger and the older generations and typifies ideal family relations is verified in many investigations. Ample proof of mutual help between adult children and parents provides further evidence of cohesion within the multi-generational family even when the household has split up.

Table 11.1. *Persons in addition to respondents belonging to the household in different samples (percentages)*

Samples	1*	2**	3	4	5	6	7
Single-person households	15	18	0	0	0	0	0
Spouse/cohabitant	67	74	91	78	86	100	100
Children	36a	52	98	68	100	75	95
	43b						
Parents	4	2c	3	20	12	2	10
Parents-in-law	1	0	2	5	5	0	
Siblings	2	1	1	6			0
Grandchildren	1	0	1	0	3	1	3
Others	1	0	2	5			3
(N)	(744)	(500)	(183)	(193)	(300)	(273)	(211)

1 = Representative sample, urban population in Finland
2 = Representative sample, urban population in Norway
3 = Couples and single mother families in Slovenian cities (answers given by women)
4 = Couples and single-mother families in the Russian town Orel (answers given by women)
5 = Married and divorced female caregivers in Rome
6 = Couples in Oldenburg, Federal Republic of Germany (answers given by women)
7 = Couples in Warsaw
a Girls.
b Boys.
c All respondents living with parents are unmarried men.
* 67% of the Finnish sample was married/cohabiting, 9% separated/divorced, 5% widow/widower and 19% unmarried.
** 61% of the Norwegian sample was married, 12% cohabiting, 8% separated/divorced, 3% widow/widower and 16% unmarried.

Social anthropologists analysing modern urban communities, argue that to some degree it is misleading to define family types on the basis of common households. They often find daughters and daughters-in-law helping with many of the household chores in order to impede or delay disabled parents or parents-in-law moving to an institution or into their own household. In such situations the multi-generational family is a condition for independent living in old age (Gullestad, 1984). Even when the elderly need nursing and supervision, the wish to live in separate households seems to be so strong that family members accept much additional stress in order to maintain this separation (Nygård, 1982).

It seems reasonable to assume that in the regions of Europe where the nuclearisation of family households preceded industrialisation and therefore goes a long way back in time, the preference for separate households between the generations in the family is stronger than in the regions where this family form is more recent. 'Intimacy at a distance' probably is a stronger value both for the older and younger generations in the Western countries than in the Mediterranean and Eastern countries.

This assumption seems to be in accordance with the conclusion Laslett (1983, p. 559) draws on the basis of many studies on the household structures in different parts of pre-industrial Europe:

> 'For us the point of importance is that the Japanese, the Russians or even the Italians and the Poles, in so far as they have adopted industrialism as a way of life, may not be in the same position in respect of the industrial culture as the West Europeans themselves. The evidence we surveyed would seem to imply that neo-local tendencies were never part and parcel of the historical social structure of these societies as they have been for the West Europeans.'

However, even in the West - as shown in Table 11.2 - for some period in their childhood a great many respondents lived in a household which included members of the extended family. Most often this member was a grandmother or a grandfather, but sometimes other members. This kind of co-residence has to some degree decreased, but has not totally disappeared.

Table 11.2. Percentage of respondents who had relatives living either in their childhood home or in their own household for at least one year

	Urban Finnish population	Urban Norwegian population	Couples in Oldenburg (FRG)
In childhood home	30	28	the question was not asked
In own household	11	7	12
(N)	(744)	(500)	(273)

Most probably the decrease is due to the growth in the economy and the welfare-state services making these kinds of co-residence less necessary. The fact that the co-residence rate between the aged and their children in the Western countries increases with age and illness of the elderly, supports this assumption (Moroney, 1976).

On the other hand, the preference for 'intimacy at a distance' between the generations in the family seems to be very strong also in the Mediterranean and the Eastern countries. Even where newly married couples first move into one of the parents' home, a separate flat for the nuclear family is the accepted model on the societal level and a major aspiration for most young couples. Also the survey from Slovenian towns support the 'intimacy at a distance' thesis. Here very few of the respondents said they would prefer to live in the same household or even in the same house as their parents, and a relatively great proportion said they would prefer their parents not to live in the neighbourhood at all.[11] Most probably the relatively high proportion of the elderly living with their children in Eastern countries may be attributed to a certain degree to the difficulties young families face in obtaining a house or a flat and not to a widespread preference for this household structure. On the other hand, though co-residence between generations might be a source of important strains and conflicts, it can be assumed that many young families might find such a situation tolerable and even desirable, due to the elderly's contribution to the household budget and their assistance in housework and care for children.[12]

From the evidence we have we may conclude that when circumstances necessitate it, shared households between generations are realised all over Europe, and family members may take on heavy burdens of care for close kin. Still, 'intimacy at a distance' may remain the *preferred* relation.

To what extent frail elderly people will prefer public care rather than be totally dependent on their children when they cannot manage on their own in everyday life, we may assume will depend on their view of having *rights* to public care services. More studies from Norway support this assumption. In a decade when public home help and home nursing services increased very rapidly, the proportion of the elderly saying they would prefer public to family care changed from a small minority to a clear majority (Daatland, 1984).

Both in the East and in the West the care of the elderly today is a subject of serious concern, and the relative shortage of public care services due to the ageing of the population has led to an increasing political interest in 'informal care'. In this situation it seems important to emphasise that a change in social policy which makes both the older and younger generations in the family more dependent on each other will most probably be experienced as a loss of welfare. Since most men have a wife as their main carer, and the main burden of inter-generational care still falls on daughters or other close female relatives, this means that such a shift in policy will first and foremost reduce the welfare of women.

Help in problem situations

In the discussion of the 'crisis of the welfare state', the increasing use of professional help to solve family problems is evaluated very differently. Sussmann (1969) argues that the use and knowledge of professionals in such situations indicates a higher level of competence than reliance on informal social networks. Others argue that the increase in the demand for professional services is an indicator of more people lacking personal linkages, or that the growth of the professional services leads to loss of spontaneity and the ability to help each other (or oneself). Sole reliance on public social services also may indicate social isolation rather than competence (Haavio-Mannila, 1976, p. 326).

In general it can be assumed that to think in terms of *either* informal *or* professional help and care is much too simplified. The provision of help and care is not a zero-sum activity so that more informal help unambiguously means less professional help and the other way round. Professional services can function as *complements, supplements* and *substitutes* for informal help and caring. Besides, because of bureaucratic and other problems in using the opportunities offered by the public care system, people in need of help often do not have the necessary skills or stamina to find what their rights and possibilities are for dealing with the welfare bureaucracy. Support and help of an informal caring network, family or otherwise, can therefore be partly a *condition* for getting access to professional or bureaucratic help and service.

Table 11.3a. Preferred type of consultants in different problem situations according to age and sex (percentages) among Swedish metal and manufacturing workers (1) and municipal workers (2)

'To whom would you mainly turn for assistance and support if you encountered difficulties in your co-life with your husband/wife/co-habitant?'

	About 25 (1)	About 25 (2)	About 40 (1)	About 40 (2)	About 60 (1)	About 60 (2)
	M	W	W	M	W	W	M	W	W

	About 25 (1) M	About 25 (1) W	About 25 (2) W	About 40 (1) M	About 40 (1) W	About 40 (2) W	About 60 (1) M	About 60 (1) W	About 60 (2) W
Parents and parents-in-law	49	60	52	23	16	24	0	2	0
Other relatives	5	7	5	6	12	16	20	31	20
Friends, colleagues	8	14	25	6	9	11	9	8	8
Professional helpers	3	6	5	18	25	29	39	16	23
Problems should be kept in the family	27	10	8	44	35	18	27	31	35
No answer/other alternative	8	3	2	3	3	2	5	12	14
Total	100	100	100	100	100	100	100	100	100

'If you have or had teen-age children who were neglecting themselves, to whom would you turn first to get help?'

	About 25 (1) M	About 25 (1) W	About 25 (2) W	About 40 (1) M	About 40 (1) W	About 40 (2) W	About 60 (1) M	About 60 (1) W	About 60 (2) W
Parents and parents-in-law	20	45	23	10	14	9	0	0	4
Other relatives	0	2	0	5	9	8	8	9	7
Friends, colleagues	6	3	4	0	7	3	0	2	4
Professional helpers	27	40	54	41	45	59	49	43	54
Problems should be kept in the family	47	10	11	43	20	16	40	34	27
No answer/other alternative	0	0	8	1	5	5	3	12	4
Total	100	100	100	100	100	100	100	100	100

Table 11.3a continued

'If you were to face financial problems, to whom would you turn first of all?'

	Age groups								
	About 25			About 40			About 60		
	(1)		(2)	(1)		(2)	(1)		(2)
	M	W	W	M	W	W	M	W	W
Parents and parents-in-law	75	73	81	21	25	48	4	4	6
Other relatives	3	3	1	8	14	5	15	14	16
Friends, colleagues	5	3	3	4	3	4	5	2	2
Social welfare office	1	5	2	2	4	7	15	11	15
Bank	4	2	4	24	12	11	26	9	10
Other, including employer	4	1	2	7	5	4	3	9	5
Prefers to handle one's own	8	13	7	34	37	21	32	51	46
Total	100	100	100	100	100	100	100	100	100

M = Men; W = Women.

To the degree that formal help and services are non-stigmatising and perceived as citizen rights, we may assume that they function more as supplements or complements than as substitutes for informal care and helping. We can also assume that one great problem of the modern welfare bureaucracies is that they often do not reach the people most in need because they lack an informal caring network that can help them to get public help. When interpreting survey-data on help-seeking behaviour, we therefore have to bear in mind these possible different and complicated relations between informal and professional care. Replies to hypothetical questions about main or first source of help in different problem situations do not say anything about to what degree this source will be the *only* source of help when such problems really arise.

Here we shall examine replies to questions about sources of help in the case of conjugal crises, problems with children and when financial problems are pressing, and we shall analyse the importance of different informal networks and how these eventually are about to change. If we take the reply 'problems should be kept in the family' as an indicator of the privatisation of the nuclear family, we find that conjugal crisis is looked upon as a more private matter than problems with teenagers or younger children. This privatisation seems, however, to be weakening, as younger people, and especially younger women, relatively seldom choose this alternative. Comparing the answers from urban Scandinavians with the answers from people living in the Russian town Orel and in Warsaw, the Scandinavian women come out as least privatised (see Tables 11.3a-e). Parents are so to speak the only helpers people in Orel and Warsaw will turn to, while urban Scandinavians have different social networks to use in such a situation. Professional help is the first choice only for a minority and there is no support in these data for the assumption that professionals more and more take over helping in this problem situation. A major trend in urban Scandinavia is that the relative importance of the network of friends is increasing, weakening first and foremost the norm of keeping the marriage problems in the family. This trend may also be interpreted as a weakening of the conjugal bond or the loyalty between the spouses. From our surveys it seems that this tendency is most pronounced among urban Scandinavian women. The importance of the bonds to the extended family in such a problem situation seems to be increasing, especially for women. Viewed in the light of rapidly changing norms of family and sexual behaviour in recent decades, the strength of the inter-generational bonds on this subject is surprising. To the degree that the generations have conflicting norms and values in this field, it does not seem to have had much influence on the confidence between parents and children and especially between women in the family.

The greater intimacy between women in the family is also supported by the distribution of the answers to a question on confidants. Female relatives are more often chosen as confidants than other female friends, and men are more often dependent on a spouse as someone to confide in, especially in the older and middle aged groups in which men have few other people to talk to about anything that troubles them. Again we get support for the assumption that the conjugal bond is more important for the emotional welfare of men than of women. In a period where marriage is becoming more unstable, this lesser dependence on the spouse and the closer connection to the family and friend networks on the part of women must be evaluated as a great advantage in terms of emotional welfare.

Table 11.3b. Preferred type of consultants in different problem situations according to age and sex (percentages) among Norwegian urban population

'To whom would you mainly turn for assistance and support if you encountered difficulties in your co-life with your husband/wife/co-habitant?'

	Age groups							
	31		31-40		41-50		50	
	M	W	M	W	M	W	M	W
Parents and parents-in-law	35	25	22	30	6	17	2	2
Other relatives*	8	20	4	11	13	13	35	49
Friends, colleagues	25	31	31	30	19	33	13	11
Professional helpers	6	11	7	11	25	10	6	9
Problems should be kept in the family	17	6	28	9	31	23	37	19
No answer	8	8	8	9	6	4	8	9
Total	100	101	100	100	100	100	101	99
(N)	(48)	(65)	(45)	(47)	(32)	(30)	(52)	(47)

'If you have or had teenage children who were neglecting themselves, to whom would you turn first to get help?'

	25-40		41-65		Total	
	M	W	M	W	M	W
Parents and parents-in-law	23	21	5	8	13	14
Other relatives	2	3	11	11	7	7
Friends, colleagues	17	12	10	11	13	12
Professional helpers	32	40	42	35	38	37
Problems should be kept in the family	13	12	21	18	18	16
No answer	13	12	11	16	12	14
Total	100	100	100	99	100	100
(N)	(60)	(91)	(92)	(97)	(152)	(188)

M = Men; W = Women.
*Of women in the age group 41-50, 7% turned to their children, among men in this age group none. In the group of 51 to 65 year old women, 30% turned to their children.

Table 11.3c. Preferred type of consultants in different problem situations according to age and sex of respondents (percentages) among inhabitants of the Russian town Orel

'To whom would you mainly turn for assistance and support if you encountered difficulties in your co-life with your husband/wife/co-habitant?'

	Age groups				
	18-30	31-50	50	Total	
	W	W	W	M	W
Parents and parents-in-law	44	25	14	20	26
Other relatives	0	9	5	4	5
Friends, colleagues	4	3	10	6	5
Professional helpers	0	0	0	0	0
Problems should be kept in the family	38	50	68	41	46
No answer	14	13	3	29	18
Total	100	100	100	100	100

'If you have or had children who were neglecting themselves, to whom would you turn first to get help?'

	Age group				
	18-30	31-50	50	Total	
	W	W	W	M	W
Parents and parents-in-law	13	13	9	13	12
Other relatives	0	2	0	1	2
Friends, colleagues, and neighbours	2	5	5	2	4
Professional helpers	6	14	23	11	13
Problems should be kept in the family	19	28	45	22	26
Difficult to answer	10	15	9	13	13
No answer	50	13	9	38	30
Total	100	100	100	100	100

Table 11.3c continued

'If you were to face financial problems, to whom would you turn first of all?'

	Age groups				
	18-30	31-50	50	Total	
	W	W	W	M	W
Parents and parents-in-law	75	37	27	29	42
Other relatives	0	15	19	10	9
Friends, colleagues and neighbours	0	16	18	14	13
Social welfare office	0	0	0	0	0
Mutual assistance fund at work	8	7	0	4	7
Bank	0	1	0	2	1
Prefers to handle it on one's own	13	22	36	26	26
No answer	4	2	0	15	2
Total	100	100	100	100	100

M = Men; W = Women.

Table 11.3d: Preferred type of consultants in different problem situations according to age and sex (percentages) among urban Finnish population

'To whom would you mainly turn for assistance and support if you encountered difficulties in your co-life with your husband/wife/co-habitant?'

	Age groups							
	26-37		38-47		48-67		Total	
	Men	Women	Men	Women	Men	Women	Men	Women
Parents and parents-in-law	16	31	8	8	5	3	10	18
Other relatives	12	19	8	25	27	62	15	33
Friends, colleagues	18	21	15	23	5	2	14	16
Professional helpers	16	18	24	21	13	15	18	18
Problems should be kept in the family	28	8	45	21	37	17	36	14
No answer	10	3	2	2	13	1	7	1
Total	100	100	100	100	100	100	100	100
(N)	(122)	(141)	(68)	(65)	(77)	(91)	(268)	(297)

Table 11.3d continued

'If you have or had teenage children who were neglecting themselves, to whom would you turn first to get help?'

	Age groups							
	26-37		38-47		48-67		Total	
	Men	Women	Men	Women	Men	Women	Men	Women
Parents and parents-in-law	13	9	6	7	1	2	8	6
Other relatives	3	12	5	9	10	16	6	13
Friends, colleagues	6	10	5	12	1	2	3	8
Professional helpers	39	55	53	45	38	40	42	47
Problems should be kept in the family	27	8	23	15	39	22	30	15
Total	100	100	100	100	100	100	100	100
(N)	(97)	(127)	(67)	(73)	(82)	(107)	(246)	(307)

'If you were to face financial problems, to whom would you turn first of all?'

	26-37		38-47		48-67		Total	
	Men	Women	Men	Women	Men	Women	Men	Women
Parents and parents-in-law	34	44	18	20	2	7	22	26
Other relatives	8	8	5	8	12	31	7	15
Friends, colleagues	8	3	2	4	3	2	5	3
Social welfare service	3	3	2	6	7	10	4	6
Bank	34	24	58	42	59	23	48	29
Other, including employer	4	4	4	2	3	1	4	3
Prefers to handle it on one's own	8	13	11	13	14	23	10	16
No answer	1	1	0	5	0	3	-	2
Total	100	100	100	100	100	100		
(N)	(159)	(180)	(82)	(86)	(96)	(140)	(337)	(406)

Table 11.3e. *Preferred type of consultants in different problem situations according to sex (percentages) among people in the Warsaw sample*

	Marriage problems		Problems with children	
	Men	Women	Men	Women
Parents/parents-in-law	29	40	18	19
Other relatives	9	10	2	3
Friends/colleagues/neighbours	4	8	3	1
Professional helpers	2	2	8	11
Other alternatives	0	0	24	22
Problems should be kept in the family	56	40	29	30
Don't know/not sure/no answer	0	0	16	14
Total	100	100	100	100
(N)	(195)	(195)	(195)	(195)

	Financial problems	
	Men	Women
Parents/parents-in-law	29	41
Other relatives	11	10
Friends	20	16
Social welfare office	1	0
Bank, employer	7	6
Prefer to handle them on my own	32	26
Don't know	0	1
Total	100	100
(N)	(195)	(195)

The importance of the parent/child relation also comes out in the question of helpers in economic matters (see Table 11.3). In the Russian town Orel, in Warsaw and in Scandinavian towns parents are far more important helpers for the younger generation than grown-up children are for their parents. Rather than interpreting this as a consequence of parents being more altruistic in relation to grown-up children than vice versa, we can assume this to be a consequence of the middle-aged and older generations being economically better off than the younger ones. Since the younger generation usually have lower incomes from their work and greater expenditure on housing and household equipment, this assumption seems reasonable. In addition, improvements in social security have made pensioners less economically dependent on the family network.

Neither in Orel, Warsaw nor in urban Scandinavia have the social welfare services become an attractive alternative for solving economic problems. To some degree friends can be said to be acceptable as helpers in economic matters in Warsaw. For those who do not think they can manage on their own or get help from formal sources such as banks and employers, the kin network, and especially the parents, seems to be the main or only alternative both in urban Scandinavia and in Orel.

To solve difficult problems with children, urban Scandinavians seem to prefer professional to informal helpers, and the informal network of the same generation seems to be as important as parents. Compared to people in Warsaw and especially in Orel (see Table 11.3) Scandinavians seem to rely more on professional help instead of keeping such problems in the family. This finding can be interpreted as an indicator of 'the proletarianisation of parenthood' being a process that has gone further in Scandinavia than in urban Russia and Warsaw. On the other hand, in a rapidly changing society, what better alternative should parents have - if they are to be rational - than to rely upon the welfare professions? At least the most serious problems for today's children and youths are in many ways different from their parents' and grandparents'. Living in a post-figurative society (Mead, 1970) means that the experiences of the older generation are of limited relevance for solving or coping with many of the most difficult problems of the younger.

As in many studies of recent years, our surveys also give some impression of the greater strains on women due to illness of family members both inside and outside the household. Even if men take care of sick family members, having to quit paid work for a longer period due to the illness of some family member still seems to be an almost exclusively female experience all over Europe. Our data do not allow us to make comparisons between countries as to how often this happens or how it is likely to change between generations of women. However, with the ageing of the population and the increasing employment of women, it seems reasonable to assume that more rather than fewer women at some point in their life course will experience strains and conflicts between the demands of working life and the expectations of fulfilling the need for care of serious or chronically sick family members.

Conclusions

The assumption that the growth of the public care services has eroded caregiving in the family does not seem to be well supported by the findings of empirical research, even if the meaning and content of family care might have changed. Many of the rights and achievements which we most value in modern society can also be seen as making the family a more fragile, though not necessarily a less satisfying, institution. It should therefore be acknowledged that many of the problems which the public care system is facing nowadays come not only from its inefficiency or injustice, but also from its promotion of social rights and of a social consciousness of these rights. In other words, modern society now has citizens who have needs not only because they have been made dependent on the state. Rather, through the not altogether perfect action of the state (and certainly because of the action of the political and interest groups which pushed for it), more people have acquired the possibility of having rich personal and private lives. The history of modern states and of their citizens lies in the oscillation between these two opposite poles: the states' initiative is often unjust, inefficient, controlling and overly homogenising, but at the same time it helps to develop a new consciousness of needs.

For what especially concerns women, the continually shifting boundaries between private and public responsibilities, implies continually shifting definitions of what kind of caregiving and caring women are expected to provide either as family members or as paid service workers. Married women today seem to be the protagonists of the so-called 'culture of services' (Saraceno, 1983). This differentiates them from their predecessors, both in dependency on services based outside the family and in their ability to articulate and represent their own and their families' needs and demands. This culture certainly varies between socio-economic groups and countries, as our comparative research also shows.

Greater economic insecurity may bring back more forced interdependence within the family and between the spouses. To suggest that this will have positive consequences, however, I think is to foster a dangerous illusion. To put it in a somewhat exaggerated form: the public care system in most European societies has *mainly* been designed supposing the male worker in his best years with no responsibility for household work and caring for dependent members in the family. It has also presumed a female service provider, a person both able to provide family care and services and to relate to the services provided by the state and the market. In a time of economic squeeze there is a danger that women, who during the last decades have moved forward from their back-stage positions and claimed more active roles in society, will be pushed further back into the family.

Notes

1. As examples of countries where the employment rate of married women is relatively low and the proportion of children in the age group 3-6 years in kindergarten is very high, can be mentioned: the Netherlands, Italy, the Federal Republic of Germany and France. In Finland and Sweden, where the employment rate of married women is much higher, the proportion of preschool children in kindergarten is much lower. Both the Eastern and the Western countries participating in the project report on lack of childcare facilities for the under 3-year-old children. In addition, most of the Western countries report on the problems for employed mothers due to the relatively short hours and inconvenient times at which many kindergartens operate.

2. From the Hungarian national report it comes out that the proportion of mothers on child-nursing leave as a percentage of all women in employment has increased in all economic sectors during the 1970s. The differences between the socio-economic groups as to the proportion which avail themselves of this leave are, however, great: almost all manual workers take this leave. Further, 70 per cent of those who left the school system after completing general school, 60 per cent of those who completed secondary school and 30 per cent of university graduates stay at home for three years with their children. From Poland it is repo.᠊᠊᠊1 that during the period 1960-78 the pattern of starting work after the maternity leave became a marginal phenomenon, while interrupting work for some few years became the dominant pattern. The factor which brings greatest differentiation into the mother's decision to continue employment after maternity leave is still education: the lower the educational level of the mother, the more likely she is to interrupt employment after childbirth.

3. In the sample from the Russian town Orel, 40 per cent of the women who took time from employment to be home with children answered that they wanted to do it, although there were other possibilities. Forty per cent said that they both had to and wanted to stay at home, while 10 per cent answered that they had to stay at home although they did not want to do so. In the Norwegian sample, the corresponding figures were 81, 11 and 5 per cent respectively, in the Finnish sample 75, 12 and 7 per cent, in the Swedish sample about 80, 10 and 5 per cent. In the sample from Slovenia, however, where only 17 per cent of the women had taken time off from employment, more than 60 per cent answered that they had to stay at home although they did not want to. Analysing the Norwegian data in more detail we find that the proportion of women who said that they wanted to stay at home is the smallest, while the proportion answering that they had to stay at home, although they did not want to, are highest among the youngest and most educated mothers.

4. The findings from the Norwegian survey reported in Note 3 can be interpreted as an indication of this change.

5. In the Finnish sample, 18 per cent of the respondents answered that their youngest preschool child was regularly taken care of 'by a family member or relative during day time' (grandparents were not a specified category), in the Norwegian sample 7 per cent answered 'grandmother'. Among the caregivers in Rome about 25 per cent of the preschool children were regularly taken care of by grandparents, in the Russian town Orel about 60 per cent, in Slovenian cities about 30 per cent in the age group 0-3 years, about 5 per cent in the age group 4-6 years. Even if the figures are not strictly comparable (due to differences in the wording of the questions), they still say something about the greater importance of the extended family in the Mediterranean and Eastern countries compared to Scandinavia.

6. The following table gives an indication of this:
'To whom one would mainly turn if one needs/needed someone to look after the children for a while' (percentages)

	(1)	(2)	(3)	(4)	(5)
Parent or parents in law	51	42	36	64	70
Own or spouse's siblings	13	11	-	9	
Other					49
Relatives	5	12	4	4	
Neighbours	9	15	-	15	38
Friends/workmates	6	6	6	1	
Paid help	5	3	15	4	8
Other/no answer	11	11	39	3	
	100	100	100	100	
(N)	(569)	(323)	(299)	(...)	

(1) Urban Finnish population

(2) Urban Norwegian population

(3) Caregivers in Rome

(4) Married and single mothers in Orel

(5) Married and single mothers in Slovenian cities (more alternatives could be named)

7. In the Norwegian sample 61 per cent in the age group 25-39 reports that they mainly turn to parents or parents-in-law for irregular childcare, while the same answer is given by 30 per cent in the age group 55-65.

8. In the Norwegian sample 78 per cent of the grandparents answer that they take care or have taken care of their grandchildren irregularly, 12 per cent give or have given care more regularly, and 2 per cent have had a grandchild living in their own household. The corresponding figures for the Finnish sample are 70, 11 and 5 per cent.

9. In the national report from the Federal Republic of Germany, we are told that the support of parents in their role by providing them with knowledge of the socialisation process has been an old tradition since the first 'Mothers' Schools' were founded as early as 1916. Parental education has become more widespread since the 1960s. The participants in parental training are still primarily women.

10. In the play group movement in Great Britain, which has developed rapidly since 1960, children from non-manual families are over-represented. The main reason for this, according to the national report from Great Britain, is assumed to be that the emphasis on child development and parents participation attracts more middle-class parents. In addition, this kind of childcare does not always help working mothers, owing to the inconvenient times on which they operate.

11. Thirty-eight per cent of the women in the Slovenian sample said they would prefer to have a dwelling in some other part of the city/town/village or in some other place than the dwelling of their parents; 47 per cent said they would prefer to have their parents living in a separate dwelling in the same street, housing area or block, 8 per cent would prefer a separate dwelling in the same building and only 7 per cent would prefer to live together with the parents. The distribution of the answers from the men is nearly the same as from women.

12. The National Report from Slovenia.

References

Abrams, Ph. (1980): 'Social Change, Social Networks and Neighbourhood Care'. *Social Work Service*, Vol. 22, pp. 12-23

Daatland, S.O. (1984): 'Eldreomsorg og eldres omsorg' (Caring for the old...). In: Wadel, C. et al.: *Dagliglivets organisering* (Organisation of daily life). Universitetsforlaget

Donzelot, J. (1979): *The Policing of Families*. Hutschinson & Co., London

Gilligan, C. (1982): *In a Different Voice*. Harvard University Press, Cambridge, Massachusetts

Graham, H. (1983): 'Caring: A Labour of Love'. In: Finch, J. and Groves, D. (eds): *A Labour of Love. Women, Work and Caring*. Routledge & Keagan Paul, London

Gullestad, M. (1981): *Barnevaktens etnografi* (Ethnography of the childminder). Arbeidsnotat RFSP Byforskningsprogram 'Naermiljo' No. 10, University of Trondheim

Gullestad, M. (1984): *Kitchen-Table-Society*. Universitetsforlaget, Oslo

Haavio-Mannila, E. (1976): 'Social Linkages Used by Migrant and Nonmigrant Families in Solving Health, Work and Economic Problems'. *Acta Sociologica*, Vol. 19, pp. 325-48

Holter, H. et al. (1967): *Hjemmet som arbeidsplass* (The home as a working place). Universitetsforlaget, Oslo

Lasch, Ch. (1977): *Heaven in a Heartless World. The Family Besieged*. Basic Books, Inc., New York

Laslett, P. (1983): 'Family and Household as Work Group and Kin Group: Areas of Traditional Europe Compared'. In: Wall, R. et al. (eds): *Family Forms in Historic Europe*. Cambridge University Press, Cambridge

Liljestrøm, R. and Øzgalda, E. (1980): *Kommunals kvinnor på livets trappa* (Women employed by local authorities). Stockholm

Lopata, H.Z. (1971): *Occupation: Housewife*. Oxford University Press, Oxford

Mead, M. (1970): *Culture and Commitment: A Study of the Generation Gap*. Natural History Press/Doubleday, New York

Mitterauer, M. and Sieder, R. (1982): *The European Family*. Basil Blackwell, Oxford

Moroney, R.M. (1976): *The Family and the State - Considerations for Social Policy*. Longman, London

Noddings, N. (1984): *Caring. A Feminine Approach to Ethics and Moral Education*. University of California Press, Berkeley

Nygård, L. (1982): *Umsorgsressursar hos naere pårorende* (Resources for caring among close relations). NIS rapport 2/82, Trondheim, Norway

Oakley, A. (1974): *The Sociology of Housework*. Pantheon Books, New York

Parker, R.A. (1981): 'Tending and Social Policy'. In: Goldberg, E.M. and Hatch, S. (eds): *A New Look at the Personal Social Services*. Discussion Paper No. 4. Policy Studies, London

Rosenmayr, L. and Kockies, E. (1965): 'Propositions for a Sociological Theory of Aging and the Family'. *International Social Science Journal*, pp. 410-26

Rossi, A.S. (1985): 'Gender and Parenthood'. In: Rossi, A.S. (ed.): *Gender and the Life Course*. Aldine Publishing Company, New York

Saraceno, Ch. (1983): 'State Interventions, the Social Sphere and Private Life. Chances for a Progressive Change of the Family's Role or just a Rollback?' Contribution to the Expert Meeting on 'Can there Be a New Welfare State: Social Policy Options toward Shaping an Uncertain Future'. Baden, Austria, Sept. 25 - Oct. 1, Euro Social R 120

Schumacher, E.F. (1980): *Good Work*. Abacus, London

Shanas, E. et al. (1968): *Old People in Three Industrial Societies*. Routledge & Kegan Paul, London

Sundstrøm, G. (1980): 'The Elderly, Women's Work and Social Security Costs'. *Acta Sociologica*, 25, pp. 21-38

Sussmann, M. (ed.) (1969): 'Crossnational Research Studies on the Family: Theoretical Problems and Approaches'. San Juan Document, Cleveland, Ohio (mimeographed MS)

Ungerson, C. (1983): 'Why Do Women Care?' In: Finch, J. and Groves, D. (eds): *A Labour of Love. Women, Work and Caring*. Routledge & Keagan Paul, London

Viklund, R. (1981): *Att arbeta i omsorg* (To work as a caregiver). Arbetslivs-centrum. Stockholm

Wanger, M. (1981): 'The Healthy Development of the Child: What Is the Role of Health Education?' In: *Psychosocial Conditions for Development in Early Childhood*. Fifth International Seminar on Health Education, Published by the International Journal of Health Education

Waerness, K. (1978): 'The Invisible Welfare State: Women's Work at Home'. *Acta Sociologica*, Supplement

Waerness, K. (1982): *Kvinneperspektiver på sosialpolitikken* (Women's perspectives on social policy). Universitetsforlaget, Oslo

Waerness, K. (1984): 'The Rationality of Caring'. In: *Economic and Industrial Democracy*, SAGE, Vol. 5, pp. 185-211

12

The Male Gender Role and Responsibility for Childcare*

Hildur Ve

In the social sciences, the debate on changes in gender roles has to a high degree centred on changes in the female gender role and on the fact that in the Western world women, and especially mothers with small children, have increased their participation in paid work in recent decades.[1] However, in this chapter the emphasis will be on changes in the male gender role, if any, and the question to be discussed is to what degree men have taken on some of the responsibilities formerly regarded as belonging to women. The data from our research project will be considered from this angle. Furthermore, some recent changes in national policies concerning paternal rights in relation to childcare will be examined.

Changes in gender roles may be discussed in a variety of perspectives.[2] From one point of view, gender roles may be looked upon as determining the distribution of *rights* between men and women. The focus may also be on the importance for both sexes of participating in society's production of commodities. From a typically sociological view on the division of labour between men and women, gender roles may be considered as giving a variety of opportunities, and experiences for learning different types of *rationality*.[3] From a psychological angle, the *effect* of gender roles may be debated, i.e. the consequences - for the development of male and female personality traits - of the fact that mothers have had the main part of responsibility for and contact with infants and small children (Dinnerstein, 1977).

The sociological perspective has its roots in liberal political traditions, and its adherents - in maintaining that all human beings

*I would like to thank the Norwegian Research Council for Science and Humanities for its financing the Norwegian part of this research project.

are born equal and have the same abilities - would claim the same rights for all members of society, male and female alike. However, men's capacity for rational action in the economic and political spheres was the basis on which the various rights were developed. Women have come gradually to be considered as deserving the same rights as men, but primarily in these spheres.

Within the second perspective, which has its origin in Marxist thought, the important point regarding the position of women has been that the way to liberation from capitalist exploitation for men as well as for women is understood to be through participation in paid labour. With a few important exceptions, followers of the liberal and Marxist traditions have not regarded skills related to childcare as having liberating dimensions (Dahlerup, 1973). Within the main stream of the liberal tradition, which emphasises both human rights and the advantages of competition between members of society, the distribution of *obligations* between sexes, i.e. obligations concerning housework and childcare, has not in any significant degree been questioned until recent years. The consequence of this has been that even though women in countries dominated by liberal ideas have obtained the same kind of rights as men concerning education and paid work, they have not been able to make full use of these rights in practice. In countries influenced by Marxist ideas, the socialisation of housework and childcare came to be regarded as the best way of liberating women from these duties. The effect of this has been that the East European countries have established childcare facilities to a somewhat greater degree than the West European ones. However, in the East European countries the question of men sharing responsibility for childcare has only recently been raised. The consequence has been that while women have been included in the workforce to a greater degree than in Western Europe, they also carry a 'double' work load compared with men.

During the last decade, the feminist movement in the Western world has fought to put the problem of equality between the sexes within the family on the political agenda. To a certain extent, the question of the sex division of housework and childcare in the family has also been raised in Eastern Europe. At the same time, the negative effects of care in public institutions on infants have also been debated, and in many countries in this part of Europe, the trend has been to make it easier for mothers to stay at home while the children are small.

In other chapters of this book, data from our research project, as well as other data, have been presented in order to show that both in Eastern and in Western Europe, even if there has been some change, women still carry the main burden of daily household chores. The authors of the different chapters also refer to the considerable feeling of injustice that this type of inequality creates among women working either full time or part time.

From the point of view of equality between men and women in the labour market, female social scientists have done research which shows that until men start to take their full share of the responsibility for childcare, the aim of real equality between the sexes will not be reached (Skrede, 1985). Data from our project as well as from other research done in the participating countries show that men have started to take a greater part in caring for children during their leisure time. However, when using the expression 'full share' we mean much more than men increasing the time they spend with their children after paid work. It means that they must be willing to *leave paid work* for a significant length of time in the same way as women do.

Men's participation in caring for small children

Nowhere in our data do we find signs of changes in men's activity patterns which would indicate such a transcendence of the male gender role as is indicated in the expression 'full share' - neither in the older, nor in the younger age group; neither in the socialist nor in the capitalist countries. It is the women who answer that they have left gainful employment for a significant length of time because of childcare. When asked who has been the chief childminder in the first years of the child(ren)'s life, and in the years before school age, 'mother' is the most frequent answer from both women and men in all age groups, and 'father' very seldom occurs. Also when asked whether the interviewed person ought to have started work at an earlier or a later date in relation to the age of their children, this is a nearly irrelevant question for most of the male respondents. The same goes for questions about whether the interviewed person stayed at home by necessity, as no other adequate childcare alternative existed, or whether they did it because they wanted to take care of their children at home.

All in all, our data confirm that most men are still in the traditional role, i.e. to become a father has very few consequences for their job situation as such. For most women, however, becoming a mother means significant changes in their relation to paid work.

In the same way as having one's own income may be considered to have become both an obligation and a right for mothers in modern society, staying at home with one's small child should be regarded for fathers both as a right and a duty. However, the fact that most men do not seriously consider claiming the right to stay away from work to take care of their children during infancy, nor do they show in other ways that they want to take full responsibility for the care of their small children, gives women no choice in the matter, and imposes upon them the problematic task of combining the care of small children with paid work. The consequence of male activity patterns is that the image of the female worker, in the eyes of employers as well as in the eyes of the male colleagues, stays within a traditional framework. In its turn, this image furthers all the stereotypes and discriminations against women workers, many of which have been revealed by researchers during the last decade.[4]

We shall go on to discuss some other negative consequences of the division of labour among the sexes from the point of view of sociological and psychological research and theory concerning differences in rationality between men and women, and in male and female personality traits.

Two types of rationality

Persons involved in caring, either paid or unpaid, for other people who are not able to take care of themselves and who might suffer or even perish if nobody takes responsibility for them have the well-being of the dependent persons as their main aim. In order to reach this goal, the careworkers must to a great degree choose their means by *identifying* themselves with those who are in need of care and trying to understand their various requirements. This type of rationality may be defined as caring or responsible rationality. In the production of goods, and to a certain extent also in the field of services, where the customers are not dependent on the workers in the sense described in caring, efficiency and profit are the basic aims, i.e. to maximise production with the least possible expenditure of energy and time. And labour power is an important part of the calculation of efficiency. This tendency is more strongly developed in the Western than in the Eastern European countries, though the idea of efficiency is gaining more attention in Eastern Europe. We may define rationality in production as technical rationality (Sørensen, 1984). This concept includes the observation that the interaction patterns growing out of the paid production of goods and services are shaped by inherent tendencies towards objectification and depersonalisation. Those who produce and those who buy the products are interchangeable. In recent years, workers' emotional stability and ability to relate to each other have been included in the efficiency paradigm, a fact which implies a tendency to instrumentalise human emotions.

In caring, the relationship between those who perform the various duties and those who are in need of them is personal in the sense that the carer must be able to identify with the situation of the dependents who may not be able to express their needs. This type of relationship may be impaired by a high degree of changes and shifts among care-workers. The mother/child relationship is the prototype of this relationship, but many of the paid jobs in the educational, health and social sectors, which constitute women's traditional fields in the labour market, have the same traits. The ability to empathise is a very important part of a careworker's job, and often also the willingness to put the dependent's well-being before one's own (see Kari Waerness's chapter in this volume). In maintaining that women are the typical carriers of responsible rationality, we do not mean that men are unable to learn this type of rationality. Men have a tendency to think and act according to a technical rationality mainly because they, to a much greater degree than women, work in social situations where this type of rationality is predominant. In other words, we consider the differences in modes of rationality between the sexes to be caused by the division of labour between men and women, and not to be a consequence of biological differences.

Historical research on women's activity patterns supports this view. The emotionally close relationship between mothers and children has developed as a result of the division of labour typical of modern industrialised societies and was unknown in earlier epochs (Badinter, 1982).

Our main point is that responsible rationality has more humane aspects than technical rationality, and that the basis of these humane aspects is the training in empathising with persons who need care in order to survive. One of the consequences of the division of labour between the sexes is that the positions in society which give the greatest access to power and control over other human beings are held by men who have been trained to think within the framework of technical rationality. Both of the founding fathers of sociology, Durkheim and Weber, warned against the dangers inherent in the economic, technological and bureaucratic developments of the twentieth century. They did not, however, seriously consider the humane aspects of women's experience and the development of responsible rationality as factors in their theories in order to avoid the dangerous consequences of modernisation. This perspective has been developed by women in sociology.

Using the Freudian theory of psychoanalysis as a point of departure, women psychologists have developed new insight into the effects of the psyche of men and women taken care of mainly by their mothers in their first years of childhood.

The unhealthy effect of 'mother-power' on male and female personality

Some psychologists maintain that the fact that fathers share to such a small degree the responsibility for caring for children in their first years, creates an image in the minds of both men and women of 'mothers' as immensely powerful, able to give and able to withdraw warmth and closeness and food (Dinnerstein, 1977). Since this image is created before children have learned to talk, it remains a part of the unconscious and so do feelings of longing and aggression towards it. In their simultaneous struggle for closeness with and independence from this early 'mother' image, women and men enter into a neurotic symbiosis, which hinders both sexes in becoming fully adult persons. The result is, however, more serious for men, in that they are of a different sex than the mother. Unlike women, they cannot in later years of childhood identify with the caring aspects of the mother, which they have consciously experienced. On the contrary, boys learn that they must not become like their mothers, nor do they in any significant way develop their ability to identify with and care for those who are dependent and are in need of care. As a result of this, they need women to satisfy their longing for closeness created in infancy, but can accept it only if women refrain from controlling them. But most importantly men come to admire toughness and powerful male figures and invest their creative abilities in attempts to share this power over women and over nature.

However, as a result of the childhood image of the all-powerful mother, from which they also strive to loose themselves and become independent, women come to accept some male premises in the relationship between the sexes in return for men's support against this frightening image from infancy. In doing this, women refrain from fully developing their ability to be responsible both for their own fate and for that of society (Gilligan, 1984). They leave this responsibility to men, and may even develop an admiration for the strong and capable male sex.

These women psychologists contend that this neurotic symbiosis between men and women only has a chance to come to an end if fathers begin to share in the nurture of small children.

National policies on paternal rights to caring for small children

We shall present our data on differences in national policies regarding fathers' rights from the sociological and psychological perspectives outlined above. This means that we consider those countries as being to a certain degree progressive which have granted substantial rights to fathers in the field of childcare. In judging progressiveness, we shall make use of the model developed by R. Jallinoja in her chapter in this volume. (Table 12.1.) There are significant differences between the countries which have introduced paternal rights concerning the length of the post-parturition leave granted to fathers, and the number of days they are allowed to stay at home with sick children. Sweden was the first country to start this trend, and is also the country in which the number of days of leave for 'sick children' for fathers is the highest. In the FRG, on the other hand, the number of days is very small in this respect, and fathers have no right to share the post-parturition leave with their wives. There are also differences as to the amount of pay given to the father during leave and the way in which this pay is organised (*Women at Work*, 1984).

Table 12.1. *Relationship between patterns of women's work-roles and national policies concerning paternal rights*

		Fathers are allowed to share the post-parturition leave with mothers	Fathers are allowed to stay at home with sick children
The housewife pattern	Netherlands	no	no
	Italy	yes	yes
The moderate sex role pattern	Norway	yes	yes
	Sweden	yes	yes
	France	yes	no
	Great Britain	no	no
	FRG	no	yes
The pattern of employed women	Hungary	yes	yes
	Finland	yes	no
	USSR	no	no
	Poland	no	no
	GDR	no	no
	Slovenia	yes	yes

However, for our purposes, the information in Table 12.1 gives a basis for discussing the very different trends in the participating countries as to the role of men and women and to the degree of equality between the sexes. The Netherlands seems to be the most clear case of having traditional roles and a comparatively low degree of equality for both men and women: according to Jallinoja's variables it may be placed within the housewife pattern, and at the same time, it is among the least progressive ones as to fathers' rights. On the other hand, among the countries placed within the pattern of employed women, the situation between the sexes in three of them may be defined as unbalanced in that they have not introduced paternal rights. They may thus be considered among the least progressive ones as regards the male gender role, while regarding the degree of employment as the female gender role, they are among the most modern ones. As mentioned above, this type of relationship between men and women implies a very heavy workload for women.

Two of the countries placed in the moderate sex-role pattern may be considered progressive regarding the male role. It may be maintained that there is a tendency towards greater equality between the sexes in these countries than in the groups of countries where the situation between the sexes is defined as traditional. It is more difficult to decide whether the degree of equality is also higher than in the countries where the situation between the sexes is defined as unbalanced.

However, equality between the sexes means more than extending certain of men's *rights* to women. If men do not take on some of the *obligations* of women, the result of women's increased participation in paid work is that men's traditional responsibility for providing money for the family is shared by women so that men have been released from part of their burdens, without taking on any great share 'of women's traditional responsibilities. This type of argument is related to the debate within the liberal tradition on gender role as a determinant of the distribution of rights.

As to the Marxist perspective on liberation through participation in the production of commodities, we maintain that this perspective is one-dimensional in that it overlooks the humanity in the type of rationality which is learned through the experience of caring for children (and other dependent persons). When looking at Table 12.1, and combining the two dimensions, we can argue that the two countries within the pattern of employed women and with progressive male role patterns get the highest score as to liberation potentialities both for men and women.

Discussion

We are fully aware that reasons for introducing paternal rights may vary from country to country. We do not think that the sociological and psychological perspectives presented above have been very influential in the work of the various law-making bodies in those countries which have granted the right to fathers to stay at home in the post-parturition period and/or when the children are ill. Public discussion in some of the countries on this issue has very often centred on the positive effects of men's sharing the responsibility of childcare with women on women's opportunities in the labour market. It may also be that the fertility problem, i.e. the very sharp decrease in the number of children born in recent decades, has made some public authorities look for many different solutions. One of these solutions might have been to grant fathers the right to stay at home with small children (Befolkningsutviklingen, 1984).

In a report from the OECD (1985) on 'The Integration of Women into the Economy', the authors wrote that 'An important innovation in some countries has been the introduction of extended leave which may be taken by either parent. This represents a move away from segregation of roles and a recognition that fathers should participate in caring for children too'. This kind of argument may be placed within the perspective of gender roles as determinants of the distribution of rights between the sexes. The argument seems to imply some notion of *obligations* on the part of the fathers, which is a step forward compared with the more one-sided discussion of rights.

We do not think that the granting of rights to fathers may change the male gender role in any significant way in the first years after the laws have been introduced. In this respect we may refer to the debate on the possible effects of law-making on the norms and behaviour of people, which has in no way been conclusive. However, from another angle it has been argued that when a new law is being introduced, it is very often the result of the development of new norms and values among the people in a country. But there seem to be great differences among the various cultures in this respect.

There is at present very little research done on the changes, if any, in father's behaviour patterns after these laws have been introduced in the various countries. The few results which have been published seem to indicate that a rather small number of fathers have made use of their new parental rights (Bernhardt, 1985). In the debate in the mass media it has been stated that many employers do not consider parental leave as an adequate reason for men to stay away from work. As has been argued by many female social scientists, these attitudes on the part of employers indicate that gender role patterns are of importance in the economic system. Only if it suits the interest of capital, will the roles be changed.

In addition to criticism from employers, male colleagues of men who have made use of this right are reported to look down upon them and mock them in various ways. This seems to indicate that male dominance is at stake, which also makes it improbable that significant numbers of men will make use of their parental rights in the near future. However, some research data from neighbouring fields may give reason for more optimistic views.

There are certain indications of differences within the social classes regarding men's sharing responsibility for caring for small children. In Sweden, work on mixed-class or cross-class families, i.e. families where the spouses belong to different classes with regard to their job, revealed some interesting patterns as to which of the parents stays at home with a sick child (Leiulfsrud and Woodward, 1986). Researchers have found that in families where one parent according to his/her job belongs to the working class, and one parent has a non-working-class job, the spouse of the former group, whether a man or a woman, stays at home. One of the reasons the working-class respondents gave when explaining the patterns developed by the spouses was that they themselves felt that they were interchangeable. They meant that their job was more easily done by somebody else than their partners' job (which was either in the social or the teaching sectors). This way of reasoning is related to the concept of responsible rationality elaborated above. In this chapter, there is no scope for discussing either the importance of the insight these respondents reveal, or the tragic fact that men and women should work in jobs which give them this feeling. Our point in this respect is that some men do develop the type of thinking implicit in their responses.

Another research result, which may also give some cause for optimism, comes from a survey conducted among Norwegian school children (Skoledirektøren..., 1985). When asked what kind of solution they might choose when becoming fathers, more than 35 per cent of the boys in the 8th grade (approximately 14-15 years old) answered that they would prefer alternating with their spouses staying at home with their children, while 15 per cent answered that they would prefer their spouse to stay at home. The others chose some kind of public or private childcare arrangement.

In the next decade we shall be able to find out whether the family patterns in the countries which have introduced this new right of fathers to parental leave will have changed so that significant numbers of fathers choose to make use of their right or the situation remains more or less the same as today. What kind of effect a possible change may have on gender roles is another matter. Men will certainly learn from their new experience as caregivers, and develop some degree of responsible rationality, but this may be a somewhat different type from the one developed by women within the present gender-role pattern. One may expect that the unhealthy effect of the powerful mother image of early childhood on the personality development of men and women may disappear if and when fathers share the nurturing role with mothers.

However, men will give nurturance and care to children in ways somewhat different from women. The interaction patterns between spouses and between parents and children will change. The patterns these changes will make is impossible to forecast. But from the sociological and psychological perspectives there is a great chance that the changes will be for the better.

Notes

1. The role concept, originally developed within the structural-functional tradition and defined as the cluster of norms connected to social positions, is in this chapter used in a less precise fashion, which includes the notion that the role 'incumbents' may be considered as rational actors: they are influenced by social expectations, but may to some extent reflect upon this influence, and may also to a certain degree choose between different means and goals of action.

2. The Danish social scientist, Drude Dahlerup has showed in her book (Dahlerup, 1973) how the discussion on women's situation has many different origins.

3. The Norwegian sociologist, Bjørg Aase Sørensen (1982), has developed this concept in relation to her research on differences in male and female behaviour in various job situations. Some related topics are also discussed in another article of hers (Sørensen, 1984).

4. The Swedish sociologist, Gerd Lindgren (1985) has discussed the subtle patterns of discrimination against women in different types of workplaces.

References

Badinter, E. (1982): *The Myth of Motherhood*. Souvenir Press, London

Befolkningsutviklingen (Population development), No. 26, 1984; NOU

Bernhardt, E.M. (1985): 'Women's' Home Attachment at First Birth. The Case of Sweden'. University of Stockholm, Research Reports in Demography, No. 28

Dahlerup, D. (1973): *Socialisme og Kvindefrigørelse i det 19. Århundrede* (Socialism and the liberation of women in the nineteenth century). GMT, København

Dinnerstein, D. (1977): *The Mermaid and the Minotaur: Sexual Arrangements and Human Malaise*. Harper & Row, New York

Gilligan, C. (1984): *In a Different Voice*. New York

Leiulfsrud, H. and Woodward, A.E. (1986): 'Women at Class Crossroads: Repudiating Conventional Theories of Family and Class'. *Sociology*, No. 3

Lindgren, G. (1985): *Kamrater, Kollegor och Kvinnor* (Comrades, colleagues and women). Department of Sociology, University of Umeå, Research Reports

OECD (1985): *The Integration of Women into the Economy*. OECD, Paris

Skoledirektøren i Bjørgvin (1985): 'Skolens holdningsskapende arbeid' (The creation of attitudes as part of the school's work). Bergen

Skrede, K. (1985): 'Velferdsstaten og kvinner' (The welfare state and women). In: *Kvinner i velferdsstaten* (Women and the welfare state). Arbeidsnotat 4/85, NAVF's Sekretariat for kvinneforskning

Sørensen, B.A. (1982): 'Ansvarsrasjonalitet: Om mål-middel tenking blant kvinner' (Responsible rationality: on means-ends thinking among women). In: Holter, H. (ed.): *Kvinner i fellesskap* (Women together). Oslo

Sørensen, B.A. (1984): 'The Organizational Women and the Trojan Horse Effect'. In: Holter, H. (ed.): *Patriarchy in a Welfare Society.* Oslo

Women at Work, No. 2, 1984, International Labour Office, Geneva

Part Four

Conclusions

13

European Family Life Patterns - A Reappraisal

Katja Boh

Introduction

Interest in changes in family patterns has been growing by leaps and bounds during recent years, and so have the number of publications on this topic. An increasing number of scholars all over the world have become involved in studies exploring the processes that families in modern societies have been undergoing. Only a few scholars though have had the exceptional opportunity to study family change in a cross-national perspective or, more precisely, within the framework of a comparative research project covering 14 countries from the East, North, West and South of Europe.

In this chapter an effort is made to integrate the findings yielded by the comparative research and to trace the tendencies in changes of family patterns in the various European states. We try to answer the crucial question whether these tendencies converge, which would mean that family patterns in European societies are becoming more similar, or the recent political and economic developments have produced differences contributing to a greater diversity in family life patterns. (For the theoretical elaboration of the divergence/convergence concept and its application to the European situation see Qvortrup's chapter in this book.)

'Hopefully comparative studies will be undertaken which are alerted to convergence as well as to divergence, without any a priori theoretical dismissal of either possibility', wrote Weinberg (1969, p. 15), and it sounded like a challenging invitation to our efforts.

Data used in this chapter come from various sources. Statistical data were used, as well as the National Reports prepared by scholars who participated in the cross-national project. Even though the authors of the National Reports approached their analyses in the respective countries from somewhat different perspectives, and in doing so had to rely on different sources, the resulting information still allowed to study some common issues.

The analysis covers the period from 1945 to the present, which is of course definitely too short to provide material for a historical analysis of family change, but nevertheless long enough to reveal their convergent and/or divergent tendencies. We are also aware of the shortcomings of the method we used in this analysis. We know that there are many more indicators which might have been used. The selection of indicators had to be adjusted to the requirements of the international comparison.

There is also much room for speculations and arbitrary decisions in our method. Empirical data rarely produce pure patterns and in many cases it is difficult to determine where to put the boundary between one and the other pattern. Still, with these constraints in mind, and with the background information provided by the National Reports, we are inclined to believe that our comparative analysis will contribute to a better understanding and offer a few suggestions as to why and where the searchlight on convergence and divergence may be turned.

Changes in family work patterns

The shift - which is a result of men's and women's work-roles - from the traditional model of the family with the husband/father as breadwinner and the wife/mother as a full-time housewife to the dual-work family in which both husband and wife are employed outside the home is considered one of the most significant changes in family patterns. Therefore we begin our analysis with trends and changes that have taken place in work and employment since 1945, particularly in the gainful employment of women.

The employment of women

A large number of women have always worked either on family-owned land or business or as workers and employees in industry, administration and service organisations, but never before have so many married women and mothers with young children gone out to work, which in turn required a reorganisation of their family life.

Judging by the *present* proportion of women in the labour force, it is possible to divide the 14 countries that participated in our project into three groups.

Table 13.1. Work patterns in 14 European countries*

	B	I	FRG	NL	GB	N	S	SF	F	H	SL (YU)**	PL	SU	GDR
Women at work	1	1	1	1	1	2	2	2	2	2	2	2	3	3
Married women at work	1	1	1	1	2	2	2	2	2	2	2	3	3	3
Part-timers	1	1	2	3	3	3	3	1	1	0	0	0	1	2

*The countries' symbols are: Belgium - B, Finland - SF, France - F, Great Britain - GB, German Democratic Republic - GDR, Federal Republic of Germany - FRG, Hungary - H, Italy - I, the Netherlands - NL, Norway - N, Poland - PL, Sweden - S, Soviet Union - SU, Slovenia (Yugoslavia) - SL(YU). For the construction of the patterns a very simple method was used. Countries where the proportion of women in the total labour force around 1980 was less than 40% were given value 1, those with a proportion higher than 40% were given value 1, those with a proportion higher than 40% value 2, and those countries with a proportion of or above 50% value 3. The GDR with 49.5% was put into this group. If the proportion of gainfully employed married women in 1975-80 was 20 to 35% value 1 was given, 35 to 65% was valued 2 and more than 65 was valued 3 (cf. Table 13.3). Countries with no part-timers in 1980 (or no information available) were given value 0, those with less than 20% value 1, with part-time up to 30% value 2, and those with more than 30%, value 3 (cf. Table 13.4).

**Only the Socialist Republic of Slovenia took part in the cross-national comparative research. Therefore statistical data and research results referred to in this and all other chapters in this book relate only to Slovenia and are not representative of Yugoslavia as a whole.

The first is the group of countries[1] where less than 40 per cent of the labour force are women (Belgium, the FRG, Great Britain, Italy and the Netherlands). In the second group are the countries with a participation rate higher than 40 but less than 50 per cent, while the third group includes countries where the participation is

around 50 per cent (GDR and Poland) or has exceeded 50 per cent
(USSR) (see Tables 13.2, 13.3 and 13.4).

*Table 13.2. Trends in women's participation in non-agricultural economic
activities (in percentages of the economically active population of 15 years and
over)*

	1930	1940	1950	1960	around[*] 1970	1980
Belgium	27	25	25	28	30	31.1
Finland	38	39	41	42	44	46.6
France	34	35	33	33	35	42.0
German Democratic Republic	-	41	35	45	46	49.5
Federal Republic of Germany	30	31	31	34	35	38.9
Great Britain	31	-	32	34	37	39.1
Hungary	29	-	28	34	42	44.0
Italy	23	-	25	18	21	
Netherlands	23	-	22	24	27	33.3
Norway	36	32	29	27	29	42.0
Poland	29	-	33	35	40	43.0
Slovenia (Yugoslavia)**	-	-	30	36	42	45.0
Soviet Union	29	-	-	48	50	51.0
Sweden	35	31	31	33	37	42.0

Census years deviating from every tenth year are: Belgium 1947, France 1936,
1946, 1954, 1962, Germany 1925, 1933, 1946, Netherlands 1947, Norway 1946,
Sweden 1945, Italy 1936, German Democratic Republic 1946, 1964, Soviet Union
1926.

Sources: ILO *Year Books of Labour Statistics, U.N. Demographic Yearbook,* 1980.
*Sources: National Reports (Supplements).
**Statistični letopis SR Slovenije* (Statistical Yearbook of Slovenia), Ljubljana,
1965, 1981.

One would expect that, because of differences in the levels of
industrial development, timing of industrialisation and differences
in the official ideologies and employment programmes, it will be
possible to identify a distinctive Western European work pattern,
and one which is characteristic of the Eastern European socialist
countries (cf. Jallinoja's chapter in this book). It turns out though
that a distinction between West and East cannot be supported by
statistical evidence. The proportion of gainfully employed women
is high not only in the Eastern socialist countries but also in some
Western and North European countries with capitalist economies.

Table 13.3. *Trend in the labour force participation rates of married women*

	1960	1970	1975-81*
Belgium	20.0	27.0	32.0
Finland	45.0	53.0	57.0
France	32.0	34.0	40.0
German Democratic Republic	-	-	84.0
Federal Republic of Germany	33.0	35.0	35.0
Great Britain	30.0	43.0	48.0
Hungary	-	37.0	52.0
Italy	18.0	21.0	26.2
Netherlands	7.0	16.0	32.8
Norway	10.0	23.0	40.0
Poland	-	60.0	73.0
Slovenia (Yugoslavia)	-	-	60.0
Soviet Union	-	-	87.0
Sweden	24.0	37.0	58.0

Source: United Nations 1980, pp. 12-15, OECD 1982, p. 71.
*Source: National Reports; E. Haavio-Mannila and K. Kati: Demographic Background of Changes in the Life Patterns of Families in the Nordic Countries. 1979. Appendix 6; *Statistični letopis SR Slovenije* (Statistical Yearbook of Slovenia), Ljubljana, 1981.

Table 13.4. *Women part-time workers (as percentages of total employment), around 1980*

Belgium	16.5	Italy	10.6
Finland	10.9	Netherlands	31.6
France	15.2*	Norway	44.9
German Democratic Republic	30.0	Poland**	-
Federal Republic of Germany	27.6	Slovenia (YU)**	-
Great Britain	39.0	Soviet Union***	2.0
Hungary		Sweden	46.2*

*All persons working less than 30 hours a week. Source for all OECD countries: Eurostat, Labour Force Sample Survey: *National Statistics* (OECD Working Party 6, 28 May 1982).
**No information available.
***USSR National Report.

The relationships become even more complex when instead of one, several indicators of female work participation are taken and combined into patterns. The introduction of additional indicators, as for example the proportion of employed married women, and the proportion of women working part-time, yields a greater differentiation of work patterns that cannot be simply explained by the East-West divide.

When these rough approximations are used to measure the intensity of women's participation in gainful employment, four patterns can be distinguished.

The first pattern, found in Belgium, Italy, the FRG and the Netherlands, is characterised by low participation of women in the labour force, and by an equally low rate of gainfully employed married women. The proportion of part-timers, however, varies from very low in Belgium and Italy to high in the Netherlands. We will call this pattern the *low-employment pattern*. If compared with the patterns developed by Jallinoja (see her chapter in this book), we can see that it corresponds to the 'housewife pattern', which has been very common among women of the older generations throughout Europe, but is gradually disappearing since younger women are becoming increasingly employed everywhere.

The second pattern, that is the *medium-employment pattern*, appears most frequently in Finland, France, Hungary and Slovenia (Yugoslavia) and is characterised by an overall employment rate of women higher than 40 per cent, an employment rate of married women between 35 and 65 per cent and a low proportion of part-timers.

In between the first and the second pattern there is a pattern which, with regard to moderate employment rates resembles the second pattern, but deviates from it in the high proportion of part-timers. Among countries represented in this pattern are Great Britain, Norway and Sweden, where part-time work is nearly as high as it is in the Netherlands (cf. Table 13.4). This is called the *high part-time pattern*, which may be compared with Jallinoja's moderate-employment pattern characterised by high job discontinuity and a high proportion of part-timers among women.

The fourth pattern is practised in three socialist countries: Poland, the USSR and the GDR. We shall call it the *high-employment pattern*, which partly overlaps with Jallinoja's 'pattern of employed women' and Dahlström's 'radical pattern' (Dahlström, 1962, p. 3). However, even these patterns are far from being homogeneous.

The patterns found in the three socialist countries are characterised by a very high participation of women in the labour force, but differ as to the proportion of part-timers, which is practically zero in Poland, is somewhat higher but still low in the USSR and rather high in the GDR.

The analysis has proved that it is extremely difficult to study employment trends on a comparative basis, and give reasonable explanations for all the differences in the dynamic of change and pattern variations in particular countries. Employment of women does not necessarily depend only on economic factors but is related to employment policies, which in turn are shaped by prevailing family ideologies, political practices, historical traditions and cultural values and norms (Shorter, 1976, p. 250; Stone, 1979, pp. 149-64; Haavio-Mannila, 1983, pp. 243-60; Gowler and Legge, 1983, pp. 138-58; Jallinoja's chapter in this book).

For example, countries in the low-employment pattern have a much longer industrial tradition than countries characterised by the other three patterns and particularly those countries for which the fourth pattern is the most common (except the GDR). In addition, historical facts and recent economic developments together with great variations in employment policies that have not been always in favour of women becoming gainfully employed have also caused differences in the development of work patterns in each individual country. How specific historical circumstances and political interventions influence employment patterns in different ways may be exemplified by several cases, as for instance by the Dutch case. In the Netherlands the increase of female employment has been slow throughout these years, and the reason why the Netherlands still belongs among the European countries with the lowest female economic participation rates may lie in recent history. 'In the Netherlands the war did not lead to a large-scale take-over by women of jobs... On the contrary, in order to prevent men from taking forced employment abroad, women withdrew from the labour market. This became a patriotic act, advocated also by the women's movement' (Clason, 1981, p. 12). It took a long time until this tendency began to change, and up to now the Netherlands has remained in the group of countries with the lowest employment rate for women, and a high proportion of women working part-time.

Employment of women is also very susceptible to transitory economic and political situations, and may change rapidly in one or the other direction, as is shown by recent experience. Very illustrative in this respect are changes which have taken place in Italy, where the feminisation of agriculture in the fifties and sixties together with the expansion of the secondary and tertiary sector employing women caused a rapid increase in women's employment. This was followed by a process of masculinisation of farming due to the industrialisation of agricultural production, and this was associated with an equally considerable decrease in the number of women employed in the industrial sector. Although the tertiary sector continued to expand, female employment in Italy decreased by 16 per cent over 13 years, the total going from 35.5 per cent in 1959 to 19.5 per cent in 1972. At the same time, women are assumed to have been increasingly employed on the black or illegal labour market. Nevertheless, during the last few years, for different, predominantly economic, reasons, the participation of women in the labour force seems to have increased again (Sgritta and Saporiti, 1980).

In Belgium, the FRG and Great Britain the growing proportion of gainfully employed women was mainly motivated by a shortage of labour. 'Therefore, an appeal was made to foreign labour for hard work (miners), and to female labour for light work which required little training', is reported from Belgium (Siercu, 1984, p. 26).

In Great Britain the rates of married women rose consistently in the fifties and sixties. There were increases approaching 50 per cent for women aged 35-54 in the fifties and 50 to 61 per cent in the sixties. In the seventies the increase seems to have slowed down, but at the same time there has been an acceleration in participation rates for younger married women (Sierakowski, 1983, p. 23; Gowler and Legge, 1983, pp. 138-58).

The low proportion of employed women in the FRG shows that a labour shortage does not always provide a stimulus to higher female employment rates. In the FRG, women, who replaced men in all kinds of jobs during the war, were pushed back home once the economic situation improved and the shortage of labour was compensated for by foreigners. The explanation for such a policy may, according to Nave-Herz (1981, p. 10) be found in the extremely traditional attitudes towards the role of the family and women, reinforced by a back-to-the-family trend as a reaction to the Third Reich in which the ideology of the state and society ranked above the family: 'The reorganization of the labour market and production went therefore hand in hand with a phase of return to the family and emphasis on the independence of the family within and towards society as a whole.'

Norway is also a peculiar case. Here, throughout the twentieth century the development of women's participation in the labour force has been somewhat different from the other European and even the Nordic countries. This may be explained by the fact 'that the increase in economic welfare did not make married women's employment necessary' (Waerness, 1982, p. 15). In Norway, traditionally a very high proportion of the economically active men (in sea transport, fishing, whaling) have lived outside the family households for long periods of the year. In consequence, the traditional role of the Norwegian housewife implied a relatively high degree of independence and social status.

Immigration of foreign labour does not seem to have influenced women's employment in France as much as it did in other countries. France has a long tradition of women's gainful work, and ever since the second half of the last century it has been increasing steadily. In spite of a strong immigration of labour from the Third World, in 1962, according to the French statistics, two out of three working women were employed in salaried jobs, and in 1975 the proportion was four out of five (Michel, 1982, p. 10).

Nowadays women's participation in labour in France is as high as it is in Finland and in two of the socialist countries in the sample, notably Hungary and Slovenia (Yugoslavia). Labour in these countries was drawn mainly from the agricultural and female reserves of labour. In the latter two countries women's participation in the labour force was also a political aim endorsed by the official Party ideology and has in many instances far exceeded the real need for labour.

The same applies to the Eastern European socialist countries with the exception of the GDR. These countries were latecomers to the group of industrialised societies, and were predominantly agricultural before the Second World War or the Revolution. The industrialisation process in these countries was extremely fast and women's work patterns changed practically overnight. In Poland as well as in pre-revolutionary Russia the non-agricultural activity rate for women was low but increased rapidly, and is today among the highest in the world (Slesarev and Yankova, 1983, p. 263). These two countries together with the GDR are also the only countries in our sample where full employment of both men and women has been maintained throughout these years.

In several countries women's work patterns are also characterised by a high proportion of part-timers (cf. Table 13.4). As a rule, part-time work is higher where overall employment rates in women are lower and vice versa, whereas it is lowest in countries with the highest occurrence of female employment. Nevertheless, even this regularity is not complete and there are many exceptions to the rule. It appears that part-time work for women, although theoretically possible in all countries, has been encouraged in some and discouraged in others for various economic, organisational and/or ideological reasons.

Part-time work is also encouraged by employers in Western countries since 'women workers, especially part-time workers, offer a number of advantages to employers who want to make a quick profit in an economic situation of long term crisis ... Women workers, especially part-time workers ... provide a suitable labour force in such circumstances, both because they are relatively cheap in employment and because they are more easily and more cheaply displaced when no longer needed.' (Wilson, 1977, p. 165.)

Socialist countries have not encouraged part-time work for various reasons, primarily economic. Unfavourable economic conditions in these countries coupled with low productivity would hardly permit a shortening of working hours and would entail a remarkable reduction in wages and salaries which the great majority of women cannot afford. The woman's contribution to the family budget is (in these countries) - except a very few cases - essential, since only with two incomes can a family maintain an acceptable standard of living.

Furthermore, socialist countries objected to part-time work for ideological reasons. As feminists in the West, the ruling Communist Parties in the socialist countries have strongly opposed part-time jobs for women because it was believed that by working part-time, women would be discriminated in comparison with men in the labour market and would thus be hindered in their emancipatory efforts.

An interesting exception among the socialist countries is the GDR, where part-time jobs are available, although not favoured by official policies, and are taken up by quite a considerable number of women. In the GDR legal provisions enable mothers with at least two children under 16 years to work part-time, and 30 per cent of these mothers make use of this option in spite of the rather well-developed network of day-care for children (Ruhl and Weisse, 1982, p. 47).

In the Western countries, too, economic disadvantages and the job insecurity involved in part-time work prevent many women from choosing this alternative (see Nave-Herz's chapter in this book). The number of women who make use of it varies according to the economic conditions of the family and the number and age of the children. It is generally chosen by mothers with young children, for whom this is the best and sometimes the only possible compromise between work and home duties. Therefore it is not surprising that women often prefer part-time jobs to full-time work. Research in Lombardy has shown that 52.8 per cent of women looking for jobs or willing to have one preferred part-time employment (Sgritta and Saporiti, 1980, p. 39). Women decide for part-time jobs even though they know they will get less money and will be deprived of resources which can be mobilised only through regular work (such as health insurance and old age pension). 'Part-time work is favoured', writes Sierakowski (1983, p. 29), 'because shorter hours reduce the stress of a dual role ... and give women an outside interest and some relief from boredom and isolation, as well as a small independent source of income.'

The fact that women give priority to part-time work wherever circumstances permit it supports the argument elaborated by Haavio-Mannila and Černigoj-Sadar (see their chapters in this book) that there has been a tacit acceptance in all societies that the wife and mother will match her employment to the requirements of the family. This same idea also underlies policy measures taken for the protection of women and mothers in both East and West. Whatever the explicit goals of these measures, they imply that there are inconsistencies between the demands of work and family, and that it is necessary to help women to combine both roles more successfully (see Nave-Herz's, Michel's, Waerness's and Ve's chapters in this book).

These few examples from various European states show very clearly that changes in work patterns among women are to a great extent influenced by political decisions, rather than by free individual choice. Employment has, for a great number of women, become not only an economic necessity but also a social norm. Women go out to work to earn their living and to improve their social position but whether they get a job, what job they get, and what kind of working arrangements they will be able to make depends first of all on the available options created by economic conditions and political considerations as well as on the woman's ability to combine her two roles.

Changes in marriage patterns

We first examined changes in work patterns and tried to identify social forces that have influenced employment opportunities for women and shaped the dual-work family patterns in various ways during the last decades. We shall continue with the analysis of marriage patterns to be followed by an analysis of reproductive patterns and forms of parenting.

In the current literature demographic changes and shifts in norms have been considered the most important factors influencing variations and changes in European marriage patterns. Demographic analyses give evidence that changes in marriages in European societies were first marked by a dramatic swing to higher incidence of marriage and to falling age at marriage, to be followed by an inverse trend characterised by a decrease in marriage rates and an increase in the age of marriage, a growing number of divorces and cohabitations.

Marriage rates were highest during the first years after the Second World War, have since then decreased in most countries and are according to recent data lower than they used to be in the 1930s (Table 13.5). The decline has taken place in all countries but at different rates and times.

Three decades ago the lowest marriage rate, in Norway, was 6.2, and the highest, in Poland, 8.3, which made a difference of 2.1. In the year 1984, however, the difference between the lowest marriage rate, in Sweden (4), and the highest marriage rate, in the USSR[2] (10.3), has doubled (5.9).

There is some evidence that the growing number of those who married and the drop in the marriage age in the first period was related to the higher standard of living and the increased state provisions for young couples to help them in the establishment of a home of their own. By analogy it could be assumed that the recent decline in marriage and the rise in marriage age might be a consequence of the increasing social and economic insecurity in European societies. It is, however, not clear yet whether this is just a temporary phenomenon provoked by the recent crisis, or it is to become a general feature of a new marriage pattern.

Table 13.5. Trends in crude marriage rates (i.e. number of marriages per 1000 population)

Country	1932	1946	1950	1959	1970	1981	1984
Belgium	7.6	9.0	8.3	7.2	7.6	6.5	6.1
Finland	6.6	13.0	8.5	7.2	8.6	6.3	6.1
France	7.6	12.8	7.9	7.1	7.7	5.8	5.1
German Democratic Republic	7.9	6.7	11.8	9.3	7.7	7.7	8.0
Federal Republic of Germany			10.8	9.2	7.2	5.8	5.9
Great Britain	7.5	8.7	8.1	7.5	8.1	7.5	7.0
Hungary	8.1	10.9	11.4	9.1	9.3	7.2	7.1
Italy	6.4	9.2	7.7	7.8	7.4	5.5	5.3
Netherlands	6.9	11.4	8.2	7.8	9.5	6.0	5.5
Norway	6.2	9.5	8.3	6.5	7.5	5.4	5.4
Poland	8.3	-	10.8	9.5	8.5	9.0	7.7
Slovenia (YU)*	-	9.7		8.7	8.2	6.3	5.8
Soviet Union**	-	-	11.6	12.6	9.7	10.3	-
Sweden	6.7	9.5	7.7	6.7	5.3	4.4	4.4

Sources: *U.N. Demographic Yearbook, Monthly Bulletin of Statistics*, Vol. XXXIX, No. 4 (1981-4).

*Statistični letopis SR Slovenije (Statistical Yearbook of Slovenia), Ljubljana, 1981, 1983.
**The Soviet National Report was used as a source.

New trends in marital behaviour show that the 'interest' in early marriage and in marriage in general has diminished, not only for reasons of social insecurity but also because a growing number of young people today postpone marriage, or they do not want to marry at all preferring instead alternative 'marriage-like' arrangements. Legal marriage, once considered as the only legitimate and appropriate form of partnership, has given way to a variety of optional non-traditional forms of 'living together'. Such arrangements are called cohabitation.

In several European countries, and particularly in the rural regions cohabitation goes far back. Couples did not marry unless the woman gave birth to one or more children to prove she was fertile. In the middle class cohabitation was rare, only sometimes practised by widows who were anxious that in case of remarriage, the benefits they were entitled to as widows would be withdrawn. The phenomenon, as it appears now, may be considered new. And this may also be one of the reasons that statistical evidence on recent forms of 'living together' is, except for a few countries, scarcely available.

Cohabitation seems to be most frequent in the Nordic countries. In Sweden 'The decrease in nuptiality rate has been accompanied by an increase in the rate of cohabitation without marriage. It is an increase in cohabitation rate higher or more evident than the decrease in marriage rate. In 1960 the percentage of unmarried cohabiting couples of all couples was 1 percent and thus 99 percent were married ... The estimate of 1979 is about 15 percent' (Trost, 1980, p. 14).

Cohabitation has become increasingly widespread also in Finland and other Nordic countries, it is growing in the Netherlands, France, Great Britain and Slovenia (Yugoslavia) but is still much less frequent in Belgium and Italy.[3]

Cohabitation is practised also in the GDR where about 25 per cent of women aged 18-35 live with their partners without marrying. Data from other Eastern European countries are rather meagre, but it may be assumed that the number of cohabitations have increased also in them. Officially unregistered cohabitations are growing. During the census interviews women called such relationships 'marriage' while men preferred to call them 'a variety of a bachelor state', as it is stated in the National Report from the USSR. This also explains the number of married women being greater than that of married men by 178,000 in 1939, by 437,000 in 1959 and by 1,333,000 in 1970. (Kharchev and Yasnaya, 1983, p. 14).

Cohabitation as a trial marriage

Increased cohabitation among the young is nowadays related to the fact that young people more often begin their 'living together' without marrying. Nevertheless, there is a strong tendency in young people to marry after they have lived together for a certain time. 'This appears more and more to be a form of life planned by those concerned as an interim solution to the legal contraction of marriage', is reported from the FRG, where in a survey 37 per cent of those asked for their motives for cohabitation stated that they intend to marry in the next three years, 36 per cent simply wanted to test the strength of their partnership and only 27 per cent lived together without thinking of marriage (Nave-Herz, 1981, p. 11).

Some authors argue that cohabitation is only a variation of marriage (Trost, 1983, pp. 225-42; Liljeström, 1985, p. 3) and that cohabiting couples actually live under marriage-like conditions. There is even a tendency to give this relationship a legal status. In some countries notably Sweden, Denmark and Slovenia (Yugoslavia) there is a tendency to legally equalise cohabitation with formal marriage.

To a large extent, cohabital unions have everywhere functioned more as a trial marriage than as a more permanent alternative to formal marriage. And, at least for the time being, there is little evidence that cohabitation will replace marriage.

It appears that there are still good reasons for people to marry. Most young cohabiting couples marry once they have children. It is estimated that 30 to 40 per cent of all children in Europe (in some countries even up to 50 per cent) are conceived out of marriage, but by the time the child is born only a much smaller proportion of mothers are not married. 'German women', it is said in the National Report from the FRG, 'do not believe in having children born in non-legalized marriages' (Nave-Herz, 1981, p. 11), and this appears to be the prevalent attitude in other countries as well. It is generally believed that a legalised bond between parents gives the child a better chance that he or she will grow up in a complete family and provides him or her with more support and security.

Divorces

The postponement of marriage and the increasing number of cohabitations especially among young people, may also be related to the high risk of divorce perceived in all European countries. While in the past divorces were difficult and practically non-existent, in the course of this century, the number of divorces has gradually increased. After a relatively short stable period immediately after the war, the inevitable period of adjustment and readjustment to common life, the following decades were marked by an accelerated increase in divorce, to reach their highest numbers in the 1980s (Table 13.6). The incidence varies between countries, but there is not a single country in Europe where divorces have not increased during recent decades. According to a study carried out in Vienna in 1977, if the trend continues in the same way, about 85 per cent of all marriages in Europe will be dissolved by divorce in the year 2000 (Wiegman, 1980, p. 16).[4]

The increase in divorce may be attributed to different factors. First there is the liberalisation of divorce laws. Ten years ago the range of variation of legal provisions in this respect was still considerable in Europe. While at that time in some countries, e.g. Hungary, Poland and Yugoslavia, divorce by mutual agreement was already admitted, in countries of Southern and Western Europe the divorce law reform was still under debate.

Table 13.6. Trends in crude divorce rates (number of divorces per 1000 mid-year population)

	1965	1975	1980-81
Belgium	0.58	1.26	1.48
Finland	1.00	1.98	1.98
France	0.71	1.16	1.59
German Democratic Republic	1.56	2.47	2.90
Federal Republic of Germany	0.99	1.73	1.78
Great Britain	0.78	2.43	2.92
Hungary	2.00	2.47	2.56
Italy	-	0.19	0.19
Netherlands	0.50	1.47	2.00
Norway	0.69	1.39	1.74
Poland	0.75	1.21	1.12
Slovenia (Yugoslavia)*	1.20	1.30	1.30
Soviet Union	1.56	3.08	3.47
Sweden	1.24	3.14	2.43

Source: *U.N. Demographic Yearbooks*, 1970, 1982; National Reports.
Statistični letopis SR Slovenije (Statistical Yearbook of Slovenia), Ljubljana, 1983.

Only less than ten years later the new divorce laws introduced in other European countries transformed the basis of divorce away from a system based on a matrimonial offence, guilt and punishment 'towards one based on irretrievable breakdown, mutual responsibility and need' (Smart, 1982, p. 137). Divorce by consent made it much easier for the partners to get their marriage dissolved.

It may though be hypothesised that even with no changes in the divorce law, but as a result of a democratisation of relationships between partners and the increased independence of women, divorces (or divorce-like arrangements) would probably have increased. Even Catholic Europe has gradually given in and introduced previously unacceptable solutions.

Data from various countries indicate that divorce affects couples at all stages of their married life, but the tendency is most common among young couples in the early years of their marriage. The high divorce rate in young marriages is explained by the high number of premarital pregnancies in this group and the inability of young men and women to cope with the emotional conflicts and financial difficulties they experience when they want to start their own households (Dominian, 1980, pp. 270-2).

There are other factors, too, which may affect divorce. The most common explanation refers to the individualisation and privatisation of marriage. Divorces are seen as a sign of rising personal expectations, a greater orientation towards personal happiness and self-realisation, and a move away from traditional values such as conformity and duty (Liljeström, 1985, p. 5).

When divorces were rare and rested on the idea of matrimonial offence, divorcees and particularly divorced women could not escape the notion of 'shame' and 'guilt'. Divorces for them had difficult economic and social consequences. 'Today, they [the divorcees] rarely encounter exclusion from social groups due to their civil status, an attitude which was quite common even in the first part of the century. To be divorced is irrelevant to one's career. It is not a stigma to conceal when new heterosexual partnerships are established, and it does not decrease the reliability of the person in the judgment of the majority' (Cseh-Szombathy, 1985, p. 75).

Patterns of marriage

To construct the marriage patterns three indicators were used for which comparable data were available. These were the crude marriage rate, the divorce rate and estimates on cohabitation.

In the table below three patterns can be recognised: the first is the *low marriage pattern* most characteristic of Italy, France the Netherlands, Norway, Sweden and the FRG, the second is the *medium marriage pattern* found in Belgium, Slovenia (Yugoslavia) and Finland, and the third is the *high marriage pattern* found in Poland, the GDR the USSR, Great Britain and Hungary.

*Table 13.7. Marriage patterns in 14 European countries**

	I	NL	N	S	F	FRG**	B	SL (YU)	SF	PL	GDR	SU	GB	H
Marriage rates	1	1	1	1	1	1	2	2	2	3	3	3	3	3
Divorces	1	3	3	3	2	2	2	2	3	1	3	3	3	3
Cohabitations	0	2	2	3	2	0	1	1	2	0	3	1	0	0

*Countries with marriage rates (in 1984) less than 6.0% were given value 1, those ranking from 6.0 to 7.0% were given value 2, and those with marriage rates higher than 7.0% were given value 3 (for data see Table 13.5). Countries with divorces per 1000 marriages less than 150 were given value 1, those from 150 to 300 were given value 2 and those with more than 300, value 3 (cf. Table 13.8).

Countries with no data available on cohabitation were given value 0, with cohabitation estimates of less than 2.0% were given value 1, those with estimates from 2.0% to 10% were given value 2 and those with estimates higher than 10% value 3. (For the estimates on cohabitation information is taken from the National Reports.) For countries' symbols see note to the table on p. 267.

**The crude marriage rate in the FRG comes close to 6.0 so it might as well be placed in group 2.

The data suggest that in some countries where marriage rates are low, or have recently decreased, and the percentage of young marriages declined, divorces are somewhat less frequent than in countries with high marriage rates and an excess of young marriages. Nevertheless, this relationship is not at all complete and there are exceptions to all three patterns. The most extreme exception is Sweden, where low marriage rates are coupled with the highest divorce incidence and cohabitation in Europe, and Poland where, on the contrary, high marriage rates are accompanied by low divorce rates. High marriage rates seem to go along with high divorce rates also in the GDR, the USSR, Hungary and Great Britain.

In addition, some regularities in the relationship between marriage rates and cohabitation may be perceived. In the first pattern, where marriage rates are low, cohabitation is somewhat more frequent, especially so in Sweden. And vice versa, in countries with a higher marriage rate, cohabitation seems to be lower with the exception of the GDR, where both the marriage rate and cohabitation are high.

Table 13.8. Divorces per 1000 marriages (1980-81)

Belgium	238[a]	Italy	135[b]
Finland	320	Netherlands	333
France	254	Norway	320
German Democratic Republic	349	Poland	125
Federal Republic of Germany	265	Slovenia (Yugoslavia)	201[c]
Great Britain	411	Soviet Union	332[d]
Hungary	355	Sweden	509

Source: *U.N. Demographic Yearbook*, 1982, Tables 31 and 32.
[a]L. Siercu, 1984, National Report.
[b]Sgritta and Saporiti, National Report, p. 166 - separated included.
[c]*Statistični letopis SR Slovenije* (Statistical Yearbook of Slovenia), Ljubljana, 1984.
[d]Kharchev and Yasnaya, 1983, National Report, p. 39.

So far the findings confirm that marriage patterns have altered. Changes are underway in all European societies which seem to give much more room for a new articulation of the concept of marriage. Partner choice and partner cohesion are undergoing considerable shifts from societal towards an individual control. The latter depends more on personality factors, interpersonal relationships and individual values and norms than on social structures and pressures. Marriage is no longer seen as a life-long relationship, and the marriage breakdown is acknowledged as a 'normal' end of a marital union, 'as a symptom of the wish of many to have a second opportunity when the first, and in traditional terms, the only attempt has failed' (Kirk, 1976, p. 20).

However, not all men and women are in the position to choose and to change their marital relationship. They may be restricted by cultural and individual constraints and not least by objective circumstances.

Cultural and especially religious beliefs may have an important impact and influence on marriage behaviour. It may be hypothesised on the basis of our data that men and women in countries with a predominantly Catholic tradition - Belgium, Italy, Poland and Slovenia (Yugoslavia) - practise divorce less frequently than people in other countries, but again there are exceptions and it does not explain the whole variety of marriage patterns and the frequency with which these patterns may be found in particular countries.

Different forms of marriage behaviour may be also instrumental in the achievement of other, for example material, objectives. Namely, people may marry, may marry young or at a later age, divorce, remarry or cohabit if, for example, this helps them to improve or maintain their standard of living. In countries where housing is still a great problem (e.g. in Hungary and the USSR), and if the housing policy gives priority to married couples, young people will marry and usually do so very young. This and some other benefits are good reasons for people to get married even though the risk of divorce may be high. On the other hand, a single mother may prefer to cohabit and not to marry in countries where social provisions favour her position (e.g. in the GDR, Sweden, Finland, partly also in Slovenia (Yugoslavia). Similar assumptions can also be made in case of divorce and remarriage.

There may be circumstances in which divorcees are tempted to marry and others in which a second marriage would be dys-functional. It was previously pointed out that most cohabiting couples marry when they have children, usually before the birth of the first child. Whether they would prefer not to marry if normative regulations and social provisions made them feel more confident is not clear. We also do not know how many cohabiting couples would marry if this would be to their and their children's advantage.

Time and space do not allow more examples which could be employed to show that marriage or marriage-like status is not only a value in itself but can, in many circumstances which people can hardly influence or manipulate, become instrumental in the achievement of other goals not inherent in marriage. These and similar, very 'practical', considerations should, in my opinion, be given more room in our theoretical thinking about family change, and especially so when we study family modernisation in a comparative perspective.

Changes in reproductive
patterns and in forms of parenting

Reproductive patterns

No other trend of family change in Europe has been as homogeneous in such a short time as the decline in births. Following the baby boom after the Second World War, birth rates in the European countries resumed their historic decline. In some countries the decline was steady and even, whereas others experienced a sudden drop in the 1950s or in the 1960s[5] (Table 13.9).

Table 13.9. Trends in crude birth rates (i.e. number of births per 1000 population)

	1950	1959	1970	1979	1982	1983-84
Belgium	15.6	17.4	14.7	12.4	12.7	11.9
Finland	24.5	18.9	13.7	13.5	13.7	13.8
France	20.7	18.4	16.7	13.8	14.7	13.8
German Democratic Republic	16.9	17.1	13.9	13.9	14.4	13.7
Federal Republic of Germany	16.5	17.6	13.3	9.4	10.1	9.5
Great Britain	16.3	16.9	11.0	12.3	12.8	13.0
Hungary	20.9	15.2	14.7	15.7	12.5	11.9
Italy	19.6	18.4	16.8	12.6	10.9	10.6
Netherlands	22.7	21.3	18.4	12.6	12.5	11.8
Norway	19.1	18.0	17.0	12.8	12.5	12.1
Poland	30.7	24.9	16.7	19.0	19.4	18.9
Slovenia (Yugoslavia)*	24.4	18.0	17.0	16.2	14.5	13.5
Soviet Union**	-	-	-	18.2	18.9	20.1
Sweden	16.4	14.1	13.6	11.3	11.1	11.3

Sources: *U.N. Demographic Yearbook*, 1983; *Monthly Bulletin of Statistics*, UN, Vol. LXXXIX, No. 4, 1985.

Statistični letopis SR Slovenije (Statistical Yearbook of Slovenia), Ljubljana, 1971, 1981, 1983. Prvi stat. podatki za leto 1985 z oceno. Zavod SR Slovenije za Statistiko.

**In the European part of the USSR the birth rates in 1980 and 1982 were as follows:

	1980	1982		1980	1982
Russian SFSR	15.9	16.6	Belorussian SSR	16.0	16.2
Latvian SSR	14.0	14.6	Ukrainian SSR	14.8	14.8
Estonian SSR	15.0	15.4	Moldavian SSR	20.0	20.6
Lithuanian SSR	15.1	15.2			

Source: National Report.

The decline in fertility goes hand in hand with changes in structural elements. Today, the majority of parents decide for one, or a maximum of two children. The ratio of first and second order to all births has everywhere increased, while the ratio of third and more births has decreased. In only three countries in our sample - Hungary, Poland and the USSR - is the average number of children per woman more than two; in all other countries it is less (Table 13.10).

Table 13.10. Average number of children per women (1980-85)

Belgium	1.7	Italy	1.9
Finland	1.7	Netherlands	1.6
France	1.9	Norway	1.8
German Democratic Republic	1.7	Poland	2.3
Federal Republic of Germany	1.4	Slovenia (Yugoslavia)*	1.9
Great Britain	1.7	Soviet Union	2.4
Hungary	2.2	Sweden	1.7

Source: A 1982 People Wallchart; National Reports.
Statistični letopis SR Slovenije (Statistical Yearbook of Slovenia), Ljubljana, 1983.

In most couples the first child is born soon after marriage, and if parents decide to have more children, they try to have them and bring them up without great differences in age (Schubnell, 1976, p. 35). Most women terminate their fertility period by the time they are 30 years old (Table 13.12, see p. 288).

It goes beyond the scope of this chapter to analyse the various causes of the decline in fertility in Europe. This question does not need to be fully considered here since it has been dealt with in Saporiti's chapter. Changes in fertility behaviour are, according to Saporiti, linked to modern life in urbanised settings, to the technology of birth control, to the changing role of women and, most important, to the changing functions of the child.

In forming the European reproduction patterns we have used four indicators: the crude birth rate, the fertility rate, the fertility rate of mothers aged 20-4, and the average number of children per woman.

So, in spite of the general trend characterised by a decline in births, reproductive patterns show differences. Extremely low reproductive values are found in two Western and high reproductive values in two Eastern European countries, which may reflect the old traditions in fertility behaviour in the European West and East.

Table 13.11. *Reproductive patterns in 14 European countries**

	FRG	NL	S	I	B	H	SF	N	GB	GDR	F (YU)	SL	SU	PL
Crude birth rates	1	1	1	1	1	1	2	2	2	2	2	2	3	2
Fertility rates	1	1	1	1	2	2	2	2	2	2	3	3	2	3
Fertility rates of mothers 20-24	1	1	1	1	2	3	1	2	2	3	2	3	3	3
Average number of children	1	1	2	2	2	3	2	2	2	2	2	2	3	3

*Countries with crude birth rates (in 1983-4) less than 12.0 per 1000 were given value 1, those with birth rates 12.0 to 14.0 per 1000 were given value 2, and those with birth rates higher than 14.0 value 3 (for data see Table 13.9).

Countries with live birth rates per 1000 female in their fertile age (15-45) less than 50.0% were given value 1, those with a fertility rate from 51.0 to 60.0% were given value 2, and those with fertility rates higher than 60.0%, value 3 (cf. Table 13.12).

Countries with live birth rates of mothers aged 20-4 less than 100.0 were given value 1, those with rates from 100.0 to 150.0, value 2, and those with live birth rates higher than 150.0 value 3 (cf. Table 13.12).

Countries where the average number of children per woman was 1.6 and less were given value 1, those with an average from 1.7 to 1.9 value 2, and those with an average of 2.0 and more value 3 (cf. Table 13.10). For country symbols see the table on p. 267.

Nevertheless, it is very difficult to speak, on the basis of this analysis, of a typical Western and a typical Eastern reproductive pattern since low reproductive values may be found also in the Eastern European countries, while higher values occur in Western countries, too.

Table 13.12. Live birth rates by age of mother (per 1000 corresponding female population) around 1980

	All	-20	20-24	25-29	30-34
Belgium	51.9	23.4	116.0	124.4	54.1
Finland	51.8	16.9	88.7	118.3	69.5
France	62.5	18.1	122.5	144.0	79.7
German Democratic Republic	56.9	51.1	175.6	100.9	36.2
Federal Republic of Germany	40.8	13.9	78.8	107.1	64.6
Great Britain	54.6	28.4	107.9	12.9	69.5
Hungary	55.8	63.0	155.9	100.6	40.6
Italy	49.0		60.6	113.6	67.2
Netherlands	49.4	9.0	74.6	139.8	66.9
Norway	54.1	23.8	107.0	120.5	63.0
Poland	74.6	32.1	177.6	133.6	66.8
Slovenia (Yugoslavia)*	63.6	56.3	176.8	112.6	51.3
Soviet Union**	55.5	15.8	155.9		63.1
Sweden	49.0	14.5	90.3	120.6	71.7

Source: U.N. Demographic Yearbook, 1981-4.

*Source: Statistični letopis SR Slovenije (Statistical Yearbook of Slovenia), Ljubljana, 1981.

**In the European part of the USSR the live birth rates were as follows:

	All	-20	20-24	25-29	30-34
Ukrainian SSR	56.5	34.9	173.8	103.6	69.3
Belorussian SSR	64.5	27.9	174.9	128.7	85.4

It is possible to distinguish between a *low reproduction pattern* that appears in the FRG, the Netherlands, Sweden and Italy and a *medium reproduction pattern* found in Finland, France, the GDR, Great Britain, Norway and Slovenia (Yugoslavia). Between the first and the second there is an intermediary pattern found in Belgium and Hungary, where crude birth rates are extremely low but all the other values moderate or even high. Only the USSR and Poland demonstrate the *high reproduction pattern*.

Pattern variations in reproduction may partly be explained by cultural traditions and by differences in marriage practices. Where women marry early, as for example in Hungary, Poland and the USSR, they are more likely to give birth to a greater number of children than women who postpone marriage to a later age.

In addition to demographic and cultural factors influencing reproduction, we are inclined to see in our data an association between reproductive values and the extent to which the state through its institutional arrangement succeeds in providing the family with resources sufficient to maintain a balance between the 'losses' and the 'gains' of parenthood. (See the discussion on the 'wealth flow' theory in Saporiti's chapter in this book.) Those resources seem particularly important which provide enhanced protection to the working mother, and help her to combine more easily her occupational role with motherhood (e.g. longer maternity leave, a well-developed network of childcare institutions). These provisions may well have limited influence, and the effects may not be dramatic. Nevertheless, fertility levels are maintained higher where these measures have been applied on a larger scale (e.g. in the GDR) than in countries where provisions remained insufficient or where family policies are less interventionist.

Forms of parenting

Equally important, although more difficult to explore than demographic trends, are the various forms of parenting in modern societies. It is true that there are still many women who avoid making deliberate choices and take the risk of an unplanned pregnancy, but on the other hand those who want to do so have the 'luxury' of choosing between parenthood and non-parenthood. Improved technical means of contraception, and increased knowledge about their use have made it possible for women as well as for men to decide whether they wish to have children, how many children they want and when. Current literature suggests that fertility motivation can be analysed 'in terms of how the value of having children interplays with the alternatives, and with the costs, barriers and facilitators in the situation to produce an actual motivation' (Rapoport, Rapoport and Strelitz, 1980, pp. 140-1).

Some authors expressed their opinion that one of the main contradictions in the European family of today has to do with the increased freedom of conjugal choice on the one hand and the constraints inherent in parenthood on the other (see, e.g., Dahlström's chapter in this book). People may decide to have a child but once they become a parent there is no way to 'get out' of this relationship, or as Rossi says (1974, p. 108): 'We can have an ex-spouse and ex-jobs but not ex-children.' One may terminate an unsatisfying marital arrangement but one cannot terminate parenthood, even though it may, at a certain point in life, become incompatible with other, for example marriage or career, aspirations.

In the past it was unthinkable that a woman would deliberately choose not to have children and even nowadays voluntary childlessness in married women is not frequent. Most women desire to become mothers (and we believe this is true also for fathers) but the very fact that they can decide about procreation, and that they sometimes also choose to avoid motherhood, even though they may be under social pressure to procreate (Bandt, 1984) must be recognised as a very important change.

One-parent families

With marriages becoming less stable, and with the growing number of single independent women who wish to parent and decide to have children without having a permanent partner, the one-parent family in its different variations has become widespread in European societies.

As Laslett (1977) pointed out, there have always been one-parent families in our societies. Men and women often died before their children grew up, fathers deserted their wives and children, and children were born to unmarried mothers. But it may be assumed that never before were such a large number of lone parents responsible for the nurturing of their child(ren) for a considerable period of time.

There are various one-parent family types. They may be caused by divorce, long-lasting separations, desertion or death of one partner. Furthermore, one-parent families may be headed by the man or by the woman. It has been the case in our patriarchal tradition that one-parent families were mostly headed by women. Men were expected to be in the public world of work, women in the home with their children. Even though this is still overwhelmingly the situation, signs that this may change in the future are visible. Although not frequent yet, it appears that more and more fathers wish to retain their children after divorce, and win custody. This shift may be recognised as another important change in parenting forms. 'Single-parent fathers', writes Jackson (1980, p. 167), 'could be amongst the unwitting and often unlucky heralds of a new sense of future parenthood'.

Cross-national comparable data on one-parent families are not very illuminating. The methodology of data collection varies from country to country, is inconsistent and unsatisfactory for identifying family units consisting of one-parent and his or her children.

First, it may be assumed that quite a large number of one-parent families do not live in independent households, but together with relatives and are thus treated as part of the extended family households. On the other hand, there are families registered as 'one-parent' who in fact are not of this type. Heads of these families may cohabit with either the biological parent of the children or another partner, but do not want to admit it because they might lose supplementary benefits (Deven and Cliquet, 1986).

This partly explains the differences between countries. Data from 14 European countries on one-parent families (mostly woman headed) convey the fact that the incidence of such family forms vary from 15 per cent in Finland to only 2.8 per cent in the USSR (Table 13.13). It may be hypothesised, however, that the extremely high proportion of one-parent families in some countries, notably Finland, the GDR, Hungary, Poland, Slovenia (Yugoslavia), are the consequence of different definitions of one-parent families, including also cohabiting couples in some countries, whereas the low percentage of one-parent families in the USSR may to some extent be explained by the greater proportion of three-generational family households in this country.

Table 13.13. Percentage of one-parent families in all families around 1981

Belgium	4.7	Netherlands	5.1
Finland	15.0	Italy	10.1
France	9.6	Norway	11.0
German Democratic Republic	12.0	Poland	13.3
Federal Republic of Germany	-	Slovenia (Yugoslavia)	14.2
Great Britain	8.0	Soviet Union	2.8
Hungary	10.2	Sweden	12.4

Source: National Reports.

Another explanation for the different frequencies and pattern variation of one-parent families may be derived from the fact that one-parent family relationships are not necessarily permanent. A significant proportion of single parents marry or remarry after they have been alone with their children for a shorter or longer period. In view of the high probability of marriage and remarriage, the one-parent family relationship may, for the majority of parents, be considered only as a transitory phase in their family life cycle rather than a permanent family arrangement.

Table 13.14. Trends in births to unmarried mothers as percentage of all births

	1960	1970	around 1980
Belgium	2.1	2.7	
Finland	4.2	5.8	
France	6.4	6.8	14.2
German Democratic Republic	11.4	13.3	
Federal Republic of Germany	6.1	5.5	
Great Britain	5.4	8.4	
Hungary	5.5	5.8	
Italy	3.1	3.3	5.1
Netherlands	1.3	2.1	
Norway	3.7	-	
Poland	4.5	-	
Slovenia (Yugoslavia)*	9.0	9.0	14.0
Soviet Union	6.9	7.3	-
Sweden	11.3	22.0	37.5

Source: *U.N. Demographic Yearbook*, 1969 and Kirk, Livi Baci and Szabady, 1976, Vol. 1 of Country Reports, National Reports.
Statistični letopis SR Slovenije (Statistical Yearbook of Slovenia), Ljubljana, 1965, 1969, 1981.

Another indirect measure of one-parent families is the proportion of children born to unmarried mothers (Table 13.14). It turns out, however, that this connection is not at all clear. In some countries, as for example the GDR, Slovenia (Yugoslavia) and Sweden, both the number of one-parent families and the proportion of children born to unmarried mothers are high, whereas in some other countries no positive correlation between the two can be found. Such is the case in Finland, where the number of births to unmarried mothers is moderate in comparison with other countries, but the proportion of one-parent families is among the highest in Europe. The same is also true for Hungary, Italy, Norway and Poland (cf. Tables 13.13 and 13.14).

Towards convergence in diversity

When all three patterns - the work, marriage and reproductive patterns - are combined, we get an 'integrated' family-life pattern. This combination allows for an analysis of the relationships between the three aspects of family life within each country, and the identification of similarities and dissimilarities between them.

Table 13.15. The family life patterns in 14 European countries

	FRG	I	NL	SW	GB	B	F	N	SF	SL (YU)	H	GDR	P	SU
Work pattern	L	L	L	M	L	L	M	M	M	M	M	H	H	H
Marriage pattern	L	L	L	L	H	M	L	L	M	M	H	M	H	H
Reproductive pattern	L	L	L	L	M	M	M	M	M	M	M	H	H	H

If the low work, marriage and reproductive patterns are marked with the symbol L, the medium patterns by symbol M, and the high patterns by the symbol H, we obtain three distinguished patterns showing the low, medium and high values respectively of the three sub-patterns.

This scheme reveals a distribution of countries similar to those found in the previous analysis with the presentation of three Western countries on the lower, and the GDR, Poland and the USSR on the highest extremes. One is indeed tempted to see real differences separating two cultural styles deeply rooted in the European tradition if some 'irregularities' did not distort the picture. The pattern characterised by the lowest values appears in three countries which geographically and culturally pertain to different parts of Europe. The FRG and the Netherlands have always belonged to Western Europe, whereas Italy has been part of the Mediterranean family tradition. The same applies to the three countries with the highest values. This pattern is found in three countries among which only two are Eastern, Poland and the USSR. The GDR cannot be included in the group of countries of Eastern Europe because neither by its territory, nor by its population has the GDR historically or culturally ever belonged to Eastern Europe.

Then the medium pattern is found in one Nordic country, namely Finland, and two countries, Slovenia (Yugoslavia) and Hungary, which were traditionally connected with Central Europe. In addition to the relatively pure patterns, also intermediate patterns can be identified in the West, North and South of Europe. Belgium, Great Britain, Sweden, Norway and France are somewhere in between the low and medium patterns, and it would be difficult to decide which group of countries they resemble more.

It would be equally misleading to interpret variations in family patterns in terms of differences in the political systems dividing Europe into the capitalist and socialist part. A close examination of the four European family patterns furnishes evidence that it is not correct to make a distinction between Western and Eastern European countries. Our data suggest that changes and variations in family patterns can be predicted neither from the duration of the industrialisation process, the stage of economic development, wealth, political ideologies nor from cultural traditions. Families in the East, North, West, South and Centre of Europe disclose similarities in some, and dissimilarities in other elements of family patterns.

Scrutiny of our data further suggest that pattern variations cannot be interpreted within the framework of the modernisation theories (for a discussion on modernisation theories see Rapoport's and Jallinoja's chapters in this book). These theories assume that work, marriage and reproductive behaviour are related in a very particular way, and that change in one life sphere entail concomitant changes in the other two. According to the modernisation theories, marriage instability is coupled with low fertility, and both are the consequence of the wife being gainfully employed.

Indeed, not much imagination is needed to see that findings yielded by this analysis do not conform to these theories, at least when relationships are studied on the macro-level of societies. Moreover, our study indicates that the trend may go in the opposite direction. We found that in countries with the lowest employment rates of women there are fewer divorces and fertility is lower than in countries where female employment is high. Countries where women are more likely to be employed have higher marriage rates, in spite of the high divorce rate, and fertility is higher than in countries where women's employment is low. Fertility is highest in countries where female employment is also the highest.

This supports our argument that changes in one aspect of family life may occur independently from developments in other dimensions of family behaviour, since these behaviours may be influenced by very specific internal and external forces which may provoke change in one, without changing behaviour in other spheres of family life. Social forces that provoke changes in the work pattern, for example, do not significantly influence the other two patterns that obviously obey different rules and regularities.

Change-promoting factors are very complex and may influence family life in various ways, with different effects in different social settings.

There is not just one or a limited number of specific causes for patterns to develop in a certain direction, but there is a very complicated interplay of cause-effect relationships. Sometimes variations may be explained only by very specific circumstances in particular countries, being rooted in the past or coming about as a consequence of recent events. Such was, for example, the economic and political crisis of the 1970s. (For the different changes this crisis produced in family life in various European societies see Sgritta's chapter in this book.) Some of these circumstances and the changes they cause may be temporary, others may have long-term effects. Some may be incidental, others carefully planned. And just because of these very specific circumstances that may affect family life in very particular ways, we hesitate to give the family life patterns names that are laden with value judgements influenced by the modernisation concept. There is no justification in either theory or empirical evidence for our patterns to be ranked lower or higher on the modernisation dimension, especially not if the modernisation process is understood as a change in a certain direction. There is no indication in our analysis that the evolution of family life patterns in European societies would follow a certain pattern to become the model for family modernisation in Europe. Not one but a variety of family patterns have emerged, have become legitimate and practised by people in accordance with their needs and living conditions. And just because the living conditions and the social forces that influence them are so different in the different European countries, we are inclined to believe that the development will not go in one and the same direction, but will lead to a still greater diversification of family patterns in Europe.

Nevertheless, there is at least one uniform trend in the overall development of family patterns, and this is the trend towards a recognition of diversity (see Rapoport's chapter in this book). Increasing gender symmetry in work patterns, more freedom in conjugal choice and a more hedonistic view of marriage and love, premarital and experimental sexuality, higher marriage instability and alternative forms of 'living together', decreasing fertility and change in forms of parenting, are but a few common consequences of what people in Europe strive to accomplish (see Dahlström's, chapter in this volume). *Convergence to diversity*, which transcends the ideological barriers, is the common underlying feature in the evolution of family life patterns in Europe. Whatever the existing patterns are, they are characterised by the acceptance of diversity that has given men and women the possibility to choose inside the boundaries of the system of available options the life pattern that is best adapted to their own needs and aspirations.

Notes

1. The participation rate in the FRG and Great Britain is 39 per cent, which places them in between the first and the second group.

2. The marriage rate in the USSR has stabilised and has been 10.3 since 1973.

3. In Finland 25 per cent of the urban population aged 25-65 years have cohabited some time in their lives and 2.5 per cent of all couples with children are cohabiting couples. In Norway most cohabiting couples are in their twenties, about 17 per cent. It is estimated that in the Netherlands there are about 6 per cent of cohabiting couples. The corresponding estimate is 1.5 per cent in Belgium, 5.4 per cent in France and 4 per cent in Slovenia (Yugoslavia). In Great Britain 3 per cent of adult women aged 18-49 reported cohabiting (source: National Reports).

4. During the nine-year period from 1965-73 the divorce rate increased by 67 per cent in Sweden (Trost, 1983, p. 230). In France the number of marriages dissolved rose from 10 per cent in 1964 to 16 per cent in 1971. The divorce rate doubled in the FRG in the 1970s and it has increased three times during the last 30 years in the GDR. In Slovenia (Yugoslavia) the number of divorces grew from 1939 in the late 1960s to 2443 in 1981, and in Great Britain the percentage of divorce petitions filed by women has risen from 39 per cent in 1947, to 73 per cent in 1977. Divorces have grown in Poland where the number of divorces rose from 8000 in 1946 to 38,800 in 1980. In the Netherlands divorces have increased nearly five times from 5643 cases in the years 1955-64 to 23,748 in 1979. The only exception is Italy where couples rarely divorce but prefer to separate. Only one in thirty marriage divorces but one in ten dissolves by separation (source: National Reports).

5. The time of the birth rate decrease varied among countries. In Sweden the steepest decrease was perceived in the 1950s when births dropped from 16.4 per 1000 population in the late 1940s to only 13.6 in the 1950s. In Finland the birth rate fell from 27.7 in the late 1940s to 13.1 in the early 1970s. In France, where fertility rates were higher immediately after the Second World War, the birth rate reached its lowest point of 13.6 in 1976. A sharp decline was observed in the FRG, where the birth rate fell from 18.2 in 1964 to only 9.5 in 1979, and in the GDR, where it fell from 17.2 to 10.8 in 1974. The same development has taken place in Hungary, where the lowest point was reached in the period from 1962 to 1964, to be followed by Italy and the Netherlands in the early 1980s.

References

Bandt, M.L., den (1984): 'Voluntary Childless Women. An option explored'. Paper presented at the Second International Interdisciplinary Congress on Women, Groningen, the Netherlands, 17-22 April, 1984

Clason, Ch. (1981): 'The Family in the Netherlands since 1945'. National Report (Vienna Centre background material)

Cseh-Szombathy, L. (1985): 'The Adjustment of the Divorcees'. In: Cseh-Szombathy, L. et al. (eds): *The Aftermath of Divorce - Coping with Family Change*. Akadémiai Kiadó, Budapest

Dahlström, E. (1962): 'Analys av könsrolldebatten' (Analysis of the sexual debate). In: *Kvinnors liv och arbete* (Women's life and work). Stockholm

Deven, F. and Cliquet, R.L. (eds) (1986): 'One-Parent Families in Europe - Trends, Experiments, Implications'. In: *Proceedings of the CBGS International Workshop on One-Parent Families*. Vol. 15 of the series 'Publications of the Netherlands Inter-University Demographic Institute and the Population and Family Study Centre', The Hague - Brussels

Dominian, J. (1980): 'Families in Divorce'. In: Rapoport, R.N. et al. (eds): *Fathers, Mothers and Society. Perspectives on Parenting*. Vintage Books

Gowler, D. and Legge, K. (1983): 'Dual-Worker Families'. In: Rapoport, R.N. et al. (eds): *Families in Britain*. Routledge & Kegan Paul, London

Haavio-Mannila, E. (1983): 'Economic and Family Roles of Men and Women in Northern Europe. A Historical and Cross-National Comparison'. In: Lupri, E. (ed.): *The Changing Position of Women in Family and Society*. E.Brill, Leuven

Jackson, B. (1980) 'Single Parent Families'. In: Rapoport, R., Rapoport, R.N. and Strelitz, Z. (eds): *Fathers, Mothers and Society. Perspectives on Parenting*. Vintage Books

Kharchev, A.G. and Yasnaya, L.V. (1983): 'Changes in the Life Patterns of Families in the USSR after World War 2'. National Report (Vienna Centre background material)

Kirk, M. (1976): 'Law and Marriage in Europe'. In: Kirk, M., Livi Baci, M. and Szabady, E. (eds): *Law and Fertility in Europe*. Ordina Editions, Dolhain

Kirk, M., Livi Baci, M. and Szabady, E. (eds) (1976): *Law and Fertility in Europe*. Ordina Editions, Dolhain

Kurzynowski, A. (1984): 'Changes in the Life Patterns of Families in Poland'. National Report (Vienna Centre background material)

Laslett, P. (1977): *Family Life and Illicit Love in Earlier Generations.* Cambridge University Press, Cambridge

Liljeström, R. (1985): 'Present Day Marriage Patterns and Parental Strategies'. (mimeographed)

Michel, A. (1982): 'Changes of the Life Patterns of Families in France'. National Report (Vienna Centre background material)

Michel, A. (1983): 'Female Marital Behaviour in French Society'. In: Lupri, E. (ed.): *The Changing Position of Women in Family and Society.* E.J. Brill, Leuven

Nave-Herz, R. (1981): 'Changing Family Patterns in the Federal Republic of Germany'. National Report

Rapoport, R., Rapoport, R.N. and Strelitz, Z. (1980): *Fathers, Mothers and Society. Perspectives on Parenting.* Vintage Books

Rossi, A. (1974): 'Transition to Parenthood'. In: Greenblatt, C. et al. (eds): *The Marriage Game.* Random House, New York

Ruhl, H. und Weisse, H. (1982): *Sozialpolitische Maßnahmen - konkret für jeden Tag.* Berlin

Schubnell, H. (1976): 'Law Effecting Contraception, Abortion and Sterilization in Europe'. In: Kirk, M., Livi Baci, M. and Szabady, E. (eds): *Law and Fertility in Europe.* Ordina Editions, Dolhain

Sgritta, G.B. and Saporiti, A. (1980): 'Family, Labour Market and the State in Italy from 1945 to the Present'. Università degli studi di Roma. Facolta di Scienze statistiche demographiche e attuariali. Roma

Shorter, E. (1976): *The Making of the Modern Family.* Fontana Collins, London

Sierakowski, M. (1983): 'Changes in the Life Patterns of Families in Britain'. National Report (Vienna Centre background material)

Siercu, L. (1984): 'Changes in the Life Patterns of Families in Belgium'. National Report (Vienna Centre background material)

Slesarev, G.A. and Yankova, Z.A. (1983): 'Soviet Women in Family and Society'. In: Lupri, E. (ed.): *The Changing Position of Women in Family and Society.* E.J. Brill, Leuven, pp. 261-75

Smart, C. (1982): 'Regulating Families or Legitimating Patriarchy? Family Law in Britain'. *International Journal of Sociology of Law*, pp. 129-47

Stone, L. (1979): *The Family, Sex and Marriage in England 1500-1800.* Penguin Books, Harmondsworth

Trost, J. (1980): 'Changing Family and Changing Society'. In: Trost, J. (ed.): *The Family in Change.* International Library

Trost, J. (1983): 'The Changing role of Swedish Women in Family and Society'. In: Lupri, E. (ed.): *The Changing Position of Women in Family and Society.* E.J. Brill, Leuven

Waerness, K. (1982): 'Changes in Life Patterns of Families in Norway'. National Report

Weinberg, I. (1969): 'The Problem of Convergence of Industrial Societies: A Critical Look at the State of a Theory'. *Comparative Studies in Society and History*, Vol. 11, No. 1, pp. 15 ff

Wiegman, B. (1980): *Das Ende der Hausfrauenehe. Plädoyer gegen eine trügerische Existenzgrundlage.* Hamburg

Wilson, E. (1977): *Women and the Welfare State.* Tavistock Publications, London

14

Methodological and Organisational Considerations

Maren Bak

The first step of what would later become the 'Changing Family Patterns' project was taken in April 1976, when a meeting of the Joint Nordic Committee for Social Research was convened in Aabo, Finland, and decided to establish a working group concerned with comparative family research in the Nordic countries. A number of preparatory meetings took place in Scandinavia, the last one in Copenhagen in June 1978, to develop a comparative family study, if possible not just a Nordic one, but a European comparative project carried out by the European Co-ordination Centre for Research and Documentation in Social Sciences (in short: Vienna Centre). The Vienna Centre convened an international meeting of family researchers in Budapest in November 1978 to develop the ideas further, and in May 1979 at their meeting in Varna, Bulgaria, the Vienna Centre's Board of Directors finally accepted the project 'Changes in the Life Patterns of Families in Europe' as one of its own projects.

Organisation of the comparative research

The co-operative model

Being aware that the social-organisational set-up for the production of knowledge inevitably has consequences for the knowledge produced, it is important to cast some light on the specific organisational model of a Vienna Centre project in comparative research.[1]

Stein Rokkan[2] has developed a typology for gathering information and analysis of data across a number of distinct cultures, societies or nations based on the cross-classification of two major organisational dimensions: the number of nations from which or about which data are gathered and the number of countries participating in the research.

Involved in the organisation of the study		Sites or units of study		
		One nation		Several nations
One nation	I	Single nation	II	Centralised cross-national study
Several nations	III	Co-operative international research in one nation	IV	Co-operative cross-national study

This scheme of models in comparative research has often been discussed in the literature. From the perspective of the present discussion only models II and IV are relevant.

Model II, which Szalai[3] has named 'Safari' research, refers to the kind of social research where one researcher/national research team travels to a number of countries to collect data, sometimes with the help of local experts, sometimes without, and then returns home to compare and analyse the results without any further discussions with, or feedback to, the countries concerned. However, the 'Safari' model is also the model of most anthropological research, which need not necessarily be connected with the notions of imperialism or with white man's safaris.

The advantages of this way of research organisation are of course numerous: the conception of the problem, the theoretical frame and the analysis are made by one person or national research team and thus do not have to contain any compromises.

Model IV, the co-operative model as practised by the Vienna Centre, involves international co-operation at each step of the research process. The conception of the problem and the construction of the research instruments are the result of the discussions of the several national research teams involved. The data collection is made by the national teams in their own countries, using, ideally, one common research instrument.

Interpretation and analysis are done nationally as well as internationally.

The organisational model of Vienna Centre projects is thus decentralised collective research. It is basically democratic and egalitarian. All the participating research teams have the same rights and opportunities to influence and steer the research process. The steering function of the Centre is exercised on the same line and level as that of other participants.

The co-operative model of international comparative research does give wide possibilities for participation and for the exchange of ideas - it counteracts ethnocentrism since each step in the research process is discussed in the whole group. But it is also extremely time-consuming and complicated to organise. Democracy takes time, and of course even more so when the participants are geographically spread over Europe, talk different languages and come from different cultures.

The practical realisation of the research presented here has been co-ordinated and developed by the Vienna Centre in co-operation with the project director elected by and from among those participating in the research. When the project became a Vienna Centre project, a Nordic scientific secretary was seconded to the Centre, entrusted with the responsibility of co-ordinating the relating family research. Jens Qvortrup held the position in the period between 1980 and 1982 and Maren Bak from 1983 to 1985. Katja Boh was elected as project director in 1979 and held this responsibility throughout the whole process.

Participants in the project met approximately twice a year throughout the six-year working period at meetings held in almost all the participating countries. Between the meetings the participants worked on the national investigations, wrote the reports, etc.

Financing of the research

The non-hierarchical structure of the Vienna Centre model must also be understood in relation to the sources of research financing. The Centre does not have at its disposal any funds of its own which can finance the research teams. Every researcher or research team has to be able to raise funds for its own part of the research and for the participation in the international meetings of the research group. The lack of a central and guaranteed source to fund the research makes it obviously very complicated to implement a commonly agreed research plan. It makes the whole enterprise vulnerable and dependent on national funds available.

In the Vienna Centre model the funding question is inevitably one of the stumbling blocks. The present project was not different from any other in this respect.

There was a very wide time gap between the first teams which obtained money for the research and the last ones, and some of the interested researchers could not raise the necessary funding at all and eventually had to withdraw. This time gap has meant that empirical data are from different years, the last ones arriving long after the initial deadline for finalising the whole project, and that the teams which had money first were already involved in new projects when the last ones were only starting.

Moreover, the national institutions providing the funds often have specific interests which are not necessarily identical with those of the international comparative research. All the researchers had to 'navigate' between national priorities and the requests of the comparative project. This situation has, of course, influenced the content of the research and hampered the comparability of the data.

Participating countries

In comparative research involving 'nation' as a variable, the criteria for selecting the participating nations have been thoroughly discussed in the theoretical and methodological literature. Depending on whether the purpose of the study is to show similarities or differences, whether it is descriptive or analytical, different principles of selection should be applied.[4]

The Vienna Centre has a basic criterion for the composition of research teams according to the very purpose of the Centre: researchers from at least three Eastern European and three Western European countries should be involved.

Apart from this criterion, it is in reality very difficult to make actual selections of countries as the methodological literature suggests. Personal scientific interests and practical and financial constraints on the researchers for participating in an international comparative research project were in the end the most decisive factors in the composition of the research teams.

The final list of participants in the project included researchers from 14 European countries, of whom the majority have been able to follow the research until the project was concluded in 1985. Project participants came from the following countries: Belgium, Finland, France, FRG, GDR, Great Britain, Hungary, Italy, Netherlands, Norway, Poland, Sweden, USSR, Yugoslavia (Slovenia).

The composition entailed differences over a number of nation-related variables: socialist and capitalist economic systems, Catholic and Protestant religions, countries from North versus South Europe, West versus East Europe, early industrialised and late industrialised countries, to mention only some of them.

The national reports

The research plan had four major parts:

- A historical description, covering the period 1945-80, of the countries involved, resulting in a series of National Reports (Phase 1).
- Conceptualisation and the development of theory for Phase 2 based on the results of Phase 1.
- Empirical research producing new comparable data (Phase 2).
- Comparative analysis and publication (Phase 3).

The National Reports analyse the developments in important societal institutions and in the family in the period between 1945 and 1980. They are based on available national statistics, case studies, etc., relating to a set of commonly decided indicators. They deal with the general economic background and developments in the labour market, social development as reflected in the degree of urbanisation, housing conditions, education, data relating to demographic changes and family structure, and analysis of social policy and its influence on the family. These indicators are analysed on different levels, on that of the family, the state and the economy. Fourteen National Reports were accomplished in this first phase of the project, containing a very rich material on family developments in Europe in the post-war period. These reports showed that in this respect similarities were more apparent than differences. They justified some of the initial assumptions of incompatible demands and conflicting values as far as the relation between family and employment and family and the state is concerned.

Conceptualisation of the empirical research

Based on the knowledge which started to be accumulated in the National Reports, the research group proceeded throughout 1980 to refine the research questions, define the concepts and develop the research instruments for an empirical investigation expected to produce new comparable data. The methodology and the research instruments, the concepts and the variables ideally should be the same and agreed upon by all participants: a Herculean and ambitious task.[5]

The question of securing equivalence of the chosen indicators in comparative research is one of the most challenging endeavours, and some scholars maintain that it is simply impossible. Katja Boh has analysed the experiences gained in establishing comparability and equivalence of concepts in the present project.[6]

'Generally, the examination of the concepts and their meanings takes quite a long time, and a number of meetings are needed until the national teams come to an agreement about which concepts and corresponding indicators are meaningful and can thus be used in a comparative setting. It is interesting to notice here that the international group working on the CFP [Changing Family Patterns] project did not encounter major problems in finding functionally equivalent concepts and indicators for which, it is assumed, there are predominantly culture-bound variables (e.g. marriage, cohabitation, domestic work, paid/unpaid work, division of work, family roles, kinship networks, meaning of work and family), but it was extremely difficult to establish comparability for a number of system-bound concepts (by system here we mean the political and economic systems). I believe that all researchers who have ever been involved in a comparative analysis of social phenomena know how difficult it is to find equivalent indicators for the so-called background variables i.e. questions employed in all studies as independent variables (e.g. type of communities, stratification variables). That is why E. Scheuch (1968) suggested that these variables be standardized. As far as I know, however, no workable solution has been proposed so far, and it seems that international research groups have to go through this tiresome procedure every time a new comparative project is being prepared.'

Life histories

Our research group endeavoured to grasp historical changes and dynamics of family life over time.[7] There was a wish to combine the insight and richness of a qualitative approach with the representative data of a quantitative study. The empirical investigation was thus first planned to consist of two parts: in-depth life-history interviews with a limited number of respondents, to be followed by a structured questionnaire addressed to a larger, more representative sample.

The in-depth interviews should give a life-cycle perspective, dealing with the life history and everyday life of the interviewed person as well as with certain aspects of their parents' life histories, with family career and working career in the focus.

Much of the inspirations in these considerations came from the Swedish team, where life-history interviews had already been carried through.

> 'In order to understand how "history" touches us, how social reforms, labour market policy, efficiency engineering schemes and concentrations of people, capital and power impinge on people's everyday life, we asked women and men to tell us about their lives. Lives which in their turn are interwoven with other people's lives so as to form life patterns.'[8]

Such intensive qualitative life-history interviews were carried out in four of the participating countries (Finland, France, FRG and Sweden). The method was, however, eventually renounced as obligatory for all participating teams for a number of financial and practical reasons. Nevertheless the life-cycle perspective continued to interest the international research group and was included in the common questionnaire.

The questionnaire

It was at this stage in the research process that difficulties arose as to timing and funding. Since preparations for a comparative Nordic project had started already in 1976, national preparations were of course far ahead in these countries compared with the countries which joined the international project in 1979-80.

The Swedish team had obtained money first for a big study dealing with equality between women and men which united the ideas of the international study with national interests. Quite naturally, however, their methodology and sample selection had to fulfil the specific interests of the national study and they could not wait for the finalisation of a commonly agreed upon research instrument which was still far off. They could just try to gear their research as much as possible towards what could be expected to be the common questions. Also the Finnish team had acquired funds quite early and had to start its research.

The elaboration of a common research instrument was accomplished in Moscow in October 1981. This so-called 'Moscow questionnaire', edited by Cristine Clason and Elina Haavio-Mannila, has been the basis for the national investigations. The full questionnaire is very extensive, its main headings covering information about:

A. the interview and its kind (six questions);
B. the interviewee and the household (ten questions);
C. housing (31 questions);
D. the parents/parents-in-law (two questions);
E. working history and life conditions (17 questions);
F. household work (nine questions);
G. parenthood and childcare (19 questions);
H. care of dependent family and household members (19 questions).

The questionnaire contained compulsory as well as optional questions and in each country special national questions were added. The questionnaire was fully structured. This did not mean, however, that each country should necessarily gather this information by means of a highly structured questionnaire. Every country could, on the basis of the Moscow questionnaire, construct its own data-collecting tool but in such a way that comparison along the lines of the coding of the Moscow questionnaire be safeguarded as much as possible.

Although so much effort was put into the accomplishment of a common questionnaire, there remained of course many problems in producing really comparable data.

The whole issue of whether questions and answers can be meaningfully translated from one language (and social reality) into another has preoccupied the methodologists of comparative research for years. Here it was solved by leaving to each national team the possibility of changing the wording and the categories of answers if the content was kept the same.

When the Moscow questionnaire was finished, the Swedish collection of data was already terminated and a first Swedish study had been published. The Finnish data collection was well underway, using a questionnaire based on the first drafts for the European questionnaire. In some countries (e.g. Hungary and Poland) the Moscow questionnaire was translated and hardly changed at all, in others quite extensive adaptations had to be made - this was, for instance, the case in Italy, where funding was very hard to obtain and the study finally was connected to a special investigation concerning social service and health personnel in Rome.

The samples

Early in the conceptualisation phase of the project, the variety in family forms was discussed as well as the differences in roles, expectations, possibilities of different family members.

It was clear, however, that the focus in this study should be on the adult members of the family. The situation of children was portrayed through the parents' interpretation and the solution chosen by the parents. Children were not considered as interviewees in this study. Regarding family forms, in some countries there was an interest in making a special effort to include alternative family forms in the sample; however, having been unable to secure comparability between all the countries involved, this idea was finally dropped.

Already from the outset of the research, it was decided to focus only on an urban population. The units to be studied were households and the sample instructions were the following:

1. The sample should be drawn from an industrial town (or suburb of a big city) which must have been built before the Second World War and have a low concentration of first-generation immigrant workers. Half of the sample should be selected according to the wife's occupation and half according to the husband's.
2. The size of samples should be at least 150 couples (or families). The units of population should consist of three groups:
   a. industrial, manual workers; both sexes.
   b. blue-collar caretakers; only women.
   c. white-collar workers; both sexes.
3. Age: the sample should consist of persons born in the following years: (a) 1920-5, (b) 1940-5, (c) 1955-60.
4. The interviewing should be personal, conducted separately for each partner.

In the Federal Republic of Germany, Finland, Hungary, Italy, the Netherlands, Norway, Poland, Sweden, the USSR and Yugoslavia (Slovenia) it was possible to fulfil the empirical part largely according to the common decisions, although each research team had to make alterations. In France only a small-sample, qualitative interviewing took place, and Belgium, the German Democratic Republic and Great Britain had to withdraw from the second phase.

In Table 14.1 an overview is given of the national samples. Some deviations from the ideal of identical samples are obvious, but it is also noteworthy that many teams were actually able to come quite close to the agreed goals.

When judging the character of the empirical data, it is very important to be aware of the fact that the Swedish, the Finnish and the Norwegian samples are representative ones (for certain groups of population), whereas all other samples cannot be understood as nationally representative; they must be judged as relating to the particular geographical area (town) and occupational group in which interviewing took place.

The National Reports, on the other hand, are based on national statistics as well and when referring to their findings, it is correct to talk of national tendencies or national characteristics.

Table 14.1. Sample descriptions

	Finland	Germany, Federal Republic of	Hungary	Italy	Netherlands
Kind of sample	Random	Random 279 married persons 1950 (1949-51) 1970 (1969-71) 1980 (1979-81)	150 families in an industrial suburb of Budapest. All interviewees finished industrial-technical school. 70 women industrial workers added in 1983. Blue collar skilled workers	300 women (married-separated-divorced-widows or single unmarried) Social service and health personnel of intermediate level	Random sample from couples married 1950 (1948-52) 1960 (1958-62) 1970 (1968-72) 1980 (1978-82)
Children of respondent	Random sample	At least one child	At least one child	At least one child	Random sample
Place	Cities founded before 1965	City of Oldenburg 135,000 inhabitants	Industrial suburb of Budapest	City of Rome	City of Assen 50,000 inhabitants
Towns and Age of respondent	25-65	20-	30-60	25-60	20-60
Sex of respondent	m+f	m+f	m+f	f	m+f (couples)

	Norway	Poland	Sweden	USSR	Yugoslavia (Slovenia)
Size of population interviewed	744 personally interviewed. 409 spouses returned questionnaire. 70 women added, personally interviewed	279 personally interviewed. Either the husband or the wife interviewed on total family situation	150 persons personally interviewed, in half of the sample the man, in the other half the woman	300	132 couples = 264 persons; partly interviewed together, partly separately; personal interviews
Time of interviewing (Moscow questionnaire finished Oct. 81)	Nov. 81-Jan. 82	April-Sept. 83	1982	Nov. 83	1983-84-85
Questionnaire or research instrument	Questionnaire based on the Swedish and the European ones drafted before Moscow meeting	Moscow questionnaire	Moscow questionnaire	Moscow questionnaire adapted to specific research in Rome	Moscow questionnaire
Kind of sample	Random sample chosen from the population 25-64 years, living in cities and towns	Selected from employment lists of enterprises/firms essential in the area; (white and blue collar) 200 married couples	Selected from 1. metalworkers union (men + women); 2. union for manual workers employed by local authorities (women)	Random sample from three districts in the town, of persons over 18 years of age; couples with and without children and single mothers	Random sample of women aged 25-55 in four local communities; if a partner was present he was included in the sample

Children of respondent	Random sample	Random sample	Random sample	Random sample	At least one child
Place	Urban	Industrial part of Warsaw	National	City of Orel 200,000 inhabitants	City of Ljubljana, 300,000 inhabitants City of Celje 50,000 inhabitants
Age of respondent	25-64	25-30/35-40/55-60	20-25/38-40/58-60	18-60	25-55
Sex of respondent	m+f	m+f (couples)	m+f	m+f	m+f
Size of population interviewed	500 personally interviewed 212 spouses returned questionnaire	200 couples = 400 persons couples interviewed together	885 questionnaires mailed and filled in	364 interviewees filled in questionnaire in presence of interviewer	330 persons personally interviewed; if couples, interviewed separately
Time of interviewing	May and Sept. 1983	1983	1980	1983	1982
Questionnaire	Moscow questionnaire similar to the Swedish and Finnish	Moscow questionnaire	Mail questionnaire finished before Moscow questionnaire	Moscow questionnaire	Moscow questionnaire

Data processing and data exchange

All the national data have been computerised. The code-books were translated into English and exchanged among the teams. On the basis of the marginal distributions and the code-books, all participants have had the opportunity to request data and tables from each other. This exchange procedure, however, turned out to be much more time-consuming and complicated than anyone had anticipated. We shall not review this whole tedious process here, just mention a few instances.

First of all it is complicated to know enough of each other's data to make sensible and correct requests, and it is time- and money-consuming to answer the requests, which eventually were not answered systematically as planned and expected. Quite often the financial sources of the project had dried up before all the requests were received and the participants had difficulties in finding the means for producing new tabulations. Some major mail strikes and general disorganisation of mail systems added to the complications, and even more so did of course the prohibition in some countries against sending data across borders before official permission was obtained.

There is no doubt that the extensive material empirical data could have been used to a greater extent and maybe also in a better way in the comparative work. A less ambitious common questionnaire covering fewer and more precise issues would have secured a comparative material easier to handle and an improved actual validity of the comparison. But that would have been at the expense of the wealth of information which characterises the data produced in the present project.

Comparative analysis and the writing of the book

The first draft of the book was already done in 1982. It planned 22 chapters covering, naturally, all the central issues of the questionnaire. The first drafts of chapters, based on the scarce data then available, were discussed in November 1982.

The actual comparative work was left to the individual authors. As there does not exist any specific methodology or technique which could be labelled comparative methodology, the chapters show a wide variety of comparative approaches.

The editors, elected by the research group, have held three meetings (November 1984, May and October 1985). They have advised the authors but have not changed the content of any chapters, this being entirely the responsibility of the individual authors.

During the writing phase it was agreed to reduce the ambitious 22-chapter volume to a more handy size, still covering the main questions of the research. However, reality modified again the ideal. Other tasks started to preoccupy the authors. It became more and more difficult for them to find time to make the necessary amendments and changes in the draft chapters, and so some of the planned chapters unfortunately never saw the light of the day.

Had all the planned chapters actually been finished, the book would have given a more complete picture of the changes in family life patterns, and the connections between state, employment and family could have been more elaborated.

Evaluation

This book is the result of more than six years of work, involving about 25 researchers. Was it worthwhile? Were the time and other resources well used? Was anything important learned and communicated?[9]

The reader of course has to give her or his answer based on the content of this volume. But for the participants the book itself is only a part of the experience - much more was learned and experienced than can be reflected here.

I have tried to distinguish between two different aspects of the outcome of international comparative research:[10] the heuristic outcome and the more strictly taken scientific outcome. What is meant by 'heuristic outcome' is the whole process of scientific exchange of ideas and theories, deepened cultural sensibility towards different ways of perceiving and constructing the world, of seeing one's own culture and social world with the eyes of other people, the experience of trying to explain phenomena which one hitherto considered so self-evident that they needed no explanation, the discovery of one's 'blind spots' in social understanding. This heuristic outcome has been worth all the hardships in which the researchers were involved, and the experiences have spread to and enriched the scientific milieu around the participants. However, when the method to accomplish

313

a scientific aim in comparative research takes the form of surveys and data exchange, the whole scientific and technical 'apparatus' securing this procedure tends to grow so complicated, time- and resource-consuming that the heuristic process suffers or comes eventually to a halt.

Notes

1. The specific organisational and methodological questions in international comparative research as well as the theoretical requirements were in focus when in June 1984 the Vienna Centre organised a training seminar on comparative family research. The papers presented there are collected in the conference report: 'Comparative Family Research. Fourth International Training Seminar on Cross-national Comparative Research'. Vienna Centre, 1984.

2. Rokkan, S.: 'Cross-cultural, Cross-societal and Cross-national Research'. In: *Main Trends of Research in the Social and Human Sciences*. Part I, Paris, UNESCO, 1970, pp. 645-89. Quoted in Veronica Stolte-Heiskanen: 'Organizational Perspectives on Cross-National Family Research'. In: 'Comparative Family Research', op. cit. p. 4.

3. Alexander Szalai: 'The Organisation and Execution of Cross-National Survey Research Projects'. In: *Cross-National Comparative Survey Research - Theory and Practice*, Proceedings of the Round Table conference on cross-national comparative survey research, Budapest, July 1972, Pergamon Press, Oxford, 1977.

4. Elina Haavio-Mannila: 'Comparative Research - Guiding Principles and Practical Experiences'. In: 'Comparative Family Research', op. cit. The article discusses different types of comparison and their methodological implications and comments on the comparability of the data produced in the present project.

5. The scheme which constituted the framework of analysis in the National Reports as well as in the empirical investigations is presented as Table 4.1 (p. 76).

6. Katja Boh: 'General problems of comparative family research'. In: 'Comparative Family Research', op. cit.

7. A very interesting examination of social histories of the modern Western family is given in Lynn Walter: 'Who are They? When is Then? Comparison in Histories of the Western Family'. In: 'Comparative Family Research', op.cit.

8. Rita Liljeström and Edmund Dahlström published in Liljeström, R. and Pahlstring, E.: *Arbetarkvinnor* (Working class women). Stockholm, 1981.

9. For a profound analysis of the kind of knowledge which can be obtained in comparative research see Jens Qvortrup: 'Is comparative research basic or applied research'? In: 'Comparative Family Research', op. cit.

10. Maren Bak: 'Heuristic aims and theoretical problems in comparative social research'. In: 'Comparative Family Research', op. cit.

Appendices

List of Contributors

BAK, Maren was teaching social science in Aalborg University Centre, Denmark, from 1974 to 1982, where she initiated an interdisciplinary research group and edited the resulting series on women's studies. From 1983 to 1985 Nordic scientific secretary at the Vienna Centre, at present a researcher at the Danish National Institute of Social Research. Her primary research fields are: life conditions of women, family, social innovations.

BOH, Katja, research associate at the Institute for Sociology and associate professor of sociology of the family at the Faculty of Sociology, Political Science and Journalism at the University of Ljubljana, Yugoslavia. Her main fields of interest are: family sociology and social policy. She is engaged in a number of projects which have policy implications. She has contributed several chapters to books, written numerous articles for social science journals and papers for national as well as international conferences.

ČERNIGOJ-SADAR, Nevenka, research associate at the Institute for Sociology at the University of Ljubljana, Yugoslavia and Senior Lecturer of Psychology at the Academy of Music. Her main fields of interest are: sociology of the family and leisure. She has published a number of articles and contributed papers to national and international conferences.

DAHLSTRÖM, Edmund, Doctor of Philosophy, Sweden, docent from 1951 at the University of Stockholm. Appointed professor at the University of Gothenburg from 1959. Main research and publication areas are: sociological theory, social structure of Sweden, class structure, industrial organisation and workplace democracy, family functions and gender relations, practical interests and the development of scientific knowledge and the Lappish minority in Sweden.

HAAVIO-MANNILA, Elina, Ph.D. in sociology in 1958, associate professor of sociology at the University of Helsinki, Finland since 1971. She has conducted research on medical and nursing professions, position of women in politics, employment and the family, on Finnish immigrants in Sweden and history of Finnish sociology. She has served in Finnish state committees on marriage law and working time, and been active in international sociological co-operation.

JALLINOJA, Riitta, Ph.D. in sociology, docent at the University of Helsinki, Finland. Her main scientific interest has been in family sociology and women's studies. Her doctoral dissertation was on the active periods of the Finnish Women's Movement, published in 1983.

MICHEL, Andrée, Doctorat d'état in sociology from the University of Paris (Sorbonne) , France, in 1959. She is currently research director at the National Centre of Scientific Research (CNRS), Paris where she founded the Research Group on Sex Roles, the Family and Human Development. She has published widely and been visiting professor at universities in Europe, USA and Canada. She is a member of the editorial board of *Current Sociology*, (GB), *The Journal of Comparative Family Studies* (Canada) and *Nouvelles Questions Féministes* (France).

NAVE-HERZ, Rosemarie, professor of sociology at the University of Oldenburg, Federal Republic of Germany since 1974. She has written several books and articles in the field of family sociology.

RAPOPORT, Rhona, Ph.D., co-director of the Institute of Family and Environmental Research, London, Great Britain. She qualified as a psychoanalyst, has had a continuous interest in health issues, and is now particularly interested in innovations in primary care and new therapies. She is a consultant to a number of bodies, including the Ford Foundation, where she is involved in their programme of affirmative action and changes in families.

SAPORITI, Angelo, educated and at present researcher at the University of Rome, Italy. His main interests are: family sociology, social policy and methodology; he has published several articles on the Italian family and recently co-authored the book *Disegno della Ricerca e Analisi dei Dati* (Research design and data analysis).

SGRITTA, Giovanni B., associate professor of sociology at the University of Rome, Italy. He has published several articles on family, socialisation and social policy. His most important publications are: *La famiglia, la società e i processi di socializzazione* (The family, the society and the process of socialization, 1975) and *Emarginazione, dipendenza e politica sociale* (Exclusion, dependence and social policy, 1984).

VE, Hildur, sociologist, associate professor at the University of Bergen, Norway. She has written articles on gender and class, socialisation, education and family. Present research interests: women's situation in the educational system in the Nordic welfare states; the expanding privatisation of education and its influence on women.

QVORTRUP, Jens, sociologist, graduated from the University of Copenhagen, Denmark in 1971. In the 1970s his main research field was the social structure and living conditions especially in the socialist societies; in recent years he has been preoccupied with comparative sociology and sociology ᶠ childhood. From 1980 through 1982 he was a scientific secretary at the Vienna Centre. He is presently associate professor at the Institute of East-West Research, University Centre of South Jutland, Esbjerg, Denmark.

WAERNESS, Kari, associate professor of sociology at the University of Bergen, Norway. She has done research in social policy and family sociology with particular emphasis on the role of women as well as the relation between informal care in the family and public health and social service.

List of Participants

Belgium:
W. Dumon, Katolieke Universiteit, Leuven.

Finland:
E. Haavio-Mannila and R. Jallinoja, Department of Sociology, University of Helsinki.

France:
A. Michel, F. Battagliola Bedos, Centre National de la Recherche Scientifique, Paris.

Federal Republic of Germany:
R. Nave-Herz, Universität Oldenburg.

German Democratic Republic:
H. Kuhrig and J. Gysi, Institut für Soziologie und Sozialpolitik der Akademie der Wissenschaften der DDR, Berlin.

Great Britain:
R. Rapoport and M. Sierakowski, Institute for Family and Environmental Research, London.

Hungary:
J. Sas and M. Herzog, Institute of Sociology, Hungarian Academy of Sciences, Budapest.

Italy:
G. Sgritta and A. Saporiti, Istituto di Statistica e Ricerca Sociale 'C. Gini' Facoltà di Scienze Statistiche, Università di Roma.

The Netherlands:
C. Clason, Sociologisch Instituut, Rijksuniversiteit Groningen.

Norway:
K. Waerness and H. Ve, Universitetet, Bergen.

Poland:
A. Kurzynowski, Socio-Economic Department, Central School of Planning and Statistics, Warsaw.

Soviet Union:
A. Kharchev, M. Pankratova, Institute of Sociological Research, Department of Family, Moscow.

Sweden:
R. Liljeström and E. Dahlström, Sociologiska Institutionen, Göteborgs Universitet.

Yugoslavia:
K. Boh, and N. Černigoj-Sadar, Institut za Sociologijo pri Univerzi, Ljubljana.

Co-ordinators were J. Qvortrup (1980-1982) and M. Bak (1983-1986). Director of the study was K. Boh.

Vienna Centre Reports
on the Project

'Changes in the Life Patterns of Families in Europe'
National Reports, in the series 'Vienna Centre Current Research
Reports'

Volume I, 1981
Finland by Elina Haavio-Mannila and Riitta Jallinoja
France by Andrée Michel
Federal Republic of Germany by Rosemarie Nave-Herz
Great Britain by Margaret Sierakowski
Hungary by Judit H. Sas

Volume II, 1982
Italy by Giovanni B. Sgritta and Angelo Saporiti
Norway by Kari Waerness
Sweden by Edmund Dahlström and Rita Liljeström
USSR by A.G. Kharchev and L.V. Yasnaya

Volume III, 1984
Belgium by Lieven Sercu
The Netherlands by Christine E. Clason
Poland by Adam Kurzynowski
Slovenia (Yugoslavia) by Katja Boh

Volume IV, 1984
German Democratic Republic by Jutta Gysi and Wulfram Speigner

'Comparative Family Research'
Reports and papers for the Vienna Centre's Fourth International
Training Seminar on Cross-National Comparative Family
Research, Finland, 16-20 June 1984.
  Report on the seminar by Maren Bak
  Is Comparative Research Basic or Applied Research? by Jens
  Qvortrup
  Heuristic Aims and Theoretical Problems in Comparative
  Social Research by Maren Bak
  Organisational Perspectives on Cross-national Family
  Research by Veronika Stolte Heiskanen
  Comparative Research - Guiding Principles and Practical
  Experience by Elina Haavio-Mannila

Appendices

General Problems of Comparative Family Research by Katja Boh

Who Are They? When Is Then? Comparisons in the Histories of the Western Family by Lynn Walter

Life-Cycle Analysis in Comparative Family Research by Rita Liljeström

Comparative Aspects of Care in Old Age by Kari Waerness

For Product Safety Concerns and Information please contact our EU
representative GPSR@taylorandfrancis.com
Taylor & Francis Verlag GmbH, Kaufingerstraße 24, 80331 München, Germany

www.ingramcontent.com/pod-product-compliance
Lightning Source LLC
Chambersburg PA
CBHW070554270326
41926CB00013B/2309